DIRK PHILIPS

Friend and Colleague
of Menno Simons
1504-1568

DIRK PHILIPS

Friend and Colleague of Menno Simons
1504-1568

Jacobus ten Doornkaat Koolman

In memory of his teachers
Prof. I. J. Le Cosquino de Bussy, 1846-1920;
Prof. Dr. S. Cramer, 1842-1913.
Professors at the University of Amsterdam
and at the Mennonite Seminary

Translated from Dutch by
William E. Keeney
Edited by
C. Arnold Snyder

Published by Pandora Press
Kitchener, Ontario
Co-published by Herald Press
Scottdale, Pennsylvania/Waterloo, Ontario

Canadian Cataloguing in Publication Data

Doornkaat Koolman, J. ten
    Dirk Philips, friend and colleague of Menno Simons, 1504-1568

Translation of: Dirk Philips, vriend en medewerker van Menno Simons, 1504-1568.
Includes bibliographical references and index.
ISBN 0-99698762-3-8

1. Philips, Dirk, 1504 - 1568. 2. Menno Simons, 1496 - 1561.
3. Mennonites - Netherlands - Bishops - Biography.
I. Snyder, C. Arnold. II. Keeney, William E. (William Echard), 1922-   . III. Title

BX8143.P45D6613 1998   289.7'092   C97-931070-9

DIRK PHILIPS, FRIEND AND COLLEAGUE OF MENNO SIMONS, 1504-1568
Published in 1998 by Pandora Press
    51 Pandora Avenue N.
    Kitchener, Ontario,
    Canada N2H 3C1
Co-published by Herald Press
    Scottdale, Pennsylvania/Waterloo, Ontario

This book is a translation of:
Jacobus ten Doornkaat Koolman,
Dirk Philips, Vriend en Medewerker van Menno Simons 1504-1568
Haarlem: H.D. Tjeenk Willink & Zoon, 1964
© 1997 renewed by Hans ten Doornkaat Koolman
Zollikerberg-Zürich (Switzerland)

English translation by William E. Keeney
Edited by C. Arnold Snyder
Copyright © 1998 by Pandora Press
International Standard Book Number: **0-9698762-3-8**
Printed in Canada on acid-free paper

Cover drawing: Christian E. Snyder, based on Cornelis Koning's engraving (ca. 1630)
Cover design: Clifford M. Snyder

All rights reserved. No part of this publication may be reproduced, stored in a retrieval system, or transmitted in any form or by any means, electronic, mechanical, photocopying, recording or otherwise, without the prior written permission of the publishers.

06 05 04 03 02 01 00 99 98 10 9 8 7 6 5 4 3 2 1

Author's Preface

I lived in Amsterdam from September, 1911 to October, 1915, with a short break when I served as minister in Crefeld. In 1913 I wrote a thesis about Dirk Philips for the German candidate's exam and later wrote a dissertation on the same subject. In 1915 I had to abandon this study and could only return to it in 1957. Thanks to Dr. H. W. Meihuizen of the Hague it developed into a book. He encouraged me to rework the material as completely as possible, rather than use it only for a few journal articles.

Many have helped me in this work. I would like to acknowledge Prof. Dr. K. Heeroma, director of the Nedersaksisch Instituut of the Rijksuniversiteit in Groningen, for reviewing and improving the text and the notes of Appendix I. Prof. H. de la Fontaine Verwey was kind enough to help me with the solution of several difficult questions. I was able to exchange thoughts about my studies with Dr. N. van der Zijpp whenever I visited the Netherlands in recent years. I have received useful suggestions from him.

I thank the officials of the University Library in Amsterdam and of the Central Library in Zurich for their cooperation. Above all Mrs. Y. de Swart-Pot, librarian of the Library of the United Mennonite Congregation in Amsterdam, has lightened my task, both in Amsterdam and in Zurich, by providing the necessary resource books. My sister-in-law, Miss A. S. M. ten Bosch, a retired librarian, was willing to work through the manuscript and the galley proofs, and has also improved the style. I thank her for the careful preparation of the index. The reader will find in the notes the names of others who have supported me through their comments. Dr. F. Blanke of Zurich, my advisor and neighbour, has followed my work with interest.

Full credit goes to those who compiled the writings of Dirk Philips, especially Dr. F. Pijper. His help came at a critical moment, for he completed this extensive work within a year. In it he demonstrates his own vision about the worth of the material. Although our views differ, nevertheless I shall never forget that Mennonite history is deeply indebted to him.

Zurich, September, 1964   J. ten Doornkaat Koolman

Translator's Preface

In 1961-63 our family was in the Netherlands under assignment from the Mennonite Central Committee. About the middle of the term I received a letter from Zurich. The writer was J. ten Doornkaat Koolman. He had read my articles on Dirk Philips in *Mennonite Quarterly Review* and *Mennonite Life*. He also learned that I was living in Amsterdam. He mentioned that he had resumed work on Dirk Philips after having to leave his research idle for years due to his health problems and the direction his career had taken him as a consequence.

In the letter he noted that he was now in retirement and was resuming his work on Dirk. He asked if we might find occasion to meet sometime while I was in Europe. Not too long after that I had to make a trip to Switzerland for the Mennonite Central Committee and had time for the side trip to Zurich where he was living.

When I arrived at the train station in Zurich, I spotted a man holding a copy of *Mennonite Life* prominently in his hands. It was J. ten Doornkaat Koolman. We went to his home and had a delightful lunch while we got acquainted and discussed our common interest in Dirk Philips.

It turned out that he was apprehensive that I was working on a more extensive biography of Dirk while I was in the Netherlands. I might then pre-empt the possibility of him publishing the continuing research he had done on Dirk Philips. I assured him that my interest was primarily in Dirk's theology and not in documenting all the points of his life and career. I also expressed a need to have a full length biography of Dirk and my happiness at seeing his work published.

Our further discussion disclosed that we shared a common assessment of Dirk's importance to the origins of the Dutch Mennonite church. We both felt that insufficient attention had been given to his contribution to the movement. I continue to think that Dirk's contribution has too often been ignored or underrated.

In 1964 I received a copy of J. ten Doornkaat Koolman's book soon after it was published. I read it with enthusiasm. It filled in a number of gaps and confirmed many issues which I had felt were probably so but had not documented.

Since that time I have felt J. ten Doornkaat Koolman's book should be made available in English because so few English-speaking people can read Dutch. Access to ten Doornkaat Koolman's material might help restore Dirk to the significance he merits. Along with Cornelius J. Dyck and Alvin Beachy, I worked on translating *The Writings of Dirk Philips* (Scottdale: Herald Press, 1992), and wrote the introductory biography to that volume. It reflects some dependency on ten Doornkaat Koolman's book. My career did not afford opportunity to work on translating ten Doornkaat Koolman's book until after my retirement in 1990. It is satisfying now to anticipate the publication of the book in an English translation.

One problem of translation from Dutch to English has to do with the use of names. I have decided to use the original Dutch or German. That also creates problems for indexing. During the sixteenth century surnames were not used in the part of Europe covered in the book. Given names were used and then some additional identification was employed to distinguish the person from others with the same given name. Where the father was known, a patronymic was added. Thus Menno Simons was really Simonszoon, shortened to Simons, that is the son of Simon. Likewise Dirk and Obbe Philips are the sons of Philip. Therefore it is not a mark of undue familiarity (as a friend of mine once implied by saying that I worked with them so much I was on a first name basis with them) to refer to Menno or Dirk rather than Simons or Philips. In fact, to use only a given name is most appropriate, especially since no modern person knows the fathers in question by name!

Other means of identification were either by occupation or place of origin. Sicke Freerks or Snijder could be identified either as the son of Freerk or by his occupation as a tailor. Jan van Leiden was from the city of Leiden and Gillis van Aken was from the German city now called Aachen.

In looking for a name in the index one should check any of the possibilities: by a given name usually, though sometimes by the father's name. In general I did not use *van*, *von*, or *de* as the location in the index since all of these are indications of one's place of origin, in Dutch, German viii

or French respectively. So in using the index, search various options. It seemed an undue clutter to cross reference all the possibilities.

I would be remiss if I did not acknowledge the help of the Mennonite Historical Library at Bluffton College. Ann Hilty, librarian, generously supplied me with space to work. She also gave me access and assistance for resources of the library where reference materials were needed. Margaret Weaver and Gerald Schlabach graciously assisted me in translating the Latin sections.

Bluffton, Ohio, October, 1996   William Keeney

Editor's Preface

Bringing to fruition this English edition and translation of *Dirk Philips, Vriend en Medewerker van Menno Simons 1504-1568* has not been an easy task. The lion's share of the thanks must be laid at the door of William Keeney, who provided the impetus for the project with his original translation of the Dutch text. Having decided to proceed with the publication of this English edition through Pandora Press, many complex individual decisions, and much more work, still lay ahead.

Early in the project Professor Keeney and I agreed that the English version of *Dirk Philips* should, as much as possible, be presented in a natural English syntax and rhythm. That is to say, when faced with inevitable choices between stark literal accuracy and normal English usage, we decided to favour the latter. The task of overseeing the production of a final English text fell to me.

Professor Keeney's translation was our basic working text, and subsequent linguistic decisions were made with his translation in hand. Special mention must be made of the skilled and careful contribution of Margaret Overduin at the second stage of revision. Her native mastery of the Dutch language and her skill in English were invaluable to the project. Carrie Snyder then contributed her linguistic and editorial skills, and Cornelius J. Dyck also offered helpful suggestions at this stage.

The manuscript, thus revised, then returned to the hands of Professor Keeney and, after his suggested changes had been incorporated, came into my hands once again. At the final stage I re-read the text again, with frequent reference to the Dutch original, making such final changes as I felt might still be necessary. The index was prepared by Professor Keeney.

The Dutch text is translated here in its entirety, with the notable exception of the appendices. The first three appendices of *Dirk Philips, Vriend en Medewerker van Menno Simons 1504-1568* (the fourth is bibliographical) had already been translated into English. They are available in: *The Writings of Dirk Philips, 1504-1568*, trans. and ed. by Cornelius J. Dyck, William E. Keeney, and Alvin J. Beachy (Scottdale, PA: Herald Press,

1992). The *Writings of Dirk Philips* (cited in this book as WDP) make an excellent companion volume for those who wish to pursue Dirk Philips' writings in conjuction with Rev. ten Doornkaat's biography. The appendices included in Rev. ten Doornkaat Koolman's book, but omitted here, can be found in WDP in the following places:

Appendix I = WDP, pp. 611-617
Appendix II, = WDP, pp. 545-548
Appendix III, = WDP, pp. 590-610

All of us involved in this project have made every effort to produce a text that is both a faithful rendition of the original, as well as a book that communicates clearly and naturally in English. In the end, it is our hope that the book which has emerged from this lengthy process will prove useful and helpful to English-speaking readers. They will find Rev. ten Doornkaat's work a valuable resource for understanding the forces, personalities, and issues that shaped the Mennonite tradition in the late sixteenth century.

Sincere thanks goes out to Rev. ten Doornkaat's son and grandson, of Zollikerberg and Hinwil Switzerland, respectively, for their kind cooperation in the completion of this project.

Conrad Grebel College, February, 1998   C. Arnold Snyder

Jacobus ten Doornkaat Koolman: Life and Writings*

Jacobus ten Doornkaat Koolman was born April 9, 1889 in Hamburg, Germany. His father was a medical doctor, and member of a prominent Mennonite family. After studying theology first in Marburg, then in Berlin, and finally at the Mennonite Seminary in Amsterdam, Jacobus ten Doornkaat Koolman received his first pastoral charge as a ministerial assistant for the Mennonite churches of Crefeld-Neuwied in 1913. The situation in the Mennonite church of that time unfortunately meant that he was unable to find a permanent pastoral post in the denomination of his birth. From 1915 on, he devoted his pastoral energies to service in Protestant churches, first in the Evangelical Church of the Rhineland.

In 1919 a bout of tuberculosis forced Rev. ten Doornkaat to take a cure in Davos, Switzerland. He would spend the rest of his life in Switzerland, carrying out a variety of pastoral activities in the Reformed Church, first in the canton of Graubünden, and from 1936 on in the canton of Zurich. From 1943 until his retirement in 1954 he served as full time pastor in the hospitals of the canton of Zurich. He was devoted to this task. Well past the age of eighty, he continued to visit the sick and to preach in Zurich hospitals.

Rev. ten Doornkaat's deep interest in Anabaptist and Mennonite history remained strong all his life. He was well-grounded in the language, culture, and history of the Dutch Mennonite church. After his move to Zurich he developed a corresponding interest in Swiss Anabaptism. He was conversant with Anabaptist sources and the scholarly literature dealing with both the Dutch and the Swiss movements. His own work was published in both Dutch and German, as well as in English translation. The bibliography of his works (see the selected bibliography below) in-

---

*Biographical information and bibliographical references have been drawn from Heinold Fast, "Jacobus ten Doornkaat Koolman, 1889-1978," *Mennonitische Geschichtsblätter 31 (1979), 106-110.*

cludes numerous encyclopedia articles as well as publications in scholarly journals. He never stopped working on historical projects. At the time of his death at the age of 89, he was working on an article dealing with the Anabaptists of the Zurich *Unterland*, a work which, unfortunately, he was not able to complete.

Rev. ten Doornkaat's scholarly interest was awakened when he was a young man, during the time of his study at the Mennonite Seminary in Amsterdam. There he had the opportunity to study with professors Cramer and de Bussy, an experience which he credited with widening his intellectual field of vision.

One scholarly thread was spun early in Amsterdam, and remained unbroken throughout Rev. ten Doornkaat's life: his interest in Dirk Philips. His research for what would become this present biography was well underway when World War I broke out in 1914. Circumstances dictated that the project had to be suspended indefinitely, not to be taken up again full time until after Rev. ten Doornkaat's retirement from the ministry in 1954. The present book, first published in Dutch in 1964, is thus a labour of love spanning a fifty year period, a testimony to Rev. ten Doornkaat's passion for Anabaptist and Mennonite history.

The careful and meticulous historical work of Rev. ten Doornkaat has stood the test of time. His biography of Dirk Philips remains the fundamental monograph on the subject. Its present publication in English, coming 33 years after its original publication in Dutch (and more than a century after the author's birth) is an event long overdue. However, it is the kind of delay and outcome that the author would have understood, and probably smiled at. Worthwhile projects encounter obstacles, and sometimes require extraordinary perseverance. It is only fitting that, however late, the fruits of Rev. ten Doornkaat's lifelong dedication to the study of the life of Dirk Philips finally be made available to an English-speaking audience.

Select Bibliography of Historical Works Published by Jacobus ten Doornkaat Koolman

I. Books

1. *Dirk Philips. Vriend en Medewerker van Menno Simons. 1504-1568.* Haarlem, 1964.

II. Journal Articles

2. "Leupold Scharnschlager und die verborgene Täufergemeinde in Graubünden," *Zwingliana* 4 (1926), 329-337.

3. "Een Onbekende Brief van Dirk Philips," *Nederlandsch Archief voor Kerkgeschiedenis* (N.A.K.G.) 43 (1960), 15-21.

4. "In de Voetsporen van de Oude Dopers in het Noorden van Europa," *Algemeen Doopsgezind Weekblad* (A.D.W.) 15 (1960), no. 17, 4ff; no. 18, 2ff.

5. "Die Täufer in Mecklenburg. Ein Forschungsbericht," *Mennonitische Geschichtsblätter* (M.G.Bl.) 18 (1961), 20-56.

6. "Joachim Kükenbieter (Nossiophagus). Ein lutherischer Eiferer des Reformationszeitalters, N.A.K.G. 44 (1961), 157-176.

7. "The First Edition of Peter Riedemann's 'Rechenschaft,'" *The Mennonite Quarterly Review* (M.Q.R.) 36 (1962), 169ff.

8. "De Anabaptisten in Oostfriesland ten Tijde van Hermannus Aquilomontanus (1489-1548)," N.A.K.G. 46 (1963-64), 87-99.

9. "The First Edition of Dirk Philips' *Enchiridion*," M.Q.R. 38 (1964), 357-360.

10. "Het *Enchiridion* van Dirk Philips 1564-1964," A.D.W. 19 (1964), no. 44. [Different article from above].

11. "Die Wismarer Artikel 1554," M.G.Bl. 22 (1965), 38-42.

12. "Noch einmal: Geburtsjahr Menno Simons," M.G.Bl. 25 (1968), 67-69.

13. "Dirk Philips 1504-1568," A.D.W. 23 (1968), no. 13.

14. "Fritz Blanke, the Man," M.Q.R. 43 (1969), 5-21.

15. "Täufer in Zürcher Zünften 1588," *Zürcher Taschenbuch auf das Jahr 1970*. Zurich, 1969, 31-47.

16. "Jan Utenhoves Besuch bei Heinrich Bullinger im Jahre 1549," *Zwingliana* 14 (1976), 263-273.

III. Encyclopedia Articles

A. Articles under the following headings were written by Rev. ten Doornkaat, and published in both the *Mennonitisches Lexikon* (1913-1967) and the *Mennonite Encyclopedia* (1955-1959).

>   Amsterdamer Taufgesinnten-Gemeinde
>   Amsterdamer Universität und Taufgesinntes Seminar
>   de Bussy, Isaak
>   Doornkaat Koolman, Jan
>   Graubünden

B. Articles under the following headings were published in the *Mennonitisches Lexikon*.

>   Vergerio
>   Weyer, Matthes
>   Wismar
>   Zaandam
>   Zendingsraad, Doopsgezinde
>   Zierikzee
>   van der Zijpp
>   Zillis
>   Zuidlaren
>   Zürich

C. Arnold Snyder

Table of Contents

Chapter I	Origins. The Franciscan becomes an Anabaptist Bishop	1
Chapter II	Bishop in Appingedam	7
Chapter III	An Immigrant in East Friesland	15
Chapter IV	Menno and Dirk at the Banks of the Rhine	23
Chapter V	The Struggle to Purify the Church	29
Chapter VI	The Earliest Writings of Dirk Philips	41
Chapter VII	Study, Travel, and Conferences at Lübeck and Wismar	47
Chapter VIII	Dirk Philips' First Treatises Printed	57
Chapter IX	Dirk Philips, Advocate of the Strict Ban	81
Chapter X	Dirk Philips as Elder in Danzig and Visitor to the Netherlands	99
Chapter XI	The Great Schism	115
Chapter XII	The Last Writings and the End	143
Postscript		165
Notes		166
Index		223

Abbreviations

A.R.G.   *Archiv für Reformationsgeschichte*, 1903 ff.

B.R.N.   *Bibliotheca Reformatoria Neerlandica*, Dl. I-X, 's-Gravenhage, 1903-1914.

CWMS   *The Complete Writings of Menno Simons, c.1496-1561*, translated by Leonard Verduin (Scottdale, PA: Herald Press, 1956).

D.B.   *Doopsgezinde Bijdragen*, Amsterdam, Leeuwarden, Leiden, 1861-1919.

M.G.Bl.   *Mennonitische Geschichtblätter*

M.E.   *The Mennonite Encyclopedia*, 4 volumes, Scottdale, PA, 1955-1959.

M.L.   *Mennonitisches Lexikon*, 4 Bde., Frankfurt (Main), Karlsruhe, 1913-1963. Bd. IV bis Lfg. 50.

M.Q.R.   *The Mennonite Quarterly Review*, Goshen, IN, 1927 ff.

N.A.K.G.   *Nederlands Archief voor Kerkgeschiedenis*, Nieuwe Serie, Dl. XLIII (1959), XLIV (1961), XLVI (1963-1964.)

N.D.B.   *Neue Deutsche Biographie*, 1953 ff.

N.N.B.W. *Nieuw Nederlandsch Biografisch Woordenboek*, Dl. I-IX, Leiden, 1911-1937.

R.E.[3] *Realencyklopädie für Protestantische Theologie und Kirche*, 3. Aufl., 1896-1913.

R.G.G. *Die Religion in Geschichte und Gegenwart*, 2 Aufl., 1927-1932, 3. Aufl., 1956-1963.

S. IV. *Huldrici Zuinglii Opera*, ed. M. Schuler et J. Schulthess. Vol. IV, Turici, 1841.

WDP *The Writings of Dirk Philips, 1504-1568.* Translated by Cornelius J. Dyck, William E. Keeney, and Alvin J. Beachy. Scottdale, PA: Herald Press, 1992.

Z. *Kritische Zwingliausgabe*, Bd. III = *Corpus Reformatorum*, Vol. XC; Bd. IV = C. R., Vol. XCI; Bd. V = C. R. Vol. XCII.

I

Origins.
The Franciscan Becomes an Anabaptist Bishop

Dirk Philips was born in Leeuwarden in 1504,[1] the younger of two brothers. His father was a priest there,[2] probably vicar at Camminghaburg or Camminghabuur.[3] The state of marriage was common for priests at that time in Friesland,[4] as an authority such as Reitsma claims.[5] At least, it was a common occurrence for a priest to live with his housekeeper[6] and it was not viewed as dishonorable and illicit.[7]

What education the young Dirk received is not known. De Hoop Scheffer guessed that the father himself instructed him and his older brother in reading, writing and arithmetic. He later saw to it that they received advanced education.[8]

[His brother] Obbe became a surgeon as well as a barber. We know from a letter of Joachim Kükenbieter to the Lutheran preacher in Hamburg, Johan Garthen, probably written from Lüneburg around Pentecost 1539, that Dirk Phillips came "from the Franciscan rabble."[9] He would have been accepted by the Lesser Brothers [Franciscans] in Leeuwarden and received a fairly decent education, for that time, in the New Galilee monastery. He studied Latin as well as writing essays and debating. At least we may assume this much from his literary work.

The New Galilee cloister had been relocated inside the city walls in 1498 during a period of unrest. The Lesser Brothers were helped by the city administration in the construction of a church and cloister buildings. The cloister belonged to the strict order of the Franciscans, the Observants. Dirk must have been exposed to their strict discipline.[10] He was probably there as a lay brother because as a "priest's child" he could not become an ordained religious. Priests and brothers led the same communal life that was prescribed by cloister regulations. Of course the priests and brothers performed different activities. While the priests devoted themselves to study and pastoral care, the brothers performed all kinds of work in the house, garden and the work place. Sometimes they had to assist the priests in their functions.[11]

The occupants of the cloister numbered around twenty. Unfortunately not a single name is mentioned before 1557,[12] and so Dirk's name cannot be found. The new religious movements must have affected the monks at the cloister also, and although they apparently were not, at least in serious measure, lacking in faithfulness to the church and the Catholic faith,[13] still some individuals must have broken the bond with the cloister. Dirk also chose freedom at about thirty years of age.

We do not know if he joined the circle of the Sacramentarians [opponents of Catholic sacramental theology] which had formed in Leeuwarden, as his brother Obbe did. This circle early on came under the influence of the writings of Melchior Hoffman, the prophet from Strasbourg, who had visited the Netherlands in 1531 and 1532. In the latter year Hoffman probably also sojourned in Friesland, although it was only while passing through.[14]

Before that, a trial of an Anabaptist in Leeuwarden had caused a stir, and certainly must have made an impression on the friends of Obbe Philips. Sicke Freriks Snijder was beheaded on the 20th of March, 1531, after he had been baptized at Emden about the middle of December, 1530 by a disciple of Hoffman called Tripmaker. We know that the death of this first Dutch Anabaptist martyr, "a god-fearing pious hero," motivated Menno Simons to search for the scriptural basis of infant baptism.[15] In December 1531, Tripmaker and seven other Anabaptists were "judged by the sword" in The Hague. This motivated Melchior Hoffman to suspend the command to baptize for two years and during that time only study and teach quietly.[16] This explains why a circle of Melchiorites lived in Leeuwarden without having been baptized. However, they were in close contact with Strasbourg. Messengers went daily to and from Melchior: "also every day we received his writings in which his visions and revelations were shared," writes Obbe in his "Confession."[17] He gives an extensive account about it and concludes with the words: "As these teachings and consolations proceeded we had no little joy and hope; we hoped that everything was true and would be fulfilled. For we were all unsuspecting, simple, and innocent people, without evil in our hearts."[18] The turning point was the action of the baker Jan Matthijs in Haarlem, who presented himself as Enoch disregarding Cornelis Polderman from Zeeland, who had been proclaimed as Enoch in Strasbourg.

Melchior Hoffman was considered to be Elijah and one of his disciples the second witness at the dawning of the New Jerusalem. "Jan Matthijs was one of those people who suddenly emerge out of obscurity at any revolution."[19] Posing as a prophet from the Old Testament he inspired devotion, surprise, and fear in his audience. The inspiration of the moment was followed by somber resolution; he was stern in his demands and commanded obedience.[20]

Jan Matthijs immediately ordered baptism to be resumed and sent out twelve apostles, two by two. Bartholomew Bookbinder and Dirk Cuyper went to Friesland.[21] They knew exactly whom they had to seek out at Leeuwarden: the circle of the Melchiorites. Fourteen or fifteen men and women met and listened to the new preaching. The messengers testified that they were sent forth with no less power or fewer wonders than the apostles at Pentecost. They comforted the audience and proclaimed that the believers needed to be afraid no longer, for no Christian blood would be shed. God himself would destroy all the tyrants and the godless. Most of those present allowed themselves to be baptized.

The following day, before the messengers travelled on, they ordained Obbe Philips and Hans Scheerder[22] as elders "by appointment of other brothers," with the laying on of hands to preach, baptize, and to lead the congregation.[23]

A week later a third messenger from Jan Matthijs, Pieter Houtzager, came to Leeuwarden, when the new elders had already left the city to evangelize here and there. Therefore Obbe stated truthfully that he had never met this Pieter.[24] According to an old chronicle Pieter Houtzager proclaimed to the small circles he was able to form, that the day of judgment was near and would soon occur. Therefore everyone had to repent and be baptized in order to be saved. Whoever was not baptized on the basis of their faith would not receive grace, and was eternally damned. He also admonished the believers not to go to church any more and to avoid everything that people do in the established churches.[25]

Pieter Houtzager baptized Dirk Philips in Leeuwarden, along with a few others. But there was opposition. Pieter got into a debate with the Sacramentarians and had to leave after two days. He was chased by the authorities all through the land and barely escaped them. When Obbe and his fellow elder returned from their journey, they had to lie low and leave the city and province soon after. This all happened between Christmas and Candlemas 1533/34, that is before February 2, 1534.[26]

Dirk Philips evaluated these great events in his life more than 25 years later: "At that time, by God's grace, we heard His Word through the preaching of God's messengers, and we repented and believed and were baptized in the name of the almighty God, Father, Son and Holy Spirit, into the Kingdom of Christ, into the temple of the living God." We may conclude from this that Dirk Philips held his baptism, administered by an apostle of Jan Matthijs, to be scriptural and binding.[27]

Obbe Philips had to flee following the proclamation of an edict by the governor of Friesland, Schenck van Toutenburg. Beside Melchior Hoffman, Pieter Houtzager, and Jacob van Campen (the Amsterdam bishop), the edict also named among others "Obbe Shearer or Barber" of Leeuwarden. A price of 25 Karolus guilders was placed on his head, as well as on those of the other "seducers."[28]

Throughout 1534 Obbe wandered through Groningen and Holland. One of the first people he baptized was Peter van Noerich, alias Gerdt Eilkeman. He was baptized "by the Dam" (Appingedam) in the house of Jan Mudder "long before the trouble in Münster began and before the disturbance at 't Zandt occurred."[29] About the same time Obbe established a circle of Melchiorites in 't Zandt. In the confession of Jacob from Herwerden or from Antwerp (executed at Deventer for rebaptism on February 17, 1535) eight persons were named who lived in the province of Groningen at 't Zandt, and there is a note that "The baptizer there was called Obbe from Leeuwarden, barber."[30]

Because staying in Groningen was unsafe, Obbe fled to Holland. After April 27 he appeared in Haarlem.[31] In the Fall he was at Delft, where among others he baptized David Joris, a glassmaker, and his wife.[32] Still later he lived in Amsterdam and befriended Jacob van Campen, who belonged to the "quiet" Anabaptists, and who tried to restrain his followers from all excesses.[33]

In 1534 the Dutch Melchiorites were stirred to unrest by the events at Münster. In January of that year some messengers of Jan Matthijs had arrived and gathered quite a following among reform minded people. Soon there were others who followed the strong leadership of Jan Matthijs and Jan van Leiden.[34]

From then on Dutch Anabaptism was overshadowed by the revolution and the fall of the city of Münster. Obbe Philips laments: If we had kept records of how it began and ended, "what books, writings, and letters they sent to us daily and what great signs, wonders, visions and revelations they received daily," one could certainly have written a book about it.[35]

Perhaps because of the propaganda from the Münsterites, which also reached the northern provinces, it became necessary for Obbe to return to Groningen. As much as possible, he wanted to gather the "quiet" people and to keep them from acting rashly. He must have met his brother Dirk in the Ommelanden. How Dirk had fared in the meantime we do not know. We can only suspect that he was compelled by the persecution in Friesland to move to safety in Groningen. Either before Obbe's departure in April, 1534, or after his return in 1535, he must have ordained Dirk an elder in Appingedam "through the desires of the brethren."[36] K. Vos believes that this took place in the house of Jan Mudder, whose wife, daughter, and son-in-law also were Anabaptists.[37] This same historian remarks that Dirk Philips must have already been married at the time of his ordination, for to become a bishop one had to be the "husband of one wife." "Thus the earlier Franciscan monk had abandoned his promise never to marry, as had Luther, and had chosen the blessing of the married state above the torment of asceticism."[38] That Dirk was indeed married is confirmed by the letter written by Hoyte to him, dated April 17, 1567 in which Dirk, *with his entire family*, is invited to come to Friesland as Jacob in Egypt.[39]

II

Bishop in Appingedam

In the years 1530-1536 the city and district of Groningen were under the tolerant regime of Karel van Gelre, an illegitimate son of the Count. When the government was compelled to intervene because of the events at Münster and Münsterite propaganda (1534), the Anabaptists in Groningen only received a fine.[1] The situation grew more serious when messengers arrived from Münster. One of the twenty-eight "apostles" sent by Jan van Leiden, Claes van Alkmaar,[2] managed to reach Groningen. The brothers appointed two representatives, Jacob Kremer of Winsum and Antonie Kistemaker of Appingedam, to accompany him on his return and to see what the situation was at Münster. They returned to the area at the end of December and brought a booklet, *About Vengeance*, written by Bernhard Rothmann, the Münsterite preacher. In this booklet the believers in the Netherlands were urged to travel to Münster and to liberate the city.[3]

What happened then, partly as a result of this booklet, were disturbances in the area of 't Zandt, which had more the appearance of religious fanaticism than of a religious movement. The lead person was Harmen Schoenmaker, who at first presented himself as the Messiah and subsequently named himself God the Father. About a thousand men and women gathered together there and for several days were thoroughly influenced by the new prophet. There was also another revolutionary there by the name of Gerdt Eilkeman, who confessed that he "was also with the Assembly from 't Zandt."[4] But the enthusiasm shown in Münster was lacking, and when the armed force sent by the governor appeared, the crowd dispersed rapidly. Harmen Schoenmaker was brought to Groningen and died in prison after being subjected to severe torture.[5]

Several months later new troubles occurred in the district, brought about by the propaganda of Jan van Geelen who, with more than 300 followers, had occupied Bloemkamp, the Old Cloister, at Hartwerd, and who had offered strong resistance to the Frisian Governor Schenck van Toutenburg and his troops.[6] Jan van Geelen asked the Groningen Anabaptists for help. Jacob Kremer and Hans Scheerder, co-elders with Obbe, were willing to do this.[7] They managed to bring together a group of seventy followers. However, a trip to Friesland was prevented by the wives, who feared for the lives of their husbands. Yet, the leaders would not refrain from the plan to take the cloister. And so they travelled to Warfum where there was a Johanniter monastery, called "Oldeklooster" [Old Cloister]. The actual leader appeared to be Jacob Kremer, but also a certain "Lippe, who travelled with Obbe, was one of the leading persons in the attack on the cloister in Groningen land."[8] The attack failed because of the vigilance of the Governor Karel van Gelre. Thirty revolutionaries were brought as captives to Groningen, but only one of them, the messenger from Münster, was executed. He was the only person to be executed in Groningen during this riotous time, proof of the government's tolerance.

One wonders which side Obbe and Dirk Philip took during these uprisings. Obbe testified twice that he had not taken part, and his brother even less so. After describing the horrors in Münster and the end of "Elijah" (Melchior Hoffman) and "Enoch" (Jan Matthijs), and after rejecting the false prophecies, Obbe continued,[9] "But God knows that Dirk and I could never tolerate such attacks. We also taught firmly against it, but it did no good for most of the crowd had already made up their minds." And further: "For a long time there was no one of the teachers [ministers] who helped me counter these false brothers and all the rioting, other than Dirk Philips; we were never disposed in our heart for such riotous zeal and false prophecies." This demonstrates that the circle around Obbe was in the minority. Their attempts to dissuade the other teachers [ministers] from revolutionary plans, for example Hans Scheerder, the messengers from Münster, and Lippe, were in vain.

Obbe also indicates where the weakness lay. They did not have the power to convince the false brothers with reasonable arguments, and "the letter of Scripture took us captive."[10] The revolutionaries, while they were their brothers, could not bear this censure and opposition. They swore death on both brothers. That the Philips brothers took such a position was confirmed incidentally by Nic[olas] van Blesdijk.[11]

> *There were some Anabaptist teachers [ministers], in West Friesland who now began to doubt because of disappointed expectations regarding the fulfillment of Hoffman's predictions, and because of other failed riots and undertakings. They started to share their misgivings. Among them were Obbe and his brother Dirk . . ., but they achieved so little with their complaints about the Münster affair, at least as long as things at Münster went well, that they aroused hatred and most of [the brethren] considered them enemies of the Kingdom of Christ.*

Dirk Philips spoke about the people who were led astray at various places. The place which Reitsma already mentioned is known:[12]

> *For what they cannot prove with the New Testament, they wish to prove with the Old Testament and the Prophets. Because of this many sects have begun; many a false religion has been established. Yes, primarily from this fountain have flowed the idolatrous ceremonies and pomp of the anti-Christian churches and the lamentable errors of the revolutionary sects which during our time, under the appearance of the holy gospel, of the faith, and of the Christian religion, have done much harm and stirred up much aggravation.*[13]

Nowhere are the Münsterites mentioned, as far as I know, but indirect references can be found.[14] For example, in *Concerning Spiritual Restitution*, Dirk complains about the tyrants who "with their strong mandates and posters, with water, fire and sword" persecute the church; and about those teachers who "with their philosophy, guile, and sharp wittedness . . . provoke the civil authorities to drive away, strangle and kill." And then Dirk goes further:

> *But in opposition to this, the people of the Lord arm themselves not with carnal weapons such as (alas) has*

> happened to some through misunderstanding, but [they are armed] with the armor of God, with the weapons of righteousness in the right hand and the left, with the helmet of salvation, . . . and with Christian patience.[15]

Dirk speaks more in other places about the "misunderstanding" of some of the brothers.[16] He also opposed the allegorical exposition of the Bible and eschatological heresies.[17]

Against these clear statements by Obbe and Dirk Philips we find accusations of several writers, new and old, who speak to the contrary, namely that both elders actively participated in the disturbances. Gerardus Nicolai in his "Insertions" to Bullinger's *Against the Rebaptizers* makes it appear as if "the rebellious rebaptizers Batenburg and Obbe Philips with their adherents"[18] not only instigated the rebellion of Münster, but also the capture of the Oldeklooster, and with the help of Gillis van Aken caused the disturbances at 't Zandt and the Warfum cloister. These reports from an otherwise so capable historian can only be explained as ecclesiastical partisanship.[19] The same applies to his comment: "Obbe was one of the principal teachers [ministers] of the 't Zandt baptizers."[20] We have seen that people other than Obbe were the leaders of the Groningen disturbances.

Obbe's brother Dirk was also accused. The Jesuit Franciscus Costerus claims in his "Toetsteen" [Touchstone] that Dirk belonged to the troublemakers of Oldeklooster.[21] This opinion was copied in the "Anabaptist Succession."[22] Vos offered an insightful hypothesis about how this report could have originated.[23] Vos writes in the above mentioned piece: "Obbe and his brother Dirk may have presented themselves as enemies of violence, [but] it cannot be denied that several of their disciples differed very much from their teachers."[24]

No, that cannot be denied, and Vos does not do that.[25] "It is certain that Obbe did associate with the revolutionaries." Then, however, Vos points out that Obbe often sent money to his earlier baptist friend, Gerdt Eilkeman, to keep him from committing robbery. Eilkeman confessed: The Obbenites were against the Batenburgers. The Batenburgers often persecuted him and in addition pressured him to leave the sect of the

Obbenites and to join them.[26] From this Vos correctly concludes that Obbe's followers belonged to the peaceful ones; their teacher had the same beliefs.

The other modern historian, Mellink, who describes the position of Obbe and Dirk Philips in the years 1534 and 1535, is somewhat ambiguous in his judgment. On the one hand he admits that Obbe kept apart from revolutionary plans during 1535, and that the Philips brothers, so far as is known, took no active part in the events.[27] On the other hand, Mellink tried to prove that Obbe was a witness to the turbulence at 't Zandt and that he was present at the attack on the Johanniter cloister at Warfum.[28]

But there is no good reason to doubt Obbe's position. A large number of Anabaptists, Obbe's fellow believers, were among the revolutionary Anabaptists. However, he opposed their plans and undertakings and must have seen with sorrow that his and his brother's warnings were futile.[29]

Burgman commented very correctly:[30]

It does makes a difference if one associated trustfully with those who later plan to rebel, or if [on the other hand] one has extended a helping hand and was a co-participant in rebellion. The first was said correctly of Obbe, just as for most of the older Mennonites, but the latter was incorrectly attributed to him.

The fall of Münster was the great turning point for the Anabaptist movement. The enchantment which radiated from the New Jerusalem had disappeared. Disillusionment followed, above all among the Dutch Anabaptists. The peaceful direction which existed under the leadership of Obbe increased in power and influence. What Obbe and Dirk previously dared to speak only in closed circles, and what had aroused opposition and hatred in revolutionary companions,[31] they now proclaimed freely. They censured Münsterite teachings and scorned the revolutionaries.[32] Those who continued to trust the Münsterite teachings—the Kingdom of God had already collapsed there—and those who expected a new prophet, could not endure this criticism. It resulted in vigorous debates leading to the separation of Anabaptist groups from one another.

There were four such groups: the followers of Obbe, called Obbenites;[33] then the actual Melchiorites (Blesdijk uses the name "Hoffmanianen" [Hoffmanites]). Opposed to them stood those that used the sword, namely the rest of the Münsterites, who were prepared to take the sword again at the first sign; and finally the Batenburgers, led by Jan van Batenburg, a bastard of noble descent, who formed a gang of robbers. The first two groups were peaceful, although they had differences which prevented them from merging.[34]

What position did Obbe take in these turbulent months? Obbenites and Melchiorites both condemned the Münsterites for setting up of the Kingdom of God by violence and for instituting polygamy, but they did not agree concerning prophecies and visions, nor over the expectation of a new outpouring of the Spirit, or about the office and administration of the sacraments. The Obbenites taught that one may expect no other Kingdom of Christ here on earth than the present one, which can be seen by everyone's eyes, that is, the church of Christ which is exposed to persecution.

If Obbe had doubts earlier about the prophecies of Hoffman and others, he now distanced himself from them for good. And whereas the true followers of Hoffman expected a new Pentecost which would enable them to teach and baptize with apostolic authority,[35] Obbe and his followers wished to follow the New Testament example: Only those chosen by the baptized members were allowed to preach and administer the sacraments, as long as their office lasted.[36] Obbe, and later Menno, viewed their functions (teaching, baptizing, and the distribution of the Lord's supper) as canonical, so to speak, and as instituted by the apostles.[37]

All this is according to Blesdijk who, as an earlier follower of Menno was well acquainted with the persons involved and their views. He granted first place to Obbe, although he frequently mentioned Dirk, his brother, as someone who agreed fully with Obbe.

Menno Simons described the circle of the Obbenites in his *Departure from Popedom* as follows:[38]

> *[After leaving the Roman Church] I sought the godfearing and found some (although few) zealous in doctrine. I dealt with the perverse, delivered some by God's help and power out of the bonds of their damnation, won them over to Christ, and left the hardnecked and stubborn peopleto the Lord.*

In August 1536 the four Anabaptist parties, differing on important points but also bound together by common doctrinal positions, were invited to assemble at Bocholt in the Bishopric of Münster.[39] The leaders from either extreme were absent, the Batenburgers as well as Obbe and Dirk Philips. According to Blesdijk, the latter were absent out of fear for their lives,[40] certainly not without justification, for at the assembly a hot argument developed, and at a certain moment it seemed as if a bloodbath would take place.

Then David Joris stepped forward. He had been ordained an elder by Obbe Philips in Delft in the Fall of 1535.[41] He was able to calm emotions and to effect a compromise that the Münsterites as well as the Melchiorites could accept. It was only an apparent victory; disillusionment followed quickly when they recovered their senses. Kühler notes: "Thanks to Bocholt the peaceful group finally separated from the 'inferior elements' and from then on was able to develop unhindered and normally."[42]

However, for the growth of the new baptist fellowship there was need for a leader other than Obbe or Dirk, someone who was better educated, who could further the movement by eloquence and style of writing. The brothers chose [Menno Simons] the former pastor of Witmarsum, who shortly after leaving the Catholic church had been baptized by Obbe Philips, and had come to reside in rural Groningen.[43] He "spent his time reading the Lord's Word and writing in solitude."[44] About a year after his baptism, thus presumably in January 1537, six to eight men came on a commission from the Obbenites and asked him to have compassion on poor oppressed souls, and put to use the talents which the Lord had given him. Menno does not give us the names of these men, perhaps because Obbe, the leader of this deputation, later became an apostate. Dirk probably was also one of the representatives. In complete agreement with the above mentioned report from Blesdijk,[45] the representatives did not come on their own authority, but "on behalf of the godfearing."[46] Menno describes them as men

> who were of one heart and soul with me in their belief and life (as much as a person can judge), blameless, separated from the world according to the witness of the Scriptures, subjected to the cross, who had turned away not only from the Münsterites, but also from all the world's sects, curses, and abominations.[47]

Menno could not decide immediately and asked for time to think about it. But after earnest prayer and after repeated requests, he accepted. He was invested as bishop or elder in Groningen with the laying on of hands "by the wish of the brothers."[48] Vos assumes that Dirk was present at this ordination,[49] but we do not know for certain. After a while, Menno began to teach and to baptize.[50]

III

An Immigrant in East Friesland

The ordination of Menno Simons took place in the city of Groningen in January, 1537. It would not have escaped notice. Witness an exchange of letters between Maria of Hungary, sister of Charles V and governor of Brussels, and the government of Groningen. In June 1536, Groningen became part of the Habsburg Netherlands. After Karel van Gelre, illegitimate son of the Duke "departed with silent drum,"[1] the city of Groningen put itself under the administration of the Emperor. On June 6 Schenck van Toutenburg, who as governor of Friesland had persecuted the Anabaptists so mercilessly, came to the city of Groningen and was installed as governor of the city and the district.[2] At the discussions with the city government the topic of the "Rebaptizers" most probably came on the agenda. The government must have pointed out that they had earnestly and explicitly fought against the Rebaptizers with their mandates[3] (Oosterwarfs-Constitution of October 8, 1535 and Ooster- and Westerwarfs-Constitution of May 3, 1536.) The governor must have been in agreement in trying to be sensitive to the feelings of the newly won province. He probably chose the diplomatic way and reported his findings to Brussels, perhaps in one of the many letters he wrote to the Count van Hoogstraten.[4]

At any rate the governess of Brussels found reason to think, from the reports of the spiritual and secular leaders, that Rebaptizers were being tolerated in Groningen. On March 22, 1537, she wrote to the city officials and admonished them to live according to the Imperial mandates. The mayors and the Council of Groningen answered immediately on April 2 and defended their position.[5] They admitted that in 1534, twenty-three or twenty-four Anabaptists had been living in Groningen. These people had either recanted or had been banished from the city for more than a year.[6]

After Groningen joined the empire these Anabaptists had returned, hoping for the grace and mercy of the Imperial majesty. The Council gave all possible guarantees that these people would conduct themselves as good Christians. The Council had made them swear a solemn oath[7] and was also prepared to consider the matter fully with the governor at his upcoming visit and to take the necessary measures, in so far as the Council could be responsible for this before God, Emperor and Empress. Naturally the people of Groningen would not tolerate foreign Anabaptists in their city. Day by day suspected persons were subjected to rigid interrogations.

It is understandable that Menno and Dirk took flight when these measures were made known. Obbe no longer was able to flee, since he was already imprisoned. Perhaps he had been picked up in a raid and recognized as an Anabaptist elder. Perhaps he was known to the authorities. It is possible that he had been banned on the basis of the Ooster- and Westerwarfs-Constitution of May 3, 1536, and could expect death by the sword now that he had returned. Obbe later escaped from prison and fled to a safer location.[8]

To what place did Menno and Dirk flee? The handiest place for escape was East Friesland. Here Count Enno II (1528-1540), a capable ruler, was governor. But because of weakness and indecision he was not very successful, either in secular or ecclesiastical politics. Twice he tried to make the Lutheran confession the reigning religion in his territory (Bremer Church Ordinance, 1529, and Lüneburger Church Ordinance, 1535), not because he favoured Lutherans, but for political reasons. The followers of the original East Frisian reformation, who originated with Dutch Sacramentarian and Swiss influence, were opposed to it. In the west of the country, above all in Emden, the majority remained Reformed. And because Enno was distracted with other cares, a certain balance was reached between the two confessions. At least they did not fight openly.[9]

This was the situation in the church when Menno and Dirk came to East Friesland in the spring of 1537. This phenomenon is something we can observe often in Anabaptist history: Whenever the evangelical churches quarrelled with each other, or if a strong Catholic church still existed next to a reformed church, the Anabaptists could easily go undercover and were left relatively undisturbed, more so than in territories where there was only one church denomination.

Menno Simons probably went to Oldersum,[10] a refuge since the time of Ulrich van Dornum for those who were persecuted on account of their faith. He did not, however, meet Ulrich personally, since Ulrich had died on March 12, 1536.[11] The lord of Oldersum was the nobleman Hero, the administrator of Oldersum and Goedens, who like his uncle protected the Reformed and persons of other beliefs against the Count and the Lutheran preachers.[12] Menno must have enjoyed a time of peace until the zeal for the house of the Lord compelled him to travel through the northern Netherlands, to strengthen the faith of the brethren. Whether he subsequently found a hiding place in the "Omme-landen" district [the district around the city of Groningen][13] or often returned from his travels to Oldersum[14] cannot be ascertained. It appears, however, that Menno maintained a place of residence somewhere, because he published some important writings in the years 1537-1543.

Dirk travelled to Norden where the situation was just as favorable for him. There the Luneburger church order was still in effect. Gellius Faber, who in 1537 had been called to Emden, was succeeded by the quarrelsome Joachim Kükenbieter (Nossiophagus), a fervent Lutheran.[15] He was supported by a Lutheran colleague, Wilhelm Lemsius, whereas two other preachers were of the Reformed persuasion. Not only did Kükenbieter disagree with the Sacramentarians, he also fought against the Anabaptists. In a well known letter to the Lutheran preacher Johannes Garcaeus in Hamburg, written before Pentecost 1539,[16] Kükenbieter wrote that he had debated with Dirk in 1537, in Norden.[17] During this disputation he had noticed that the Anabapitsts not only deviated from Lutheran doctrine by their adult baptism, but that they also believed a "horrible" doctrine about the incarnation of Christ, while their concept of the Lord's Supper agreed with that of the Sacramentarians. On the other hand, he admitted that they were not rebellious and honoured the government. His comment about Dirk: "He misleads the people with his hypocrisy," we can read as a backhanded compliment to his opponent.

From this we can ascertain that Dirk did not remain silent in Norden. Because the evangelical church was divided, he was successful in spreading Anabaptist views. And he was not alone there, but was accompanied by a number of Obbe's followers who had settled in Norden. It is possible that Obbe himself, after his escape from prison at Groningen, passed through Norden, but we do not know for sure. According to Kükenbieter, Obbe lived in Rostock in 1539. Some of his adherents, driven out of Norden because of their heresy,[18] fled to Rostock and urged the remaining Anabaptists at Norden to follow their example.

In my opinion Dirk had already left Norden earlier and had found a domicile in Emden or in that area. I imagine that he was Menno's second in command whenever Menno travelled to the northern Netherlands for any length of time. Dirk himself would not have risked such a trip. At least his name was not mentioned in any of the placards nor in the hearings of the imprisoned Anabaptists.

Kükenbieter complained that it was very difficult to identify the sectarians. They changed not only their clothing but also their names to be less visible.[19] That is probably true. In the early years after the fall of Münster, many who sought a secure hiding place were doing this. It was a favourite practice especially among the Davidjorists. However, I do not agree with Pijper's conclusion[20] that Dirk Philips "in deep secrecy and using an alias went about his work for several more years (in the Netherlands)." As far as we know none of the elders did that, for it is not in keeping with the commandment for absolute truthfulness. That Obbe Philips later, after his defection, chose another name is, however, easier to understand.[21]

I also cannot agree with Pijper when he writes:[22] "Dirk Philips was apparently often a witness to the martyrdom of one of his fellow believers." Witnessing such events would have placed his life in too great a danger.

Dirk escaped a grave danger by his emigration to East Friesland in 1537. In the beginning of 1538 Jan van Batenburg was imprisoned. He was taken to the castle Vilvoorde in Brussels and when he was tortured there on the rack he gave the names of the "principal baptizers." He named David

Joris, Hendrik Krechting, Obbe, and his brother Dirk.[23] Fortunately the arm of the inquisition did not reach across the borders of the country. Obbe had departed beyond the jurisdiction of the Emperor.

But now the congregation of the "quiet Anabaptists" suffered a severe blow. Obbe Philips, who already lived in Rostock and had gathered around him a circle of like-minded persons, had begun to doubt the justification of his mission. He realized that he had erred when he had followed the prophecies and visions of Melchior Hoffman and his followers and, above all, when he let himself be ordained as an elder by the apostles of Jan Matthijs. In his *Confession* he later wrote:[24]

> *We certainly felt the laying on of hands. We certainly also heard all the words, but we neither felt nor heard the Holy Ghost, nor received any power from above, but rather many cunning words which had neither power nor force, as we found out sufficiently afterwards.*

He had certainly not thought so at the time, and only later substituted insight and conviction for the past, but his statement clearly shows what Obbe's objections were when he separated from the Anabaptist congregation. He wrote that he had warned Menno and Dirk and had set forth the reasons which drove him to his conclusion: His commission was unjustified, and he had let himself be dragged along by the fiery preaching of the apostles of Jan Matthijs; he had been deceived.[25] According to the "Successio," using information from the *Confession*, Obbe had invited Menno and Dirk to a meeting, presumably in East Friesland, and had told them about his change of mind. He had also suggested that they do the same.[26] In any case, Obbe had a need to confess his guilt to his colleagues, namely, that he had laid hands on [ordained] them; he certainly wished that they had never wanted or accepted this office. "They might then have done what they wanted, and may as yet do what they will."[27] When Obbe wrote his *Confession* Menno and Dirk were still alive, but Melchior Hoffman had already died in the prison at Strasburg.[28] Hoffman probably died before the end of 1543.[29]

When did Obbe leave? The "List of Elders" states that he had left by 1540: "Then Obbe Philips defected."[30] Burgmann has argued that the separation must have taken place before 1542.[31] Obbe "had committed himself to silence" without actually being banned.[32] The ban was applied to him later, at least before 1554.[33]

How shocked Dirk Philips must have been by his brother's doubts, by his vain attempts to bring his fellow elders over to his own point of view, and finally by the complete separation! After all, Obbe was not only his brother, he had also been his leader. He had ordained Dirk as bishop, and they had struggled together through the difficult times of the disturbances. Dirk had also borne the name of Obbenite with pride. Now he had to choose between the church and his brother. There must have been an inner conflict. But already then Dirk appeared ready to be his own man, holding firmly and not wavering from a decision once taken. "One must abandon everything for Christ Jesus' sake, that is, father, mother, *brothers*, sisters, wife, children ..."[34] This word from his Lord gripped him; he wanted to be obedient to Christ. Inevitably, the decision that Dirk had to make had an influence on his character. The obstinance which characterized him later stemmed from it. Obedience to the word of Scripture had withstood the test.

On September 24, 1540 Count Enno II died in Emden. His widow, Anna van Oldenburg,[35] was a convinced Protestant and became more and more influenced by the Reformed stream. She called Johan à Lasco to be leader of the East Friesland church in 1543. He would look after ecclesiastical affairs from then on, and directed the church with a firm hand.[36] Based on the correspondence between the Reformed preacher Hermannus Aquilomontanus and Heinrich Bullinger, the Antistes at Zurich, it appears that more Anabaptists had settled in Emden and its surroundings than is known to us from other sources.[37] Menno himself lived in Oldersum after 1542 and it is my guess that Dirk Philips must have been close to him.[38] David Joris also lived undercover in East Friesland in 1543, for during that year the written debate with Menno took place,[39] having the fateful consequence that a very large number of Menno's followers transferred to the Davidjorists.[40]

It must have been clear at the court in Brussels that East Friesland had become a refuge for the Anabaptists. In 1543 Maria of Hungary admonished the Countess Anna in two epistles to take severe action against the Rebaptizers.[41] Johan à Lasco, who saw trouble ahead, was more in favour of dialogue and persuasion, following the example of Bucer [in Strasbourg], rather than enforcement and execution. He tried to talk with the Anabaptists. After he had an argument with the followers of David Joris,[42] a debate with Menno followed on January 28 to 31, 1544 in the church of the Franciscan cloister in Emden. Johan à Lasco and Menno only agreed on minor points, but differed about the meaning of the incarnation of Christ, baptism, and the calling of ministers. It seemed to Menno, however, that they parted as friends.[43]

Although I cannot prove it, I suspect that Dirk was present at the discussion. After all, he later accompanied Menno at similar discussions, perhaps functioning as a secretary. Being an expert with the pen and somewhat lettered, he would have been the right person to take notes of the debates. Otherwise, I can scarcely imagine how Menno would have been able to write later about the subjects they discussed.

Shortly thereafter another writing came from Brussels for Countess Anna and her councilors, "a sharp letter" in which they were accused of having offended the divine and imperial majesty. The regentess demanded, in the name of the Emperor, that the heretics be expelled immediately, otherwise they faced severe punishment.[44] The government in East Friesland hastily issued a strong mandate. The zeal of the officials was extremely great, and if à Lasco had not intervened, it would have been a great disaster for the Anabaptists. He persuaded the Countess to let him and his colleagues first examine the suspected persons. Depending upon this examination, they were to be expelled or could remain. Not only did David Joris and the most prominent of his followers deem it safer to flee, Menno Simons and Dirk Philips also thought it better to go elsewhere.[45]

The position of the Countess' government was legally established in the Judgment and Policy Ordinance of 1545.[46] It recommended a careful inspection in the cities, in each village and office, also in the estates of the noblemen. A distinction, however, was made between the "Mennisten" [Mennonites], who had to be examined by the superintendent and were allowed to remain if they accepted instruction from Holy Scripture, and the

Davidjorists and Batenburgers, who were not to be trusted and for whom an examination was useless. These people naturally fled, if they were unable to mislead the local authorities. The Mennonites were tolerated in some places by the authorities, in spite of the threats of the new law. As an explanation for this, the Policy Ordinance was meant in the first place to satisfy the imperial government. Besides, the power of the Countess was limited; she could not impose her will against that of the Council of Emden and the nobility.

IV

Menno and Dirk at the Banks of the Rhine

I have assumed that Dirk Philips stayed in East Friesland close to Menno Simons and that when Menno left for any length of time, Dirk assumed leadership of the Anabaptists. It also seems probable to me that he left East Friesland together with Menno in the Spring of 1544 and accompanied him on his trip to the Rhineland.[1] After the "Succession" describes the defections of Obbe Philips and David Joris, it says that Menno Simons and Dirk Philips "stayed with the others and sowed the seed of madness daily."[2] In other words, the author was convinced that Menno and Dirk stayed together after 1540, which supports my hypothesis. It is clear, however, that after his ordination Dirk always took second place, first in the shadow of his brother Obbe, and then in Menno's. Through his work and his loyalty he was a support to both. Only one time, in the argument with Kükenbieter in Norden, did he assume independence; otherwise he kept himself in the background. He did not dare travel to Groningen, Friesland, and Holland, as Menno did. He avoided the spotlight at all costs. It was as if he felt inferior.

For that reason I cannot agree with the harsh judgment Kühler makes about him. Kühler says that Dirk never was the genius Menno was.[3] And, he writes,

> *In 1539 Menno could follow his own impulses without being influenced by Dirk Philips, but by 1547 Menno's good time, when he only followed his own direction, was over. More and more he came under the influence of his ambitious fellow elder and had to submit to Dirk's stronger will.*[4]

Menno himself, to the contrary, called Dirk "our trusted and very loved brother," and that in 1550.[5]

When Menno and Dirk travelled to the Rhineland, they arrived in a new environment for the first time. East Friesland could still be considered an outpost of Dutch culture and church life. Of course, they were refugees who had left their country on account of their faith, but they could still feel somewhat at home there. They understood the language and had learned to express themselves fairly well in it. As cultured Frisians both were also able to speak Dutch.[6] However, now on the Lower Rhine they lived as exiles, and it was very different from what they were accustomed to.

But there were also positive things. They lived under a mild regime. In Cologne the ruler Herman von Wied decided to push for a reformation in the evangelical spirit in 1543. He had appealed for help from Bucer and Melanchthon. Following Bucer's example, he wanted to have the imprisoned Anabaptists instructed by preachers and, if possible, converted.[7] The situation was also tolerable for the Anabaptists in the lands of Duke Wilhelm V of Julich, Cleve, and Berg. He did, however, have to drop his plans to allow a moderate reform in his lands, along the lines of Erasmus, following his loss in the war with Emperor Charles about the possession of Gelre. He had to proceed cautiously.[8] All the same, he could not prevent acceptance of reform in a city such as Wezel, which enjoyed exceptional freedoms,[9] nor the wishes of the more independent nobility and shires who wanted to oversee church matters themselves.[10] Because of this small Anabaptist circles could exist, and Menno Simons was also in a position to visit congregations on the Maas.[11]

Menno did reside in the diocese of Cologne, but probably not in the city. As far as we know, no Anabaptist congregation existed there. The government kept a strict watch and opposed every evangelical movement.[12] Nevertheless, besides living in the Maas valley, Menno also stayed in the "Niederstift" [an area of Cologne], close to Odenkirchen, and in Kempen. Apparently he had contact there with the local elders Theunis van Jüchen of Sasserath and Michiel Oistwart. He also baptized a mason, Tewes Ruebsam, in Kempen on November 11, 1544. Theunis' confession, which was delivered to the bailiff of the monarch Wilhelm von Rennenberg, was composed entirely in the spirit of Menno.[13]

We don't know where Dirk Philips worked when he stayed with Menno in the Rhineland, because of lack of information. However, my guess is that he lived in the land of Cleve. I can back this hypothesis with three points.

1. An old report tracked down by Rembert, used by him and copied by others, says that "Adam Pastor worked in Goch with great results, so that many upper class people were converted to the new doctrine, especially many members of the guild of wool weavers."[14] Rembert also states that Adam Pastor worked mainly in the land of Cleve.[15] However, this does not agree with the reports known to us,[16] nor with the report of Hamelmann, quoted by Rembert himself.[17] Perhaps we may assume that this report does not refer to Adam Pastor, but to the work of Dirk Philips. After all, he was asked to take leadership in the discussion with Adam,[18] undoubtedly because he was the local or regional elder.

2. Furthermore, Dirk's letter to the "Brethren" about the divinity and humanity of Christ, written between 1547 and 1550, suggests that Dirk stayed in the land of Cleve.[19] The circumstances painted therein, especially the fact that Calvinists and Zwinglians are mentioned, indicate that the Anabaptists were living in an area where they encountered different groups of reform-minded people.[20] This strengthens our guess that Dirk resided in the dukedom of Cleve.

3. The booklet by Dirk Philips, *[Concerning] The New Birth and the New Creature*,[21] was criticized by the Lower Rhine spiritualist Matthijs Wijer, also called Matthes Weyer.[22] This person lived in Wezel, where he died on April 25, 1560 at the age of 39. His brother, Johannes Weyer, from 1550 the doctor of Duke Wilhelm of Cleve, was the well known opponent of witchcraft.[23] Matthes wrote him a letter with the heading, "The difference between repentance and rebirth, according to that booklet by Dirk Philips about the new creature, published in print."[24] From the fact that Matthijs Wijer knew Dirk Philips' booklet and wrote to his brother about it, I conclude that Dirk was known to them. Perhaps they had met him earlier in the land of Cleve; at least they must have heard about him.[25]

I return to the report of the *Succession*, which says that "between the years 1542 and 1547, Menno Simons and Dirk Philips sent out several teachers: Adam Pastor, Henrich van Vreen, Antonius van Cologne, Gielis van Aken, and Frans Reynckcuper."[26] We see immediately that two of these elders came from the Rhineland: Antonius van Cologne[27] and Gillis van Aken.[28] After they were recommended to Menno and Dirk by their congregations as trustworthy leaders, they received the laying on of hands.

In the area of Julich the Dutch elders met other Anabaptists native to that area, and their field of vision expanded. They discovered that the baptizing movement not only had caught on in the north among the evangelicals, but that there was a great movement which extended from Switzerland and South Germany to Moravia. Lambrecht Kremer[29] (Lembgen or Lemke) in Oppergelre and Zillis (Zelis, Zyllis)[30] in the Eifelgebergte, but especially Theunis van Hastenrath were some of the teachers (ministers) in Julich.[31]

Theunis appears to have been an especially zealous man. After the death of the elder Leitgen he accepted the office of teacher and elder,[32] and baptized in Visschersweert in 1545.[33] Later he took part in the discussion at Goch in 1547 and travelled throughout the whole country. He even risked the wilderness of the Eifelgebergte and preached in the marshes, between the mountains, in the bushes, and behind hedges. In 1550 he was interrogated at Gangelt (Amt Millen) by the duke's visitation committee, was imprisoned by the end of January of the following year, and five months later, on June 30, 1551, was burned in Linnich on the Roer.[34]

In 1546 the Catholic opponents of Herman von Wied prevailed, with the result that he was excommunicated, and in February of the following year left his office. Menno did not wait for the outcome, but moved farther to the north. During the years that followed he probably lived in the area of the Hanseatic cities.

Duke Wilhelm of Julich, Cleve, etc., was preoccupied with other business during the years after 1543, so the Anabaptists were able to live fairly undisturbed in his lands. This changed when a new visitation occurred in 1550. The Anabaptists, frightened out of their fairly safe residences, were forced to go to remote areas or move out of the country altogether. If my guess is correct, that Dirk Philips ministered in the region of the Lower Rhine, he must have remained there until about 1550. I will deal with his activities and his first writings in connection with the quarrel about the Trinity, the ban, and shunning.

V

The Struggle to Purify the Church

A: The Break with the Davidjorists

In 1542 the Anabaptist Roelof, who let himself be called Adam, entered the scene with a vigorous attack on the Davidjorists. At the home of Dr. Hieronymus Wilhelmi, treasurer of the city of Groningen, he was able to inspect the *Wonderbook,* and put together twenty-five articles in which he disputed the teaching of David Joris.[1] Among other things the *Wonderbook* said that Jesus was the bodily Christ, and David Joris the spiritual Christ. Pastor's articles were circulated, translated into Latin and French and sent to monarchs and heads of state, specifically to Brussels and Antwerp.[2] David tried to defend himself and pleaded innocence in twenty-five articles.[3] He was not very successful, for the title of the broadside that Adam Pastor distributed to the world was as follows: "These are the Articles of David Jorisz.'s Teaching, etc." It created the impression that it was written by David himself, and because it agreed at certain points with Roman Catholic doctrines—infant baptism, attendance at mass, and the devotion to images—the opponents of David did not even want to read his published defense, the "Great Innocence."[4]

Adam Pastor—he was actually named Roelof Martens and originated from Dorpen in Westphalia[5]—had been a pastor in Aschendorpe. He was an extraordinarily learned and clever theologian. He was more learned than the other elders; even Menno and Dirk were not his equal in debate.[6] After he was ordained an elder in 1542,[7] he travelled tirelessly here and there in Westphalia. Later he evangelized in Gelderland and Overijssel.[8] Before 1550 he seems to have lived in Odenkirchen for some time.[9] The report that Pastor "frequently stays in the vicinity of Julich and in the bishopric of Cologne,"[10] makes me think of his stay in Odenkirchen and surroundings.

Odenkirchen was an estate which belonged to "Kurkoeln" and lay close to the border of Julich.

David Joris already had his hands full warding off attacks from Adam Pastor when shortly thereafter he was engaged in a written debate with Menno Simons. He felt attacked by Menno who, without naming him specifically, warned against him (the new seducer) as well as his ungodly practices.[11] David challenged his opponent with an angry letter which Menno answered in his plain language. Unsparingly, he called David an antichrist, a son of perdition, a false prophet, etc. In conclusion Menno declared that he would not answer any more letters from this apostate. The cunning David then turned to the followers of Menno with a letter (May, 1543), directed particularly to the ministers in East Friesland, where both of them were living. The Anabaptist ministers followed the example of their leader and did not consider the letter worthy of an answer. However, the members of the congregation thought differently. They were influenced by the imposing attitude of David Joris. Perhaps they were enticed by the possibility of escaping persecution by keeping up the appearance of being good [state] church members, even though they were secretly Davidjorists.[12]

Blesdijk tells in a detailed and somewhat ceremonious way how a discussion came about between him and his friends on the one side and Menno with his people on the other. We can read between the lines that Blesdijk, who around 1536 had belonged to the followers of Menno, took the initiative because he and others, who in recent years had transferred to the Davidjorists, were despised as apostates by Menno and his adherents. They asked for and received permission from their master, who already in 1544 had left for Basel and led a luxurious life there under the pseudonym of Johan van Brugge, to invite Menno and his fellow elders to a public discussion. This discussion took place in 1546 on an estate near Lübeck.[13]

Unfortunately the account of this discussion, which was published shortly thereafter, has not been preserved.[14] From the writings of Blesdijk, which appeared in the same year, we can learn who was present in Lübeck and what was discussed.[15] The opponents of Blesdijk were Menno, Dirk, Gillis van Aken, Adam Pastor, and Leenaert Bouwens, although Bouwens had not yet been ordained an elder.[16] The subject of the argument was whether a Christian was allowed to participate in the church worship and infant baptism of Catholics and Protestants, even though he considered these external ceremonies to be wrong. Blesdijk defended the position of David Joris, that what counts is an inner belief and a heart inclined to God. If that is the case—but that is however known only to God and his holy ones—then one is free with regard to external things and one can allow the misuse of the ceremonies. And with regard to infant baptism, Christ did not command the baptism of children, but he also did not forbid it.

Understandably Menno and his fellow workers opposed this view, and the discussion must have been intense. After the general discussion, Blesdijk talked with Gillis in particular another four hours in the presence of Leenaert Bouwens. At least they heard his arguments and Blesdijk answered all the objections, and could have gone on and on.[17] Whether Dirk himself participated in the debate is not known, but Blesdijk does complain about the attitude of Menno and his people. While no one could charge him with any unreasonableness or discourtesy, he said, his opponents treated him in an unfriendly manner.[18]

Adam Pastor continued to fight the Davidjorists in later years. In his *The Difference between True and False Doctrine* he even devoted a whole chapter, the twelfth, to the doctrines of various false brothers: Münsterites, Batenburgers, and above all the Davidjorists.[19]

We notice later in dealing with some of his writings how Dirk Philips received a clear perspective on the dangers of the Davidjorist doctrine through this meeting with Blesdijk.

After Blesdijk had finished the argument with the adherents of Menno—he ended with an important summary of the doctrine of his master[20]—he departed for Basel and was rewarded for his faithful services: David gave him his daughter Tanneke in marriage.[21]

B: Disunity about the ban and avoidance. Pastor impure in doctrine.
The separation from the Davidjorists was scarcely completed when new difficulties emerged. This time it was in the heart of the Anabaptist church. About 1546,[22] probably after the meeting with the Davidjorists at Lübeck,

a difference of opinion arose in the church about several important issues. Here follows Menno's lament:[23]

> *For Christian love and peace have certainly become very weak for the past four years by very shameful arguments and disputes about the undiscoverable ground of the divinity of Christ, and the Holy Spirit, in addition also about angels and devils, about the ban, which among many has become very thin, very weak, as is common when all such disputes hold sway. May the Lord not reckon them as sinful who have started this process.*

I would like to get back to this last point, the ban, which according to Menno had become very "thin," that is, it was not obeyed strictly enough according to the prescriptions of the New Testament. All kinds of questions were raised by the church in connection with the ban: Under which circumstances must it be applied? How far must one go in shunning a banned brother or sister? How should one act if someone who has been excommunicated is found in need?

But there were also other issues which kept them busy, issues of a more dogmatic type, concerning the divinity of Christ, the Trinity, and the Holy Spirit. It was exactly concerning these dogmatic question that Adam Pastor and Frans Reines Kuiper seem to have had a falling out with Menno Simons and Dirk Philips. After they had oral or written arguments about these things, a meeting was planned for Emden in 1547.[24] In addition to the above named elders, present were Hendrik van Vreden, Antonius van Cologne, and Gillis van Aken.[25] Various points were on the agenda according to the *Succession*. In the first place shunning was dealt with, that is, disassociation from all who had been bannned.

In 1541 Menno wanted the ban to apply exclusively to those who had already been separated from the congregation for false doctrine or an immoral walk. He hoped the ban would lead to repentance. He required shunning only so that church members would not be infected by sin and so that they would be motivated to live pure lives.[26] The question was raised at Emden as to whether spouses must avoid each other when one of them had been banned. In the *Succession* it is mistakenly stated that Menno allowed spousal shunning without question.[27] But in the letter of November 12, 1556 to the congregation in Emden, partially quoted by *Succession* at another place, Menno writes[28] that in 1547 Dirk Philips and he had decided with the other elders that one should recommend spousal shunning as "the general rule," that is, as the safe way, but anyone whose conscience could not allow it would not be forced; rather, one had to treat such a person with love. Thus no law was established but each case had to be treated separately according to the circumstances. And the people in Emden would certainly still have remembered what was decided in their city![29]

The second point on the agenda according to Dirk Philips was outside marriages, that is, marriages of church members with unbelievers. Dirk wrote in the preface of his last booklet *About the Marriage of Christians*, compiled on March 7, 1568,

> *We often had difficult and troublesome controversies about this subject during the time of our service, and more than twenty years ago with seven teachers and ministers came to a unanimous decision on the basis of God's Word. Our present judgment still stands, which by God's grace we hope to explain further here.*[30]

Here Dirk almost certainly alludes to the meeting in Emden in 1547, but the question is whether or not he was in error. Perhaps his memory played tricks on him and it was not in Emden but in Wismar, for there also seven elders spoke in an assembly about marriages outside the church.[31] Or, if this issue was on the table at the Emden conference, perhaps Dirk's views elicited no response from the other elders, for the subject was not recorded in the minutes.

On the other hand, the last point, the incarnation of Christ, was treated extensively. "Menno fought powerfully against the (usual church) doctrine of the incarnation," as it was put forth by Adam Pastor and Frans Reines Kuiper.[32] It is known that Menno and indeed also Dirk Philips followed the doctrine of Melchior Hoffman regarding the incarnation of Christ.[33] Menno in particular laboured over this doctrine in debate with Protestant theologians. Jesus, the eternal son of God, entered time and became a man. Central for Menno is the word of John (1:14): The Word has *become* flesh. The Word took no flesh from a human mother, but became human in Mary by God's creating power, changed into human flesh. It had to be this way because otherwise Christ could not guarantee complete grace and deliverance. Still, Christ was a completely human person, the invisible having become visible. What had been beyond suffering, now was capable of suffering.[34]

Adam Pastor opposed this doctrine. In his *The Difference between True and False Doctrine* he devoted a separate chapter to the incarnation of Jesus Christ.[35] According to him, "the Word became flesh" did not mean that the Word was changed into flesh, but that the Word came into being; it revealed itself. This took place by the power of the Almighty and not by the power and work of a man. And so Jesus received his body from Mary and was correctly called the fruit of her womb. Therefore, Jesus was begotten by the Holy Spirit or by the power of God or by God's Word. Consequently he received more than the flesh of Adam. He also had the Word of God, the divine nature in his innermost being, and he demonstrated this by a sinless life. To the objection that the sinful flesh of Adam is unable to redeem human sin, Pastor answered that Christ himself did not sin. And what the sinful flesh of Adam was not able to do, the sinless Word and the divine nature in him were able to accomplish.[36]

These concepts must have seemed untrue to Menno and Dirk. After all, it appeared that Adam Pastor did not believe in the divinity of Christ and that according to him the Holy Spirit was none other than a power of God, not the third person of the Godhead.[37] This is what Adam Pastor alluded to in the beginning of *The Disputation Concerning the Divinity of the Father, the Son, and the Holy Ghost* when he wrote, "I still confess now what I confessed five years ago in Friesland."[38] The disputation took place in Lübeck in 1552. Thus the divinity of Christ and the Holy Spirit must already have been dealt with in Emden and not, as the *Succession* had it, only in Goch.[39] And so it is easier to understand that Menno beseeched Adam Pastor on behalf of the unity of the brotherhood not to speak in public about these quarrels.[40]

C: Adam Pastor banned as a heretic.

The danger that threatened the church was so great, namely, that it might be infected by the heresy of Adam Pastor, that the final decision could not be postponed. Therefore an assembly was held in the same year (1547) in Goch.[41] Since Adam Pastor appeared as the accused in the case, Theunis van Hastenrath sat on the board of elders to make a full seven.[42] He acted as the representative of the Anabaptists from the land of Julich, while Dirk Philips, from the land of Cleve, was the representative from that district.[43] Dirk was appointed leader of the meeting. Apparently a report of the disputation was prepared. It may not have been printed, and has been lost.[44]

If we want to know what was discussed at the conference, then we must use the quotations from "de disputatie met Dirk Philips" ["the disputation with Dirk Philips"] which Gerardus Nicolai provided, keeping in mind that Nicolai wrote as a fierce opponent of Adam Pastor. [According to Nicolai,] Adam denied the true divinity of Christ and said he was only "a pure person from Mary."[45] He also kept repeating a phrase many times: Jesus said, again Jesus said, etc., to diminish our saviour Jesus Christ. Further, Jesus Christ is in no other way God, than God's hand, God's finger, God's voice, yea, only a characteristic of God. He is God's spoken Word which became flesh and after that was called the Son of God.

From this it follows that Pastor, when he called Christ God's Word, by no means meant to say that Jesus Christ was with the Father eternally, another person equal to the Father. And when it was argued that Paul calls Christ the splendour of God's glory and the exact image of his being (Hebrews 1:3), then Adam and his followers answered that man was also called an image of God (Gen. 1:26) and is indeed not essentially God. Consequently Christ, because he bears the title of exact image of God, is not essentially God. To compare man and God's son as equals is, according to Nicolai, blasphemy.[46]

When Nicolai says that Scripture teaches us to worship Christ as our saviour, indeed that all the angels of God shall worship him (Heb. 1:6), it is likely that this argument was also brought up in Goch, for Nicolai quotes the following answer of Pastor from the *Disputation*: Worship only means to show respect and to bow the knees. Hebrews 1:6 is borrowed from Psalm 95:6[47] and does not mean anything else but to bow before Christ and to fall down before him. And with regard to the word saviour, *God* is our saviour (I Tim. 1:1; 2:3). It was not difficult for Nicolai to show with many Bible texts that the Father must be honored in the Son and that Christ was called saviour by the apostles and was considered equal to God.[48] Presumably Dirk Philips also had a sharp reply for his opponent.

In conclusion Nicolai quoted some sentences from the *Disputation with Dirk Philips*, which were either read or copied incorrectly: The spoken Word was changed into flesh,[49] therefore the humanity of Christ is God's Word and called Son of God only after his birth from Mary. In connection with this Adam said to Dirk: "If you thus separate the humanity of Christ as if it does not belong to the Godhead, or is not God's Word, you destroy your own basis for the incarnation of Jesus." In this same context, another statement is even clearer: "The Word that became flesh" became less rather than more important; indeed, [the Word] became flesh of a person.[50] Understandably such concepts encountered heavy opposition.

Dirk and Adam disputed long and hard, accompanied by their supporters, but they could not reach an agreement. The result was that Adam, who held firmly to his false doctrine and found backing among many listeners, was cut off by the old Baptizers along with his followers, banned as a heretic, and surrendered to damnation.[51]

Who pronounced the ban on Adam Pastor? The *Succession* claims that Dirk Philips did it.[52] Most of the early Dutch historians accepted this report and for that reason, painted Dirk in a very unfavorable light.[53]

I will once again try to demonstrate that Dirk Philips was unjustly accused of "serious rashness," and even "intolerable arrogance."[54] Certainly some meetings between the elders preceded the pronouncement of the ban and Menno, the acknowledged leader of God's church, must have participated actively in them. Then the assignment was given to Dirk, as chairman of the debate and as leader of the opposition, to enforce the separation. This would explain why Nicolai wrote, "Adam Pastor with all

The Church 37

his followers (was) banned by the early Anabaptists and condemned [as a heretic]."[55]

We now consider what Pastor himself wrote about the punishment. He attributes the primary blame to Menno.[56] He considered the ban unjust for the reasons listed in the letter of the ban,[57] as well as for the manner in which the banning occurred. One of the reasons mentioned was that Adam was of the opinion that the Father alone is truly God and that Jesus Christ is the one whom he has sent (John 17:3). Adam was convinced that by this confession he would enter into eternal life and not death.[58] In the letter of the ban his opponents quoted Philippians 2:6ff.: "Christ Jesus, though he was in the form of God, did not regard equality with God [as something to be exploited]," which Adam explained as follows:[59]

> *The form of God signifies nothing more than the figure or image of God. He did not put aside this form of God, but he did not consider it exploitation to be equal to God, that is to say, to be in the likeness of God upon earth. And yet He served, although he was the Lord and Master. Thereby he demonstrated his humility: he was in the likeness of man, in the form of man, yes in the likeness of the flesh of sin.*[60]

Menno and the others emphasized John 1:1 again and again: In the beginning was the Word, and the Word was with God, and the Word was God. Adam, however, insisted that this did not point to the preexistence of Christ, but that it was a spoken word of God just like the words of creation, "but I was banned for it."[61] If he was banned for belief in God the Father, and in Jesus Christ who was called the Son of God, then God, Christ, and the Apostles would still accept him.[62]

But Pastor also rejected the way in which the ban was applied against him. He believed that insufficient attention had been given to his objections. They should have debated longer, and if they were unable to come to any conclusion this time, the debate should have proceeded at another time. "Banning is no proof,"[63] he said. The point is that one "wins over" the other, that is, convinces the other with reason. And should this appear impossible, then the differences should be subjected to the judgment of the congregations.[64] He regarded the congregations sensible enough to pronounce a judgment on the matter.[65] Menno, however, did not want to dispute any longer and contended that this was not the custom in Christ's church. But that was an evasion, said Pastor. By saying this, Menno only wanted to reach an agreement regarding the letter of ban that already had been issued. Adam pointed to the consequences of such a practice: Whoever decides to ban rashly and quickly will stay in the congregation; but whoever is conscientious and thinks carefully about what a severe punishment the ban is, will be cut off.[66] This was a prophetic word, if we pay attention to the banning quarrels later on!

As previously shown, Dirk Philips alone cannot be held responsible for the banning sentence imposed upon Adam Pastor. We have to take this as a decision of the assembled elders, in whose name Dirk pronounced the sentence.

Finally we may consider the quote from the *Admonishing Confession about the Threefold, Eternal and True God, Father, Son and Holy Spirit*, written by Menno Simons in 1550: "May the Lord not account it as sin to those who have carried out the ban."[67] De Hoop Scheffer used this phrase as a weapon against Dirk Philips. He concluded that Menno rejected responsibility for the ban against Adam Pastor, and distanced himself from the strict regulation of his fellow elder, although he consented to it.[68]

By comparing the two existing manuscripts of Menno's treatise with the printed edition known to us, I have become convinced that the manuscripts have the better text. They were written in a dialect colored by Lower Saxon, whereas the text of the print has been adapted to the Dutch. The manuscripts read,[69] "The Lord not count as sinful those who have exercised the ban" (Hamburg) and "The Lord forgive them who have brought about the ban" (Amsterdam).[70] I believe I am justified in holding this latter text as the original, and can say on that basis that Menno condemns those who advocated the false doctrine about the Trinity, but he also offers them God's forgiveness.

Finally I have a quarrel with the opinion of De Hoop Scheffer, who denies that anyone was banned in the earliest Anabaptist congregations because of heretical doctrines.[71] Menno says explicitly in the *Loving Admonition* of 1541 that the ban must be applied to those who, whether through false doctrine or by leading a vain and carnal life, already have placed themselves outside of the fellowship of the saints.[72] Münsterites and Batenburgers, but also David Joris and Obbe Philips, were banned because of false doctrines. The ban used against Adam Pastor was not an exception, as De Hoop Scheffer suggests.[73] In *A Clear Response to an Article of Gelius Faber* (1554) Menno wrote, "if we had had little regard for the divine ordinance of the ban how loud they would have shouted that we were all revolutionaries and Arians."[74]

Two years later (1549) Menno put another elder under the ban: Frans Reines Kuiper, who in Emden in 1547 had turned against Menno's doctrine of incarnation and who then leaned toward the Catholic faith. In 1554 he received a pardon from M. Hippolytus Persijn, president of the court of Friesland, after he had disavowed Menno's doctrine.[75]

Two other elders, Hendrik van Vreden and Antonius van Cologne, had already separated from Menno in 1550 "as Kuiper declared in his confession."[76]

Even though banned, Adam Pastor remained active as an elder with preaching, baptizing, and administering the Lord's Supper.[77] In 1550 he went from Odenkirchen to Well on the Maas (at that time in Gelder territory), where he was under the protection of the lords from Vlodorp.[78] The question of whether he had many followers is debated. Nicolai only says that he won over many followers at the debate in Goch and that his disciples were also banned.[79] In the *Succession,* on the other hand, it says picturesquely, "he persisted with teaching as a foul water that was poured out and ran so long until with time it disappeared."[80]

Menno felt compelled to warn the church against Adam Pastor and his false doctrine and therefore composed the *Confession of the Triune God* in which he did not name Adam, but lamented in the preface that they had disputed, argued, and sighed long enough. At the end he admonished the members to "permit no glosses, no new theories, nor expositions of any persons, *whoever they may be*. . ."[81] In the postscript he mentioned the possibility that Adam Pastor's apostles might come north to propagate Adam's ideas.[82]

Dirk Philips combatted Adam Pastor's doctrine by composing a song of twenty-two verses[83] in which he assembled texts from the Old and New Testaments relating to the divinity and humanity of Christ.[84] In my opinion the song has no poetic value, but Dirk thought it would be useful in convincing simple people in the congregation about the importance of a good biblical understanding of the nature of Christ.

VI

The Earliest Writings of Dirk Philips

The first fruits of Dirk's pen are preserved only in manuscripts. They are the "Letter to some Brethren about the Divinity and Humanity of Jesus Christ,"[1] and the "Confession concerning Separation" [*Bekentenisse van de afzondering*].[2]

The conference in Emden and the debate in Goch, both in 1547, continued to cause unrest. People were very worried, especially in the land of Cleve. The issues raised by Adam Pastor's different views were vigorously discussed in the various Anabaptist circles. The evangelicals, that is, people who had founded small congregations in different places on the Lower Rhine, were also troubled by these questions. Dirk called them Calvinists or Zwinglians. By Calvinists he probably meant the refugees from the Waal, who had located in Wezel in 1545.[3] Dirk viewed as Zwinglians the representatives of an evangelical persuasion who were favoured by the chancellor of Cleve, Dr. Olieslager, who was more a follower of Erasmus than of Luther.[4]

Between 1547 and 1550 a disputation took place concerning the divinity and incarnation of Christ. The Calvinists attacked the followers of Menno and Dirk because they suspected them, as well as Adam Pastor, of being impure in the doctrine of the divinity and humanity of Christ. The Anabaptists were assisted by the well-known Antonius van Cologne, and by a certain Govert who, however, died shortly afterward. Something extraordinary happened. The brethren were of course no match for the scholarly knowledge and skill in debate of their opponents. But their teachers, on whose support they had counted, sided with the opposition and corrected their confession, probably concerning the doctrine of the incarnation. And so the defense of the brethren was weakened. A little later they directed a letter to Antonius in which they made an appeal to Dirk Philips, who had received some notoriety by his opposition to Adam Pastor. To pacify the brethren Antonius sent the letter to Dirk with the request that Dirk answer it. He apparently did not want to have his fingers burned.[5]

In his answer, Dirk gave the brothers a concise confession concerning the divinity and humanity of Christ. He did this by placing in the center the true divinity and the true humanity of Christ in accordance with the old Christian confessions,[6] heavily emphasizing the eternal generation of the Son.[7] With regard to the incarnation of Christ he confessed as he and Menno had already done at Goch,[8] that Christ had appeared in time, pure and sinless, conceived by the Holy Spirit, born of the Virgin Mary, not receiving his body from her. Thus he is God and God's son, *propius, unigenitus et primo genitus* [truly God, the only begotten and first born];[9] but being born in time as a person, he is a holy person, the Son of God and of humanity. One must take care to differentiate when speaking of the divinity and humanity of Christ. The Word became flesh and nonetheless remained the Word of life, true wisdom, truth and eternal life.[10] Although Christ originated with God entirely and fully, one should not confuse him with God himself. For God has no beginning and no end, but Christ as a person came to be in time; God prepared him a body.[11] Still the entire fullness of God dwells in him,[12] and God was in Christ reconciling the world to himself.[13]

Dirk would gladly have written more extensively about this important issue, but he lacked the time. He promised his readers to do that later, God permitting. He kept that promise, although not as soon as one would have expected. In the so-called *Faith Book*[14] and later in the treatises *[Concerning] the Incarnation of our Lord Jesus Christ* and *Concerning the True Knowledge of Jesus Christ*[15] he dealt with the divinity and humanity of Christ. The first printing of the *Faith Book* appeared in 1557.[16] Perhaps it had already been composed before that time because a copy in Lower Saxon exists that reproduces an obviously older text.[17] But I doubt that the two other writings circulated in the church as "written booklets" before they were printed.[18]

Another set of issues originating from the meeting in Emden in 1547 is mentioned in the second writing by Dirk Philip, unpublished but certainly known to Anabaptist historians,[19] "A Confession about Separation Briefly Summarized, How Far I Shall or Should Avoid the Apostate." On the basis of the signature, "D. P., your brother and fellow servant in the Lord" we see that it is a report for an assembly of the elders. Where and when such a conference was held we do not know. Only the fact that Menno's "Some Questions"[20] agrees with points 3-7 of this writing by Dirk Philips, and that Menno clearly refers to it,[21] makes us certain that the treatise from Dirk must have been composed in 1549 or earlier.

That Menno wrote the "Clear Account of Excommunication" in 1549 is supported not only by Nicolai,[22] but Menno says so himself in the *Instruction Concerning [Apostolic] Excommunication* of 1558: "Around the year [15]49 I wrote about the same thing in a booklet," namely that for each matter of discipline three admonitions have to be given prior to the ban.[23]

On the basis of these writings it appears that the greatest of difficulties arose from the application of the ban–who deserves the ban?– and especially concerning shunning–how far should it extend? Should spousal shunning also be required? Was all this caused by a curiosity for theological problems among lay people, or by renewed study of the Bible, in which members of the congregation were encouraged to inform themselves?

The elders were inundated with countless questions[24] and Menno complained that "for several years very difficult splits and quarrels occurred on account of the ban, by which Christian love suffered a great set back and still suffers."[25] Dirk also found that sometimes remarkable evasions were used and foolish questions were raised.[26] He dealt with points which, as reported, Menno also addressed. Dirk was more concise, and in general he was more strict with regard to shunning, although in some instances he left room for maintaining some contact with a banned member of the congregation. He tried to show "the safe and trodden path."

1. He rejected eating with an apostate, although he granted that it could happen on occasion in an inn.

2. Dirk deemed it to be wrong to conduct business with an apostate even if it took place through the intervention of a third party. It is better to forego any selling and buying and to give no cause for vexation.[27]

3. On the question of whether to greet banned persons, Dirk held fast to 2 John 10 and 11 ["do not greet him"], and did not allow that the intention of the passage was simply not to receive such persons or to welcome them with the kiss of peace. The ban was instituted by God for the recovery of apostates. Therefore, shaming such persons and honouring them with a greeting are complete opposites. Dirk admits that it would be a sign of freedom not to withhold the greeting from a banned person, but according to the example of Paul, a Christian must refrain from freedom in order not to give any offence to a weaker member.[28]

4. The question of spousal shunning was fundamental in Dirk's position regarding the ban. Because the ban is a general command of the Lord, and because "God is no respecter of persons," shunning must be applied to all human relationships, including marriage and the family circle. After all, judgment on the apostate is given by the entire congregation, and the wife or the husband, the father and mother or the child are all involved.[29] Therefore the innocent partner must honour the sentence and shun the banned person. It is done in the best interest of the shunned person. But Dirk does allow exceptions within the context of the Emden resolutions (1547). One ought to take account of the reasons for the banning, the nature of the apostate, and the nature of the saintly ones. One must also consider the weak consciences and ask the Lord that they might come to a clearer insight through his Holy Spirit.[30]

5. May one help an apostate who is in trouble? This was the most extensive answer in the entire treatise, probably because Dirk wanted to forestall all kinds of unnecessary and foolish objections. The believer may not neglect the ministry of compassion if the apostate encounters difficulties. Mercy must be shown to the poor and miserable of this world.[31] And in the case that one encounters an apostate who needs help, then after serious prayer one must do what one's heart says and not be concerned with the criticisms of others.[32]

In the last two sections of his essay Dirk addresses several issues which do not deal directly with the ban but which are of interest from an historical point of view.

6. The word *heilig* [holy or saint] may not be added to the names of the apostles, prophets, and other servants of God, as is the custom of the Roman Catholic Church. One should follow the example of Jesus Christ himself and the Bible, which is that one uses common names.[33] Dirk did not wish to dispute about it with anyone. It is strictly forbidden to call churches and images holy, and inns may not bear the name of the Holy Spirit.

7. One may not indicate the days of the week with heathen names (Monday, Tuesday, etc.), but following Holy Scripture call them the first day, the second day, etc.[34] Dirk finds here nothing to discuss: The Bible has forbidden it. A Christian must obey or suffer a bad conscience.

It is easily understandable that the earliest writings of Dirk Philips were not printed. They were written for a particular situation, and furthermore, Dirk himself felt that the style and the ideas left something to be desired. Later on he showed that he was a good writer and had insightful ideas, but he had yet to study and practice writing religious articles.

VII

Study, Travel, and Conferences at Lübeck and Wismar

It is impossible to determine a fixed residence for Dirk Philips during the years 1550-1554. Kühler guesses that Dirk already had his headquarters in Danzig about 1550, a supposition which is not supported by any data.[1] What Mannhardt wrote about a stay of Dirk Philips in Danzig also does not rest on facts. He guesses that Menno was in Prussia several times, either alone or accompanied by Dirk Philips and Hans Sikken, between 1547 and 1552.[2] Menno declared in the debate with Martin Micron in Wismar in 1554 that "No one except I alone baptized in these eastern cities."[3] This does not exclude the possibility that Dirk accompanied him on trips to the east, but there is not a single report about it.

I hazard another guess, that Dirk stayed in Emden and its surroundings after he fled the land of Cleve. It might seem that this was too dangerous, because of the count's edict of 1549 forbidding Anabaptists of any persuasion to stay in East Friesland.[4] The edict served in the first place to justify the count's government before the Emperor. It appears that the edict was not strictly enforced.[5] The nobility, who were partially favourable toward the Anabaptists, opposed it and the Emden city government also offered resistance. Therefore Menno could go there and have a discussion with Frans Cuiper in 1549 to prevent his apostasy.[6] And Dirk could also have settled in Emden or in the surrounding area. His intention appears to have been to devote himself to quiet study. He made no trips to his homeland. He also did not function as elder and leader of the Emden congregation, although he would certainly have maintained contact. It is really remarkable that we seldom or never hear of *"aankomelingen"* [new members] to whom Dirk administered baptism, at least during Menno's life. Only after Menno's death are several mentioned. Apparently Dirk left baptizing to the other elders.

In fact there was another person doing the practical work in the Emden congregation, a Leenaert Bouwens of Sommelsdijk.[7] He was born in Overflakkee, South Holland, in 1515 and in his early years was a member of an oratorical group. He had learned to be a good speaker, but he also had the need to play a role and he kept a gracious table. He was the most successful of all the travelling preachers and brought more than ten thousand Anabaptists into the church. We do not know when he joined the Anabaptists, only that he used his gifts already very early and took part in the debate in Lübeck with Blesdijk in 1546. He lived at 't Falder in the neighborhood of Emden.[8] In 1551 the congregation in Emden, together with the Groningen and Frisian congregations, wanted him ordained as elder.[9] It was probably someone other than Menno who laid hands on Leenaert, perhaps Dirk Philips. In the letter to Leenaert's wife, who feared for the life of her husband and made an appeal to Menno to revoke the ordination, Menno said that not he, but the congregation without his foreknowledge had called Leenaert to this office, and that Leenaert, apparently driven by his conscience, had accepted the call. How then could he (Menno) advise against it and oppose it![10]

Leenaert immediately went to work with zeal. In the first period, from May 1551 to 1554, he visited Anabaptist circles in East Friesland, Groningen, and Friesland. He likely travelled mostly by boat in order to get from one place to another. He repeatedly baptized in Appingedam during this period, demonstrating that Dirk Philips had withdrawn from his office as bishop. He baptized in many Frisian congregations, showing that Menno lived far from Friesland at that time. In fact Menno was hiding in the Hanseatic cities on the East Sea at that time.

If my assumption is correct, that Dirk lived in Emden in 1550 and the following years, then it was probably there that he first came into contact with the Flemish Anabaptists. The martyr Hans van Overdam, who was imprisoned in Ghent and burned at the stake on July 9, 1551[11] wrote at the end of his confession, "I pray that you, through the brotherly love which you have for me, send this letter to Friesland, namely to Emden land" and a few lines further: "When this letter is read, send it on to Antwerp, so that it can be sent to the congregation at Emden."[12] When a severe persecution broke upon the congregations of South Flanders around 1550, many fled north to Emden, among other places.[13] Claes de Praet, taken prisoner in Ghent and put on trial there in 1556, was baptized in Antwerp in 1552. He probably fled shortly after that, to "Emden Land" in fact, where he remained a long time working as a merchant. There must have been quite a few Ghent citizens with whom he associated.[14] And so in those years Dirk had the opportunity to get to know the Flemish Anabaptists. It appears that he appreciated them and that they trusted him too.

In 1552 Dirk was invited to participate in a gathering of elders with Adam Pastor at Lübeck. Adam was not at peace with the ban pronounced against him at Goch in 1547. He viewed the ban as an unjustified act because he had not been given enough opportunity to defend and justify himself. He was shunned by the brothers and this hurt him.[15] Therefore he tried again and again to make contact with Menno and requested a new meeting. He appealed to Menno's writings in which Menno challenged his opponents to dispute with him.[16] He held Menno to his word; Menno had written him that the eternal wisdom of God would judge all human words.[17]

Although Menno initially refused this request,[18] he finally gave in. A meeting was planned for Lübeck, probably because Menno had found a refuge there. Adam later published a report of this debate:[19] "A Disputation Concerning the Divinity of the Father, of the Son and the Holy Spirit."[20] This publication is, of course, not a word for word report. Some time later, perhaps with the help of notes made by Adam's "relatives,"[21] it was reconstructed and began with an explanation "Concerning the cause of this disputation."[22] Then follows the account of the debate in which the opponents take turns introducing new subjects and so lead the debate further. The opponents were only indicated with letters: M[enno], D[irk Philips], G[illis van Aken], E[bbink],[23] B[ouwens]. A letter "B" was written before the name of the first four speakers. According to Cramer this stands for Bishop, which seems probable to me.[24] It was mostly Menno who had objections to remarks by Pastor.[25] Dirk had only a few objections, demonstrating his biblical knowledge and quick wit, but they were immediately countered by Adam with proofs from the Bible.[26] Pastor handled the issues of the divinity and the humanity of Christ and of the Holy Spirit in the same manner as he had in Emden and Goch.[27] I will give attention to one single point: the doctrine of the Trinity. This was nowhere explicitly mentioned. At least the word "Trinity" [*Drieëenheid*] is missing where the matter itself was certainly touched upon. Adam asked,

> Where do we find written "Almighty Son" and "Almighty Holy Spirit?" And that they are not three Almighty Beings? And that the three are one Almighty God? And further, where is it written that three persons are one being?[28]

Also when it came to baptism in the name of the Father, the Son, and the Holy Spirit, the opponents agreed that these names signify three separate beings, but they did not say that these three were one. Pastor, on the contrary, certainly believed that the Father is an independent being, and also the Son; however he thought that the Holy Spirit was no independent or personal being, but only a breath or inspiration of God.[29] Because Pastor did not accept the divinity of Christ and denied that the Holy Spirit was an independent being, he could never assent to the doctrine of the Trinity.[30] For this reason he can correctly be called antitrinitarian, although I would rather use the term "unitarian" to describe him.

From Adam Pastor's writing we can conclude that the debate at Lübeck ended without a reconciliation. Both parties kept their original positions and the separation was final.

I already mentioned several treatises in which Dirk contended against the doctrine of Adam Pastor without using his name.[31] "The members of the brotherhood avoided anything that would make them suspect of heresies such as the denial of the Trinity."[32]

I have found some more accusations which may have been aimed at Pastor. In the foreword to *[Concerning] the Incarnation of our Lord Jesus Christ* Dirk wrote,

> *We would like to briefly record our faith in Christ Jesus, the only begotten Son of the living God, so that anyone can see, read, or hear that we belong to Christ Jesus and believe in his divinity and humanity; namely, that we are neither heretics nor Jews (even though the world calls us heretics and Jews) but are simply Christians and confess all that Scripture teaches and declares concerning Christ Jesus.*[33]

At the end of this writing Dirk says, "Whoever does not confess the eternal divinity and the true humanity of Jesus Christ is an antichrist."[34] And finally, in *Concerning the True Knowledge of Jesus Christ*, Dirk states in the introduction,

> *These are the perilous times of which Christ and the apostles prophesied, namely, that many false Christians will arise and lead many astray . . . Because I see and hear that there are many who undertake to belittle Christ Jesus—the one denies his true divinity, the other does not confess his true incarnation in accord with Scripture, a third rejects his blessed teaching—therefore the love of my Lord and Master Jesus Christ compels me to record my confession.*[35]

At the conference in Lübeck, or shortly thereafter, Gillis van Aken was suspended as elder because he had committed adultery with female Anabaptists. Dirk Philips took part in the decision.[36]

The sad experiences of those years gave Menno cause to complain in his letter to Leenaert Bouwen's wife:

> *The spiritual fathers have become betrayers of our souls; the watchmen, blind leaders; and the shepherds, wolves. The walls of Jerusalem have tumbled down; the stones of the sanctuary are trampled underfoot at the corners of every street. [. . .] Our inmost souls are grieved at the need of our brethren, especially when we see the great*

hunger and thirst of many sincere hearts, the accursed seduction by the false prophets and the destroying sects and similar woeful destruction.[37]

With these pitiful words Menno depicts the situation of the brotherhood about 1552.[38] He probably is referring to the final separation from Adam Pastor and the suspension of Gillis. Perhaps he also was thinking of the unceasing propaganda from the Davidjorists and of the attack by Gellius Faber in his booklet, *A Reply of Gellius Faber to a Very Acrimonious Letter of the Anabaptists*, that had just appeared in Magdenburg in 1552.[39]

In 1554 Gillis was restored to his office as elder. Menno, Dirk and the principal elders gathered in Mecklenburg "at a secret place" and dealt with the matter about Gillis. When he confessed his guilt and promised to turn over a new leaf, they forgave him and accepted him again as a brother.[40]

I place this assembly of the elders in the spring of 1554 after the disputation between Menno and Martin Micron, and after Menno and his followers, as well as the Reformed, found it necessary to leave the city of Wismar because of the mandate of February 18.[41] Apparently the elders returned later to Wismar secretly, and held the well-known conference. According to an old report,[42] seven elders gathered there to discuss several important issues. Present, among others, were Menno, Dirk, Leenaert, and Gillis. I cannot say with certainty who the other elders were.[43] The discussions resulted in nine articles.[44]

The limits set in the articles are unclear here and there, a consequence of the difficulty of finding adequate formulae which all those attending could affirm, given the differences in their thinking.[45]

Which articles would Dirk Philips have emphasized? I think immediately of the first article that deals with "outside" marriages, that is, concerning marriages between a member of the congregation and someone of another faith. This was a subject that was important for Dirk, for he wrote in *About the Marriage of Christians*[46] that he had spoken about it many times (in the congregations), had testified to it in the assembly (of elders) and also had written about it many years before.[47] He wrote that during the time of his service he had had much quarreling and trouble about "outside" marriages. He had unanimously agreed with seven ministers more than twenty years before on the basis of God's Word,[48] and "presently our judgment still is . . ."[49] He likely was referring to the conference of Wismar.

Kühler thinks that "outside marriages" must have happened only sporadically,[50] and Wessel only refers to one place during the time before 1554 where Menno warns against marriages with unbelievers in the same spirit as Dirk does later in the *Restitution*.[51] In any case, at Wismar they debated about "outside marriages" and a compromise was reached: Outside marriages must be punished with the ban and shunning until the banned party was proven to be leading a Christian life. In that case, the members were free to stop shunning him/her and to receive the member back into the congregation. After the members had observed the situation for a time, after a time of testing so to speak, re-acceptance could follow, even if the unbelieving spouse did not join the congregation.[52]

Dirk's influence is also apparent in the second article, for in paragraph two of his "Confession about Separation" he demanded that any business with a fallen member must be avoided, while Menno sounded more accommodating and only forbade the "companionship" which would result from it.[53] In any case, in the second article it was determined that doing business with a "fallen one" is sin, unless that person is in need.

Menno's milder view triumphed in the third article. It was the view already set forth at Emden (1547).[54] In Menno's letter (December 15, 1558) "to some brothers ... reporting about separation among married couples,"[55] he makes mention of a former decision of the elders (Emden 1547) and made again "in part" "by our dear b[rothers] Dir[k] Ph[ilips], Le[enaert] Bou[wens] and us" in the presence of many elders, in which we were advised to act cautiously with shunning in marriage and to consider weak consciences. Naturally this pointed to the decision of Wismar. In article three it was further determined that one must examine carefully whether the opposition to shunning in marriage stemed from conscience or from the flesh; that would soon become clear. Also the possibility was considered that should the spouse of a "fallen one" want to be admitted to the congregation, then one should act according to the combined articles 1 and 3.

I can be brief about the other articles from Wismar because they do not relate directly to what Dirk taught and strove for in particular. I only point out that divorce was allowed only when the banned partner had committed adultery. Otherwise the innocent one was obliged to live as a single person. In the same spirit Dirk wrote later in his "Omitted Writing about the Ban and Avoidance"[56] that Christ had commanded that adultery should be the only reason for divorce. Believers do not act against this command of Christ, however, when on the basis of the ban they separate from their husband (or wife). For this separation does not happen in order to take another in marriage, but rather in prayer for the gift of abstinence they wait until the banned one repents and can be taken back into the congregation.[57]

The articles from Wismar show us that the congregation had already received some insight as to what to do about excommunicated members. If a member of the congregation were married to an unbeliever and the latter commited adultery, showed no repentance, and persisted in the sin, then the innocent person was free to remarry "except that they shall take the advice and decision of the congregation." If an unbeliever wanted to divorce a member of the congregation because of his or her faith, then the believer must remain unmarried. However, if the unbeliever remarried or engaged in an adulterous relationship, then the believer might also remarry "by counsel of the elders of the congregation."

No sharp distinction was made at Wismar between the congregation and the elder. Now the one, then the other was to have authority over the moral behavior of the members of the congregation.

Article nine is even less precise in definition: "No one may travel on his own accord from congregation to congregation to act as a preacher unless he is delegated by his own congregation or by an elder."[58] So here we find the identical principle that applied to the "free ministry" of Leenaert Bouwens in 1565 and was decided upon by the ministers and elders in that year.[59] Then followed a time of transition. But congregations and elders were of almost equal importance in Wismar.

It seems possible to me that in Wismar, Dirk came into direct or indirect contact with his brother Obbe, who was occupied there as a "barber" (Master Albrecht) and was expelled from that city fourteen days after Easter in 1554. Obbe probably belonged to a small group of Anabaptists who were banned by Menno because they listened to Lutheran preachers.[60]

Menno used the interval at Wismar in the winter of 1553-1554 to answer his fellow countryman Gellius Faber in response to his diatribe which appeared in 1552.[61] Menno replied in a voluminous book that came from the press in the spring of 1554 in Lübeck.[62] Gellius had challenged Menno on the fact that the Anabaptists were not united but had split in many directions. "The one is Mennonist, the other Adam Pas[tor], the third Obbist, the fourth Dirkist, etc." Menno responded, "We are not so divided as he proposes, for Dir[k] and we are entirely one [and] hope by God's grace that we shall remain one into eternity."[63]

VIII

Dirk Philips' First Treatises Printed
(The Tabernacle of Moses and the Book of Faith)

Menno had hoped to be of one mind with his friend and fellow worker Dirk "eternally." Kühler believes he can sense a change in Menno around 1554. "The softness and tenderness disappeared to make place for something hard and self-righteous." He finds the key to this change in the just mentioned writings of Menno against Gellius Faber.[1] This Dutch Mennonite historian means to say that Menno became increasingly influenced by his fellow elder, and bowed before his strong will.[2] Is this idea fair? I think it is a biased view. We have seen that Dirk was in Menno's shadow until Wismar. He was never prominent, not even in Goch where all he did was carry out the decision of the gathering of elders. In addition, Dirk gave way to Menno concerning the leadership of the churches and travel to distant areas. Although he may have visited the Prussian churches before 1549 in the company of Menno–which seems improbable to me–he must have left the administration of baptism to Menno.[3] Certainly Menno often sought Dirk's advice and appreciated it. But at the conference of Wismar, Menno definitely held the leadership and mediated between the conflicting views of the brotherhood.

The fact is that after 1554 Dirk gained greater independence. His importance increased and he began to act on his own. Gradually his influence on Menno increased and he was able to convince him with strong arguments of the need to maintain a stricter ban.[4]

A contributing factor was that Dirk became a writer around 1554 and was perceived as being a person of authority.

How can this development be explained psychologically? After studying arduously—Dirk had researched the writings of Anabaptist predecessors and of contemporaries, had also studied the books of Menno and, to a lesser extent, those of the reformers—Dirk felt inspired to write large theological treatises and was pleased to discover that he could do it. His self confidence grew.

Menno's physical strength diminished. "In old age he become lame, therefore in his last writings he always added: your dear brother, the cripple."[5] He also had other physical ailments.[6] He felt that he was getting old and that his end was nearing. Dirk, being eight years younger than Menno and not having taken as many dangerous and tiring trips, was in the prime of his life. As Menno had to give up more activities, Dirk became busier.

When Menno fled from Wismar and found shelter with Bartholomeus van Ahlefeldt, Dirk probably accompanied him or moved there from Emden some time later. Menno was fortunate to secure a place for himself and his people near Wüstenfeld, where he also established a print shop.[7] It is probable that Dirk's first booklets were printed there, in Fresenburg.[8]

There are two reports which mention earlier printings. Schagen mentions that an *Enchiridion* of 1544 existed,[9] and Blaupot ten Cate even names two publications from 1544 and 1562;[10] but these are fabrications. I agree with Sepp:[11] Both Schagen and Blaupot ten Cate were mistaken. While we do read on the title page of the well-known *Enchiridion* of 1564 "now newly corrected and enlarged,"[12] this does not refer to the mysterious publications of 1544 and 1562, but to the first printing of the *Enchiridion* in 1564, of which I found two exemplars, one in Amsterdam (Universiteits-Bibliotheek) and one in Zurich (Zentralbibliothek).[13]

Another question is whether Dirk's writings were already in circulation before 1556[14] as "handwritten booklets,"[15] and for this we have an answer. In 1555, a trial took place in Amsterdam that concerned seven people, among them a certain Otto Barentszn. van Zutphen, mr. Vulder,[16] who knew Latin. He was never rebaptized and never attended a communion service. Otto had sent for a booklet with a clasp from the wife of a certain

Henrick Janssen, who apparently was an Anabaptist teacher (admonisher). Otto thought at first that Henrick himself had written the booklet, but he heard later that *Dirk Philips* was the author.[17] This is one indication that a booklet written by Dirk existed in 1555, and was being circulated in the church. The other example is as follows. A booklet exists with three treatises by Dirk Philips, written in a fine seventeenth century hand.[18] In addition to a letter to the brothers about the divinity and incarnation of Christ, it contains: a) "Confession of Our Faith," b) "Concerning Spiritual Restitution," and c) "The Church of God." These treatises are in Lower Saxon, and the text deviates repeatedly from the Dutch translation.[19] Dirk must have done the translation himself, for "he felt free to make important alterations in the text which a mere translator would not do."[20]

One wonders whether Dirk normally wrote in Lower Saxon, circulated these writings in the church, and then later translated them into Dutch for printing. This does not seem likely, for sometimes he wanted to address Dutch readers in particular, and at other times he was forced by circumstances to put a piece together quickly.

When did Dirk begin writing? I think that even the "written books" must be dated after 1550. Of the printed books, "The Tabernacle of Moses" dates from 1556,[21] "A Short Confession and Profession" ["Confession of Our Faith" in WDP] from 1557,[22] and "Concerning the True Knowledge of God" from 1558.[23] In the same year "A Loving Admonition ... Concerning the Ban" ["The Ban" in WDP] appeared, completed on February 5.[24] In 1559 "The Sending of Preachers" was printed.[25] The treatises, whose printing date I have already mentioned above, namely "[Concerning] the Incarnation of Jesus Christ"[26] and "Concerning the True Knowledge of Jesus Christ,"[27] appeared around 1557.[28] "[Concerning] The New Birth and the New Creature" was printed before 1560, for it was opposed by Matthijs Wijer who died on April 25, 1560.[29] However, this treatise cannot be considered to belong to the earlier writings as Pijper suggests,[30] because it placed value on footwashing, which played a role in Dirk Philips' thinking only in later years.[31] Contrary to Pijper,[32] I think the "Defence or Reply (About Avoiding Idolatry)"[33] should be dated fairly late, because it quoted the treatise "(Concerning) The Church of God" which was published after 1559.[34] In addition, the treatise was written during a time of renewed persecution and alludes to the defection of many believers due to persecution.[35] I date the treatise as appearing around 1562. Finally, there exist two other booklets which belong together: "Concerning Spiritual Restitution" and "(Concerning) The Church of God."[36] In most of the separate publications they are printed with a continuous signature.[37] The author shows the connection between the booklets in the following words: What the figure of Noah symbolizes, we have explained "in our confession about baptism," as well as earlier in "The Spiritual Restitution."[38] "(Concerning) The Church of God" was written after both the "(Confession Concerning) The Ban" and "The Sending of Preachers," and thus appeared after 1559.[39] Therefore, we would be correct in assuming that these final two treatises appeared in 1560 or 1561.

Testimonies by Dirk Philips' contemporaries back up my conclusion that Dirk began to publish the products of his study fairly late.

a) Matthijs Wijer in Wezel died in April 1560. He wrote to his brother Dr. Jan Wijer about "The confession of Dirk Philips About the New Creature."[40]

b) Nic. Blesdijk noted in his biography of David Joris, written in Basel in March, 1560:[41]

Whoever wants to describe more completely the development and present position of the sect of the Mennonites must read all the works of Menno as well as those of Dirk Philips and the other leaders.[42]

c) In January 1562, various heretical books were found at the home of Isaac Stollaert in Antwerp "such as from Menno Simons, Dirk Philips and others," that were not only intended for his own use, but also were to be distributed among the people.[43]

d) Georgius Cassander, an irenic-minded opponent of the Anabaptists, did a serious study of their doctrine. In 1562—or at least before January 1563—he shared the following in "The Baptism of Infants":

After the death of Menno, Dirk Philips took over the leadership with no less zeal, with similar popular eloquence, but with greater scholarship and knowledge of the Classics, which is evident in several booklets published in recent years.[44]

e) The martyr, Jan Gheerts, burned at the Hague on December 15, 1564 was asked by the president of the court if he had read books by Menno or Dirk P. He affirmed this and named "'The New Creature' by Menno and '(Concerning) Spiritual Restitution' by D.P."[45]

f) A witness above suspicion is Guy de Brès. In his *The Root, Source and Foundation of the Anabaptists or Rebaptizers of our Time, etc.,*[46] he repeatedly cites from Dirk Philips' confession about baptism and from the principal articles about faith ("The Faith Book" of 1557).[47] He once cites the booklet "Concerning the Incarnation of Jesus Christ,"[48] and in general further cites Dirk's books.[49] Furthermore, Guy de Brès mentions explicitly that Menno's companion, Dirk Philips, teaches the same among us *today*, namely that the Word was the Son of God before the incarnation.[50] In addition, at another place: Philip Dirk, your pastor and shepherd, following all the others, also slandered the holy ordinance of God [baptism].[51]

In my opinion, these proofs from the years 1560-1565 sufficiently demonstrate that Dirk's treatises had only recently received recognition, and therefore had appeared in print only a few years earlier.

The lack of any earlier reports also points in the same direction. In 1556, Bernardus Buwo, a Reformed preacher in Eilsum (East Friesland) published the following booklet: "A Friendly Dialogue of Two Persons Concerning the Baptism of Young Unaccountable Children, etc."[52] The author rejected Menno's doctrine of baptism found in the *Foundation Book*. He also mentioned Adam Pastor, who wanted to indicate when the man-made institution of child baptism began, but was not successful.[53] However, he does not mention Dirk Philips and his writings anywhere, and he certainly would have done so had Dirk's treatises been printed already.

Finally, I would like to report that Dirk's books also are listed in the Index of prohibited books. In fact, they are listed in the index which Alva added to the older Indices in 1570.[54] *In prima classi: Philippus Dirixon, qui suos Anabaptismi foetus inscribit literis D.P. [In the first class: Dirk Philips, who signed his Anabaptist writings with the letters D. P.]*[55] In addition, the following were named separately: "(Concerning) Rebirth and the New Creature,"and "A Short Admonition and Instruction."[56]

As examples of the first printed treatises, I will discuss "The Tabernacle of Moses" and "The Book of Faith." I will deal more with literary-historical problems than with theological content..

Hoekstra has commented that the apologetical purpose of Dirk Philips' writings often obscured his true intention which, on closer examination, does surface.[57] The "Tabernacle of Moses" was certainly apologetical, but who were Dirk's opponents? According to the general view of earlier authors, Dirk opposed the Münsterites and Bernhard Rothmann in particular.[58] However, careful analysis of "The Tabernacle of Moses" and "(Concerning) Spiritual Restitution" shows that Dirk did not primarily write against Rothmann, but that his criticism was directed toward other groups. Unfortunately, he made it a practice not to mention them by name or surname, but to indicate their identity only cautiously.[59]

Errors had arisen inside and outside the Christian church[60] and unrest was created by a peculiar exposition of the Tabernacle of Moses.[61] Dirk wanted to write a pure biblical exegesis based on the letter to the Hebrews (chapters 9 and 10).[62] The holy and the holy of holies signify the law and the gospel. In Christ all is fulfilled that was present in the law as a figurative foreshadow. However, Dirk could not entirely avoid using metaphors. The need of the church and the misunderstanding of some of the brothers necessitated a broad treatment of this subject.[63] However, Scripture does not occasion the strange expositions of the tabernacle written by some. They divided Christians, according to their maturity, into the courtyard, the holy, and the holy of holies. They called Christians of the two former divisions the children of Esau, and those of the latter they called the children of Jacob. They also thought of other names: the children of Esau were called militant, or carnal, first born children of God; children of Jacob were called conquerors, victors, and spiritual, born again children of God.[64]

All this was too much for Dirk. According to his interpretation, Esau represents the Jews and Jacob foreshadows the true Christians.[65] Dirk was further irritated by the assertion that true Christians had become victors in the struggle against sin, and that those who had received the Holy Spirit could no longer sin. Dirk absolutely rejected the idea of mortal perfectionism. Every Christian must struggle against sin and against the world, against Satan and against his servants. Christians are exposed to temptations (for human life is a struggle on earth); therefore, one must fight the good fight. No one is free from sin, but the sin is not accounted to the Christian, who has been forgiven by the innocent death of Jesus Christ. The distinctions being made between the first born and the born again children of God did not accord with the teaching of the New Testament. There is but one birth from God: The new birth or rebirth. All those who are reborn, or are spiritual children of God through God's grace, must grow in righteousness until they have become mature in faith.[66]

In the second part of "The Tabernacle of Moses,"[67] which stands apart from the first, Dirk dealt with a few contradictory words from the Bible which opponents had raised.[68] He succeeded in solving the problems [he said], because he did not use the Scripture "with unwashed hands."[69] There were those who misinterpreted the words of the patriarch Jacob, "I have seen God face to face," and concluded that a person could come to complete knowledge of God in this life, and would need no more instruction in faith. The Word of God had been written in his heart and he was illuminated by the indwelling spirit. Therefore the proclamation of the gospel could be suspended in this present world. Dirk was indignant over such contempt for the gospel.[70]

If one compares the treatise "The Tabernacle of Moses" with the writings of Rothmann, "The Mystery in Scripture about the Kingdom of Christ" and "Concerning the Day of the Lord through the Church of Christ in Münster" (Feb. 1535),[71] then it becomes clear that Dirk did not try to contradict Rothmann's booklet. According to Rothmann, the tabernacle was a figure for Christ with all that was His. Christ was in the courtyard when he suffered on earth and penetrated the holy and the holy of holies. That was what He meant by the words: I am the way, the truth and the life. Following the example of Christ, the believer must advance from the courtyard into the Holy sanctuary, and this transition is characterized by baptism. In the Holy sanctuary, one is enlightened; one has been cleansed and stands before God, and may enter into the most holy and dwell there in possession of eternal life, thus also of sinlessness.[72] Rothmann spoke in passing of three types of believers: the weak and sick, the spiritual, and the perfected.[73] But this partitioning of Christians was not the same as that which Dirk opposed. In addition, Rothmann offered views concerning the spiritual exposition of Scripture and about the restoration of all things.[74]

Although Dirk Philips perhaps knew about Rothmann's booklet, he did not indicate it. However, at the conclusion of "The Tabernacle of Moses" he warned against the wrong use of Scripture: Prophecies about future things should not be applied to this world, for doing this deceives many. By such a misunderstanding they are brought to the point where they want to supersede the apostles in wisdom. One could view this as an allusion to Münster.[75]

Rothmann's predecessor for his exposition of the "The Tabernacle of Moses" was Melchior Hoffman.[76] He established the basics of the dogma which Dirk attempted to refute.[77] Hoffman spoke mainly about fighting and conquering in the "Ordinances."[78] Those who have accepted the call of Christ—which is a work of the Spirit—enter the courtyard and must fight. They must lay aside whatever hinders them, and the sin which cleaves to them, and live upright lives. This is the first stage. If they persevere in the fight, enter into Christ, and live entirely in God's will,[79] then they will reach the second stage, which is the Holy Sanctuary, and they will belong to the conquerors. They then come to the Sabbath or to the genuine rest, where they are the elect of the Lord[80] and can no longer sin.[81] They remain in God's eternal temple; they are in the midst of paradise, like sun children, as it were.[82]

Hoffman gives a similar description of the progress of the Christian out of the world and into the promised kingdom of God in "The Explanation of the Captive and the Free Will."[83] He also speaks about struggle and achieving the victory.

Likewise, in Hoffman's writing we discover some reference to the distinction between the first born and the reborn children of God. The first or "literal" birth[84] is connected with the way of the Christian. The first born are those who find themselves in the courtyard and are genuinely enlightened.[85] They believe in Christ and persist in the struggle until they have gained the victory. Then they shall receive the other birth of the spirit.[86] Those who believe in the name of Christ Jesus are given the power to become children of God, to experience rebirth and to inherit the eternal kingdom. This takes place in the Holy Sanctuary, in the new heaven of God where they are truly new born children of God.[87] As a consequence, they can no longer sin, for genuine rebirth eternally keeps them from falling.[88]

Again, Hoffman and Dirk's other opponents claimed that after Pentecost the apostles did no longer sin, indeed, that they were ever unable to sin. For this idea we must return to Hoffman. The reborn are similar to the apostles after Pentecost: They are completely justified and can no longer sin.[89] Because the apostle Paul had not received the Holy Spirit, he stood lower than the other apostles; he was still in the courtyard.[90] The carnal Levite and Esau were symbols of the first born apostles, just as the disciples were before the death of Jesus Christ.[91]

Although Esau is named here, Hoffman did not make a distinction between Esau's children and Jacob's children as two different groups of Christians. However, David Joris and Hendrik Niclaes made allusions to that effect. According to a report from one of his followers, David Joris had explained the hidden significance of the names Esau and Jacob.[92] Hendrik Niclaes dealt with the figures of Esau and Jacob in chapter 9 of "The Gospel of a Cheerful Message about the Kingdom of God and Christ." Esau, the first born, did not inherit the divine promise and the covenant that God made with his elect people. Therefore, God does not establish his covenant with those who are born according of the flesh and are earthly or carnal, but with those who are born of the Spirit, spiritual or heavenly.

The other son, Jacob or Israel, who was born of the Spirit, increased in power and understanding, and surpassed his brother in wisdom and spiritual knowledge. He conquered the earthly or carnal nature, received the blessing of his father, and became the inheritor of the promises of God and of the revelations of his fathers.

[According to Hendrik Niclaes], a great mystery is hidden in these two births. The first born with his earthly nature sought the promises of Christ and yet achieved nothing, while he who was born of the Spirit remained quiet and, through the wisdom of the Holy Spirit, received the blessing which was promised to the seed of Abraham. At the same time, he became superior and shall reign with God. He himself shall bring forth the name Israel or Christian.[93]

The first printing of "The Gospel of a Cheerful Message" did not appear before 1555,[94] but Hendrik Niclaes, who stayed in Emden from 1540 to 1560,[95] had personally propagated his doctrine and also had spread his treatises, probably in manuscript copies and of course secretly.[96] It seems possible to me that Dirk met with him, or with his followers, and that his influence stirred up unrest in the Anabaptist church.

I should also explain the second part of "The Tabernacle of Moses," in which Dirk speaks about some contradictory texts in Scripture. Erasmus in his "Ratio" discussed Biblical texts that appeared to contradict each other, and the subject was a popular one.[97] Hans Denck wrote "Who Truly Loves the Truth" (1526).[98] Andreas Althamer, a Lutheran preacher in Nurenberg, responded to this booklet without mentioning Denck's name,[99] and Sebastian Frank gained his reputation by translating and reworking Althamer's writing.[100] The contradictory texts which the opponents cited, and which Dirk refuted, agree fairly well with no. 23 and no. 22 in Denck's booklet.[101]

The assertion of Dirk's adversaries—that a person can come to a complete knowledge of God in this life, and for this reason no more instruction is needed, nor preaching of the Gospel—puts before the historian a difficult problem. I was unable to find anything like this mentioned in the work of secular writers. These thoughts most resemble some statements of Sebastian Franck in his letter to Campanus[102] where he stated that faith is not learned out of a book or from a person, but is taught by God in the school of the Lord under the cross.[103] Further, one must explain Scripture following the conviction of conscience. God has hidden his wisdom under the cover of literal parables so that only those who are taught by God may understand them.[104] I believe Dirk was aiming at followers of Franck who had developed Franck's ideas further.

The third text which the spiritualists quoted was to be understood spiritually (Rev. 21:23). The sun and the moon are images of Scripture and of external worship, and these will pass away or have already passed away. The glory of God and the Lamb are put in their place, which is to say, the inner enlightenment of the spirit of God and of Christ who is Spirit and light.[105]

To the contrary, Dirk leaned on the authority of Scripture and admonished his readers to hear the eternal Word of God. God certainly wrote his law upon the heart when he taught believers to know Christ, but they must also encourage each other to follow the right path. The word from Revelation may not be applied to the present world, for it will only be fulfilled upon Christ's return. Dirk pointed to the danger of wanting to anticipate the future. In doing so, many had been deceived; that was what had happened at Münster. People used words from Isaiah and Revelation to justify fallacies based on a misunderstanding.[106]

From this encounter with spiritualism we see clearly that Dirk did not approve of that direction. Rather, he favoured the church taking a more dogmatic view.[107]

When reading the usual description of Anabaptist history, one can get the impression that the Anabaptists dealt mainly with practical issues, but that they were fairly indifferent to more theological problems. However, in "The Tabernacle of Moses" we see how the most divergent questions aroused interest in the community, leading to debate and dissatisfaction.[108]

Dirk Philips hoped that his explanation would clear up the division and that peace would be restored among the brothers.

The second booklet that I wish to discuss is "A Brief Confession of God, the Father, Son, and Holy Spirit with a Statement of Christian Baptism and the Proper Practice of the Lord's Supper."[109] The index mentions that "The book was previously named The Faith Book"[110] which is the name I prefer to use. Whenever Alenson quoted something out of this booklet,[111] he referred to it as "The Foundation Book," but whether he meant by this only the "Book of Faith" or the entire *Enchiridion* is unclear. The martyr Joos de Tollenaar wrote to his daughter Betje in 1589, "When I die, I would like your mother to give you as an eternal memorial a Testament and Dirk Philips' Foundation Book ... read them often, for they contain many wonderful admonitions."[112] Also, J. de Buyser who, in his "Christian House Book"[113] copied whole articles from the *Enchiridion*, mentioned as his source both Dirk Philips' "Foundation Book," and the "Hand Book," without making any distinction between the two.

Was the "Confession about Baptism and about the Lord's Supper"[114] published separately, perhaps as a "written booklet" as Pijper suggests?[115] This is unclear, because in other places Dirk refers to the "Confession about the Lord's Supper"[116] and to "The Confession concerning Baptism."[117] I read it as a sloppy citation. But it is not impossible that Dirk first wrote the treatise about baptism and the Lord's Supper, and that later, when he printed the whole, he placed the subjects under one title. The first is "Confession of our Faith,"[118] which contains the orthodox doctrine of God the Father, the Son, and the Holy Spirit. However, for someone with a good understanding, it is clear that Dirk did not deny the doctrine of incarnation.[119]

The other piece is called "Our confession about creation, deliverance, and the salvation of humankind."[120] The author gave a good summary of this doctrine. By nature we are sinners and children of wrath, and we deserve the punishment of God, but we are consoled by the grace of God who was revealed to us in Jesus Christ. We seize this grace by faith. Faith is the work of God in an individual by which he or she is renewed internally.

By faith we know the love of God; from this knowledge springs our love for God which is shown through good works and the keeping of God's commandments. However, this is possible only when one leaves the world and refrains from papist ceremonies, and ceremonies of other churches; in short, when one refrains from all false worship. The Anabaptists wanted to use the sacraments of baptism and communion according to the teachings of Christ and the example of the apostolic church.

Dirk introduced the chapter about baptism with a solemn statement.[121] Christian baptism must occur internally and externally: Internally with the Holy Spirit and with fire, and externally with water. External baptism is a witness to spiritual baptism, a demonstration of true repentance and a statement of belief in Jesus Christ.[122] Emphasis was made repeatedly that internal baptism must precede the external. A condition for baptism with water is rebirth.[123] That is why Dirk stressed that we are not saved by the power of the element (the water), but by the power of the blood and of the Spirit of Christ.[124] Still external baptism may not be neglected, for it is an ordinance of the Lord.[125]

Contrary to Luther's views, that baptism and the Lord's Supper are signs of God's grace and that this grace is extended through the sacraments, Dirk Philips emphasized that God's grace and his covenant with all believing Christians are not bound to external signs, but only to Jesus Christ. This is the only and true sign of grace. Baptism and the Lord's Supper are certainly signs in the sense that the Lord thereby displays all that he has done for us: His grace, his suffering, and his dying. Both baptism and the Lord's Supper are public evidence of God's love, and of the blessings of our Lord Christ Jesus. Nevertheless, Christ is and remains the true, and only, means of grace, and all external signs point only to him.[126]

The author opposed infant baptism using arguments similar to those used by Menno.[127] A child's salvation does not depend on baptism, for the sin of Adam has been taken away by Jesus Christ. Who may accuse the children, for whom Jesus Christ has poured out his precious blood? On the other hand, there still is something good in children although they have inherited the sinful inclination of Adam. This "good" is the "simple, submissive, and humble nature" by which they please God (nevertheless all derived from pure grace through Jesus Christ).[128] "For the simple, undeveloped dogmatic theology of the Dutch Mennonites (*Doopsgezinden*), these two views formed one whole."[129]

Dirk based his work mainly on the writings of Menno. Whether he had read other authors cannot be proven, with the exception of the *Chronicle* [*Chronica*] of Sebastian Franck. But what Menno had spread over various treatises,[130] Dirk worked on independently and then put into a systematic order, thereby showing his talent as a writer.[131]

In the first part, Dirk followed the traditional argumentation as was already found in Hans Krüsi's booklet about faith and baptism.[132] I am more interested in the fact that apparently the "Confession of Baptism" was used by the martyr Thomas van Imbroich, executed in Cologne on March 5, 1558.[133] Thomas was born in Imbroich (district of Monschau) in 1533 and grew up at St. Troyden in the bishopric of Liege. By vocation a printer, he came to Cologne in 1553, joined the Anabaptist congregation, and was baptized by the elder Zillis. He probably became a deacon for the Overlanders (Upper Germans).

Two days before Christmas he was arrested and repeatedly subjected to interrogations. The confinement was not strict, and he had opportunity to write a defence to the government of the city of Cologne.[134] In it he opposed the usual accusations and suspicions: That the Anabaptists were revolutionaries, and that they would use force if they became numerous enough. After that follows the actual "Confession" which repeated Dirk Philips' statement fairly literally.[135] Sometimes he abbreviated or summarized Dirk's thoughts in his own words, and sometimes Thomas inserted a few sentences in which he addressed the "honourable lords."

In addition, Thomas used Dirk Philips' treatise for the second part, "Defensiones oppositionum."[136] He made a choice from among the many objections to which Dirk responded and limited himself to the texts of Matt. 19:14 (Jesus blesses the children) and John 3:3-5 (Jesus' discussion with

Nicodemus). The answer to the first objection agreed closely with the arguments presented by Dirk.[137]

The matter of circumcision combined material from several other pages of Dirks writing.[138] The second objection on account of John 3:3-5 was refuted with the same arguments which Dirk himself used.[139] In this connection, Thomas expanded on the possibility that almighty God could give children faith, and here showed that he was again using Dirk's thoughts.[140] At the end, Thomas apologized for perhaps becoming too verbose, but wrote that if the lords wished more extensive answers he was prepared to give them.[141] The signature stated: Thomas von Imbroich, Y[our] g[racious] w[illing] subject.

The similarity between the treatise "Concerning Baptism" and the "Confession" is so striking that one must suppose that Thomas read and used Dirk Philips' booklet in prison. Of course, it remains an open question whether both had known and copied a writing from a third party, but I have not been able to document this possibility.

How did the "Confession Concerning Baptism" come to Cologne, and into Thomas' hands? Perhaps the German teachers who visited Menno in Wüstenfelde in 1556 brought the manuscript with them. One of them was a certain Heinrich, and it seems probable that this was Heinrich Krufft of Cologne.[142] However it is also possible that the booklet was printed in 1557, and was sent by Dirk to former friends in the Rhine land. Whatever the case, the similarity between the "Confession Concerning Baptism" and Thomas' "Confession" is irrefutable.

Dirk names Luther twice in the second part of his "Concerning Baptism."[143] Dirk clearly took the first two sentences of the first citation from Menno's "A Basic Confession of the Poor and Miserable Christians" (1552).[144] The rest of the argument is a literal translation from Luther's "Preface to the Prophets."[145] Dirk borrowed his other quotation of Luther entirely from the *Chronicle* of Sebastian Franck,[146] with the omission of some words that were not essential. The quotation from Erasmus' "Apology to the Bishop of Seville"[147] is likewise to be found in Franck.[148]

Therefore, it appears that Dirk, as well as Adam Pastor,[149] and Menno,[150] used the *Chronicle* as a sort of encyclopedia. It is understandable that these men gladly used such a resource in their study, and that they took it with them when they had to move from one place to another.

In the third part of the baptism booklet,[151] there is still another citation that may be from Franck: "There are some who have the nature of the spider and turn everything that is good into evil; yes, who change honey into poison."[152] Frank used this saying repeatedly,[153] but it may have been a generally known proverb.

The third part presents us with many difficult questions. Dirk again gave no names or writings so that we are forced to solve these puzzles as best we can. He first complained that baptism was very much looked down upon by some as a mere outward ceremony.[154] He was probably referring to the Davidjorists and the House of Love (Hendrik Niclaes). Nicolai reported extensively about them: They held the Sacraments to be useless (they called them external ceremonies), artificial, childish and fleshly things which belonged to the past.[155]

Dirk's defence was that baptism is God's command. For this reason he would hold firmly to the institution of the Lord and the practices of the apostles.

But the opponents had still other objections. Mockingly they asked what baptism was, and why the Anabaptists took persecution and suffering upon themselves even while they confessed that salvation did not depend upon external signs. They further asserted that external institutions such as baptism and the Lord's Supper could be made superfluous by faith and love. Just as Moses abandoned circumcision in the desert, so Christians may act according to their own insight regarding these outward signs.[156]

I have indicated in an earlier chapter[157] that David Joris permitted his followers to participate in the ceremonies of the state churches even though he was convinced of their uselessness. Hendrik Niclaes taught along the same lines.[158] The Libertines or Franckists had the same opinion, according to Nicolai.[159] They claimed that they loved God with their hearts, but at the same time they denied Him. In addition, they said that one did not need to expose oneself to mortal danger on account of confessing the truth.[160]

Nicolai is not very logical in his explanation. "One time he calls the Franckists predecessors and forerunners of David Joris and Hendrik Niclaes; then again he says that the 'French Libertines' stem from those two arch-heretics."[161]

Because Dirk refers here to faith and love which abolish the ceremonies, it seems to me most probable that he was pointing to the prophet of the House of Love.[162] It was not difficult for Dirk to oppose these erroneous doctrines from his biblical standpoint.[163] Certainly salvation is dependent upon the grace of God and not upon outward signs. But out of obedience to God's Word and according to the example of Christ, baptism must be administered and received. Indeed, Moses did abandon circumcision due to circumstances in the desert[164]–after which followed an important explanation characterizing the biblical perspective of the Anabaptists.

> *In principle, we do not obey figures and images, nor the incompleteness of the Old Testament, but we should follow the real, complete essence and spirit of the New Testament. We are not under the law, but under the gospel. We are not disciples of Moses, but of Christ. The law, images and shadows of Moses are not hereby put down, but we see and understand everything according to the spirit and true essence of the New Testament.*

In addition, Dirk argued that the omission of baptism does not happen from necessity, as in the wilderness regarding the circumcision. Also, as far as defending infant baptism and participating in it is concerned, one ought to know that it has been changed by the Antichrist into an idolatrous ceremony.

In conclusion, Dirk emphasized again that the doctrine of baptism that he had composed agreed with Holy Scripture. The Anabaptists only wished to live quietly according to their faith, to obey the government in everything that did not conflict with the will of God, and to seek, if possible, peace with all people.

At the end of the *Faith Book* Dirk dealt with the doctrine of the Lord's Supper.[165] He knew that in the Reformed churches this doctrine had led to many quarrels, and he did not want any part of that. In his introduction, he suggested that the Lord's Supper was instituted by Christ as a memorial of his suffering and death. The words of the Lord's Supper have to be understood spiritually. Only then do the various biblical verses have true meaning. Faith is essential, namely a faith that conforms to Scripture, for without such a faith human thought takes over.

1) Dirk first unfolded the doctrinal significance of the Lord's Supper.[166] He supported his exposition with the sixth chapter of the Gospel according to John, but did not neglect the ideas of the synoptic gospels. He opposed the bodily presence of Christ in the bread and wine, and approved of a spiritual conception of the Lord Supper. To back this up, he stated five reasons:

a) On the basis of John 6, Dirk proposed that "eating" signifies "believing," and that "drinking" is the same as "trusting." Christ is the true bread of heaven that is consumed. The bread of heaven is God's Word, and the Word has become flesh and is offered to us. These three words of Scripture are the food of life for the person who has faith. Whoever believes and trusts in Jesus Christ, who was crucified and died for us, that person eats and drinks the spiritual flesh and blood of Christ. Spiritual food must be received spiritually. It is clear that when Christ instituted the Lord's Supper and spoke about eating his body and drinking his blood, this was meant symbolically, or spiritually. Dirk appealed to John 6:63: "The spirit alone gives life, the flesh is of no avail; the words which I have spoken to you are both spirit and life."[167]

How did Dirk arrive at this point of view? It is obvious that he had studied Menno's writings about the Lord's Supper.[168] Menno quoted texts from John 6, and discussed the spiritual significance of the eating of the bread, and the drinking of the wine; even John 6:63 is mentioned explicitly.[169] Dirk also consulted other sources, although he avoided citing them. It seems likely that he was acquainted with Cornelis Hoen's well-known letter on the Lord's Supper.[170] Hoen was the first to translate "est" [is] as "significat" [signifies]. However, he had added that Christ wanted to give of himself when he said: "This is my body."[171]

I believe that Dirk had even more help from Sebastian Franck.[172] In particular, Franck had quoted many sayings from Augustine which did not agree with later Roman Catholic doctrine. For example:

> That the body and blood of Christ is only a spiritual food and drink to feed the heart of a believing soul, and that the body of Christ is not received with one's literal mouth, but with the hand and the mouth of the heart, spiritually, by faith.

Further:

> Just what do your teeth and belly receive the minute you have eaten? Only by faith is Christ food and drink. Only he who believes in Him, eats Him.[173]

b) Christ himself clarified His words, "Take, eat, this is my body," by adding "that *shall* be given for you."[174] The very body of Christ sat with the apostles at the table, shared the bread and the wine, and spoke the words of institution. His physical body, received from the Holy Spirit and born from the virgin Mary, was offered for us on the cross. But the apostles ate and drank ordinary bread and wine, and they were assured of salvation as are all believers.[175]

c) Judas also ate of the bread and drank of the wine, but he did not receive the flesh and blood of Christ. What God gives us in these holy acts, faith alone receives. That which the sacraments signify externally, God works in the elect by his Spirit. Fellowship with Christ did not exist for Judas as for the other apostles, for he was in the fellowship of Satan before, during, and after the Lord's Supper. The word of Paul (I Cor. 11:27) applies to any unbeliever who participates in the Lord's Supper: "He sins against the body and blood of the Lord because he eats the bread of the Lord without knowing the Spirit, without faith, without love for Christ and the brothers, and without discerning the body of Christ."[176]

d) Scripture often uses images symbolically (Christ as the door of the sheepfold, the true vine, the rock).[177] In Scripture, a sign is often named after the meaning of things. Thus at the Lord's Supper, Christ called the bread his body and the chalice his blood, because they signified that he gave his body and poured out his blood for us so that through the power of his sacred offering, in spirit and by faith, we might have eternal life. Dirk was amazed that people could be so ignorant as to believe in transubstantiation, even while they understood that Jesus spoke much more extensively about the eating of his flesh and the drinking of his blood in John 6, more so than at the Lord's Supper. He spoke about spiritual eating, which is believing. Luther and his followers did not deny this. Nevertheless they wanted to hold on to the physical presence of Christ in the elements of the Lord's Supper.

e) Jesus Christ became completely human, although without sin. But he rose from the dead and now sits at the right hand of God, where he will sit until the last day when he will come to judge the living and the dead.[178]

Luther said that Christ was physically present in all created things; therefore, he is also present in the bread and wine of the Lord's Supper.[179] Dirk saw this as a lie and a falsification of Scripture. Although Christ's divine power is present in all things (Heb. 1:3 and Col. 2:3), his physical self and human personality are neither in all creatures nor at all places, but alone with the Father in heaven.

Based on these five reasons, Dirk rejected the presence of Christ in the Lord's Supper. He continued to believe that Christ was seated at the right hand of God in divine glory and in a human form, but that he was with his disciples, the true Christians, in spirit until the end of the world.

2) Proceeding from the text of I Cor. 10:16, Dirk discussed the significance of the Lord's Supper as a meal of fellowship during which believers commune with Christ.[180] Spiritual fellowship begins with faith, which one receives through the grace of God. Faith is renewed and strengthened by baptism and the Lord's Supper.[181] Whenever Christians gather at the Lord's Supper in unity of faith they remember Christ's gifts of righteousness and sanctification.[182] Communal eating and drinking point to fellowship among believers. Here Dirk quoted the well known parable from the Didache[183] which was also found in the Münster "Confession

Concerning Both Sacraments" and in Menno's work.[184] If there is to be true fellowship with Christ, then Christians must be one in heart and soul, and serve, help and comfort one another.

Baptism was of primary importance in Dirk's teaching, as was the fellowship with Christ which is brought about by faith. If there is no fellowship, the Lord's Supper accomplishes nothing, and becomes a meaningless, outward exhibition.

3) The Lord's Supper is a meal of remembrance,[185] but not in the general sense that the memory of Jesus Christ (humankind's beneficiary) lives on. Rather, the ceremony instituted by Christ has a specific content. We must commemorate the bitter suffering and innocent death of Christ, and remember that his body was offered for us and his blood was shed for us.[186] Such a commemoration has practical consequences for the life of faith: We learn to fear God and to hate sin. When we consider that the only Son of God suffered and died for our sins, we are brought to humility and self-knowledge, to the true fear of God, and are filled with a thankful heart for what Christ has done for us.

4) When passing the cup Christ said,[187] "This cup is the new covenant (testament) in my blood."[188] Although Dirk seemed to know that *diatheke* means both "testament" and "covenant," for the sake of his argument he preferred to read the meaning as "testament." He drew two conclusions:

a) A testament does not take effect until the testator has died. A death is involved. Just as the Old Testament was put into effect by the blood of calves, so the New Testament is confirmed by the blood of Christ.

b) Anyone who draws up a will is not personally present in it, but the wish of the testator is present, and through this the will receives its power. Dirk used this argument to show that although Christ is in heaven,[189] his spirit is near to his own and works in them. Therefore, Dirk concludes, the doctrine of the "blind and perverted world" which claims that Christ is physically present in the symbols of the Lord's Supper, does not agree with Holy Scripture.

5) In the last section,[190] Dirk gives some practical hints on how to celebrate the Lord's Supper in the proper manner.

    a) The Lord's Supper is held in a Christian congregation which gathers in the name of the Lord. The death of Christ must be proclaimed and the significance of the Lord's Supper explained, always in agreement with Scripture.

    b) Only "the friends of God" may participate in the Lord's Supper, namely those who have accepted the Gospel, who have been baptized upon their confession, and who lead a Christlike life. They find strength through their fellowship with Christ and all believers.

    c) Because the Lord's Supper is a communal meal, it may not be celebrated alone, as happens in other churches.[191] Furthermore, the minister must celebrate the Lord's Supper with the congregation,[192] for this follows the example in the New Testament. The bread must be broken, and the bread and the cup distributed and received by each Christian. That is, a wafer alone may not be used nor may the cup simply be held to the lips of the communicant.[193]

    d) On the basis of I Cor. 11:28 ff., the writer admonished participants in the Lord's Supper to examine themselves. They must believe that Christ is the head of the congregation. They have received grace and life from him, and they must follow him. Christians are members of a body (the congregation) and they must live in unity, ministering to each other with material and spiritual gifts. This is what it means to treat the body of Christ with care.

Here Dirk attached an allegorical exposition of the Jewish Passover which is less important to us. I will only mention this: The Israelites were not supposed to leave any part of the Passover lamb; whatever remained had to be burned. In the same way, we also must eat Jesus Christ, our Passover lamb, fully and entirely. That is, we must listen to all of his teachings, and keep them, and not do as some do, who pick and choose teachings they like. Every word of God and of Christ ought to be accepted in faith, and we must persist in this until the end. Dirk acknowledged that there is much in Scripture that is difficult to understand. Therefore, we must pray in the name of Christ for the gift of the Holy Spirit which will enlighten us.

Up to this point the article on the Lord's Supper is more theological than devotional. When Menno dealt with the same subject, he wrote more emotionally and personally.[194] However, on one of the last pages, Dirk spoke of the comfort the Lord's Supper provides.[195] We are inwardly refreshed; we are assured of God's grace and of fellowship with Christ. We are justified before God, participants in eternal salvation.

In an epilogue Dirk denied that he was a *swermer* (radical).[196] He recalled that according to Scripture, Christ is physically in heaven at the right hand of God, but he is with believers in spirit, and the words of institution must be understood spiritually. That is the only correct scriptural meaning.

Dirk studied various writings and constructed his treatment from them. He did this, I believe, in a capable manner, and delivered a judicious work that certainly contributed to the instruction of the church of God.

Dirk's criticisms of Lutheran conceptions and practices of the Lord's Supper show that he had lived in a Lutheran environment and observed the Lutheran church. He probably came into contact with the Lutheran church mostly in the areas of Lübeck and Wismar, and somewhat less in East Friesland.

IX

Dirk Philips, Advocate of the Strict Ban

From the earliest days of the Anabaptist movement the ban was viewed as necessary for forming a congregation of true Christians according to the example of the New Testament. Felix Mantz, on the basis of Christ's commandment (Matt 18) and the doctrine of Paul, demanded that public sinners be excluded from the congregation.[1] The elders assembled at Schleitheim, "whose scribe is supposed to have been Michael Sattler,"[2] also dealt with the ban in their articles. Sincere Christians wanted to unite into a congregation separated from the world and its works. Therefore, the brother or sister who fell into sin or unwittingly stepped out of line had to be admonished according to the commandment found in Matthew 18, and would be banned if he or she would not listen to the congregation.[3] The ban was the means by which God's church, which Menno had gathered after the catastrophe in Münster, would be kept pure. The ban also prevented the dangers emerging from the Davidjorists and the doctrine of Adam Pastor.[4]

Menno hoped that practical questions about proper procedures and application of the ban had been satisfactorily answered at the conferences in Emden (1547) and Wismar (1554), and by his article "A Clear Account of Excommunication" with its attachment "Some Questions" (1550).

Around 1555, more trouble faced the brotherhood. Ministers in congregations north of Amsterdam (the Waterland) resisted the zeal of Gillis van Aken. Menno visited the congregations twice to follow up and to "establish them on the old foundation."[5]

Shortly thereafter, a serious quarrel arose in Franeker about the implementation of the ban. Menno received an urgent written message from five brothers "known to be of good reputation" in which they requested his opinion about the issues at hand. Menno's answer was dated November 13, 1555.[6] He wanted to apply the ban with fatherly kindness, in true love, according to the teaching of Christ and the apostles; he did not want himself to be influenced by other's teaching and beliefs. He stood on the foundation of his own faith, as taught by Holy Scripture. It is "an especially valuable letter in which he warned against improper zealousness."[7]

However, Leenaert Bouwens was one who stirred up unrest everywhere. He was gripped by the ideal of the pure church and would not tolerate any leniency. Whoever sinned must be removed from the circle at any price. God's command must be obeyed unconditionally. Leenaert banned a member of the congregation in Emden—we do not know for what reason—and demanded that his wife, Swaen Rutgers, shun her husband.[8] However, she objected to Leenaert's charge[9] and apparently found support from a part of the congregation. Her defenders turned to Menno for help and received a letter from him dated November 12, 1556.[10]

In this letter, Menno held to the decisions taken in Emden and Wismar, and his judgment was that if the innocent spouse could live unhindered in her faith and was bound by her conscience to her banned husband, one should not ban her nor force her to abandon her husband. "May the compassionate Lord prevent me from agreeing to this," Menno wrote.[11]

His letter had the contrary effect. Instead of calming the situation, the letter angered Leenaert. Swaen Rutgers, who had been given time to reconsider, was now "surrendered to the Devil and banned."[12]

The two parties formed a sharp contrast. The Waterlanders and the Franekers stood on one side, and Leenaert Bouwens and his followers stood on the other. Both wanted a church without spot or wrinkle (Eph. 5:27), but they disagreed about how to answer the practical questions: When and how the ban should be used, and what were the consequences for relationships among the members (shunning)?

The moderates wanted to have each application of the ban preceded by the threefold admonition found in Matthew 18:15-17.[13] Here Menno had one reservation: Some sins were punished by the government, such as murder, witchcraft, arson, theft, and such criminal matters. Whoever had committed these sins must be cast out of the church immediately, because otherwise the sweet dough of the church would turn into awful sour dough for the entire world. However, the carnal sins which the apostle summed up in Ephesians 5:3-5 and Galatians 5:19 ff., may not be punished without the three preceding admonitions. Thus teaches the Holy Scripture.

The secret of the confessional was honoured by the moderates. If a brother had sinned in secret, shown remorse for it, and confessed the sin to a member of the congregation, his confessor was not allowed to speak about it. Otherwise the danger existed that someone who sinned in secret would be too ashamed to come to confess the sin and would have to go through life with a feeling of guilt.[14]

If someone stumbled because of weakness, acknowledged it before the congregation, and repented, members were not allowed to be hard on such a one, for "whoever stands, see to it that he does not fall." Not the weak, but rather the wicked had to be cut off.

With regard to spousal shunning, the moderates held to the decisions taken in Emden and Wismar, and wanted to respect "a sick conscience"[15] or "a bound conscience,"[16] "although the decision makers said that each case had to be carefully examined to determine whether the objections really arose from the conscience and not from some other source."[17]

To the contrary, proponents of the strict ban, under the leadership of Leenaert Bouwens, wanted the sentence of the ban passed without preliminary warnings, not only against criminals, but also those who were guilty of the sins described in Ephesians 5 and Galatians 5. In addition, the banned member had to do penance outside of the church. Only then could the member be received back again.[18]

Leenaert and his followers did not agree that secret sins could be confessed and forgiven in a confidential meeting. Every offence, every transgression of God's commandments, must be made known to the church and judged by it, lest the church become polluted. Therefore, members who did not reveal to the congregation the sin shared in confidence should be threatened with the same punishment as the transgressor.[19]

The same harshness had to be shown to those who had fallen because of weakness, had confessed it openly, and shown repentance. Such persons had to be banned, with all the consequences.[20]

The extremists were most unrelenting when it was a case of spousal shunning. They would not permit any exception, and did not make allowances for a person's conscience. Marriage vows were less valid than obedience to the Word of God which required strict separation.[21] Only then was the purity of the church assured.

What position did Dirk Philips take in these controversies? Was he still influenced by Menno, and did he mediate as Menno would have? Unfortunately, the answer is "no." In the years immediately preceding the quarrel about the ban, Dirk had spiritually distanced himself from Menno and had gone his own way. He devoted himself to study and prepared the first printed booklets for publication. To do so, he probably lived close to Menno at first, but the fact that his name was not mentioned in connection with the meeting that was held with Zylis and Lemke in Wüstenfeld at the end of April, 1556 leads me to suspect that he had departed Emden by then.

In Emden, Dirk allowed himself to be convinced by Leenaert about the truth of Leenaert's position and, as far as I know, approved the ban on Swaen Rutgers.[22] This happened in the winter of 1556-1557. If we can believe Nicolai, then Leenaert and Dirk exchanged thoughts with Menno either orally or in writing for a considerable time, and only then began to push for the ban without the threefold warning. It is possible that Menno tried to restrain Dirk by reminding him in a letter to the congregation in Emden (November 12, 1556) that in 1547 and 1554 they had decided to apply separation in principle, but not to force it on anyone who had conscientious objections.[23] Nevertheless, Menno's letter was to no avail. Dirk had joined the strict party and held firmly to the strict ban to the end of his life.

An assembly of the elders was called to settle the differences. It probably took place in Harlingen in the Spring of 1557.[24] I will omit details and refer to Kühler's statement that "we will never know exactly what was discussed at the assembly."[25] It must have been disappointing for Menno that his old friend Dirk agreed with Leenaert and tried to win him over to the same viewpoint. The assembly, under Leenaert's leadership, put pressure on Menno which finally caused him to switch and accept the strict rule of shunning in marriage.[26]

Dr. van der Zijpp writes, "It remains a mystery how Leenaert was able to convince Menno in Harlingen."[27] Indeed, there was a change in Menno's attitude between November 1556 (the case of Swaen Rutgers), and a few months later when he gives his permission to strict shunning. How does one explain this?

Menno was confronted in Harlingen with ideas he had always supported, that is, that one must love Christ more than husband, wife, father, mother, or child, and that the word of Holy Scripture must be obeyed precisely. Menno admitted that in 1541 when he had written his first booklet about the ban, he had not been so "enlightened" as to be able to distinguish the various aspects of this issue.[28] He not only instructed others, but had been instructed by others. Here he alludes to the fact that he had received better insight through Leenaert and Dirk.[29] But the instruction he had received from the Holy Spirit he deemed most important. Like every servant of God, he had tried to penetrate deeper into the hidden truth of Scripture. He had earnestly reflected on the matter of the ban, and had finally come to the conclusion that the congregation should not tolerate in its midst members whom God himself had excluded through his Spirit and Word.[30]

In light of this it is unjust, in my opinion, to speak about a change in Menno regarding the ban. Rather, one could see his view as progressing from the basic principle of keeping the congregation pure, the bride of Christ who must be found without spot or wrinkle.[31]

As a consequence of the Harlingen debates, the division between the extremists and the moderates (Franekers and Waterlanders) became final.

Although Leenaert and Dirk banned the leaders, Hendrik Naaldeman and Joriaan Heyns, the break occurred without placing the ban on the congregations (1557).[32]

Dirk Philips had less difficulty than Menno in adjusting to the strict ideas of Leenaert, as they corresponded to his linear thinking and his systematic spirit. It appears that he spoke with various members of the church in Friesland about the issue of the ban before or after the assembly in Harlingen. He said[33] that he had spoken with them about shunning and instructed them from Holy Scripture at the request of his own party (they were called the Godfearing ones), and also at the wish of those who still had doubts. It seems that he convinced them, for they thanked him for the instruction they had received. Later they switched to the opposition party and slandered Dirk verbally and in writing.

After the gathering at Harlingen Dirk travelled to North Holland, probably to warn those churches against the influence of the Waterlanders. In 1557 he visited the congregation in Hoorn and ordained a new elder, Jan Willems, who had been called by the congregation when he was barely 14 years old.[34] On the one hand, this fact shows how highly Willems was regarded by the congregation; on the other hand, Dirk was a welcome balance against the elder Jacob Jans Scheedemaker, who was active in Waterland, and against Joriaen Heyns and Hendrik Naaldeman, who were called in by the Waterlanders for help.[35]

A brief overview will suffice concerning the differences with the Upper Germans (Overlanders); Dirk dealt with them only later. After 1555, alienation increased between the Dutch and the Upper German elders. An assembly of church members and elders met in Strasburg in August 1555, to consult about the doctrine of Christ's incarnation at the request of the "Hoffmanites" and the brothers in the Netherlands.[36] The majority of South German Anabaptists explained incarnational doctrine differently than did the followers of Melchior Hoffman and Menno Simons. Hoffman's doctrine of the incarnation–also embraced by Menno and his followers– was rejected as useless, and because quarrels about the ban had already begun, the article concluded with this note: "Rather than by word of mouth, we want to punish a godless life and all appearance of evil with a more Christlike and Godly walk."[37] When the rumour about the difficulties in Franeker reached the Upper Germans, a delegation came to Menno in Wüstenfelde at the end of April, 1556. The delegation was comprised of Zylis, Lemke,[38] and a certain Heinrich, probably Heinrich Krufft.[39] Herman van Tielt from Wismar and Hans S. came from the east.[40] No agreement was reached. It cannot be determined whether Menno shared a written explanation of his ideas regarding the ban at this time, as Krahn guessed,[41] or whether this first happened after the meeting in Cologne (1557), as De Hoop Scheffer assumed.[42]

After the Harlingen conference Leenaert, accompanied by Menno and others, tried to win the Upper Germans over to his point of view at an assembly in Cologne in the summer of 1557.[43] But only a very few representatives came to this assembly; even Dirk Philips was absent because he was still travelling in the Netherlands. In any case, a general assembly at Strasbourg was being planned for the near future, and therefore no definitive decision was taken at that time. The Dutch elders were confused about the forthcoming Strasbourg assembly and about the answer which it would give. Internal differences among the Upper Germans, the questions of the ban and shunning—in particular spousal avoidance—were discussed and a written answer was drafted.[44]

It was acknowledged that the ban was a necessary means for keeping the congregation pure, but the goal was to bring the fallen brother or sister to repentance and conversion. The Upper Germans asked the Dutch brothers—and this was to be taken as brotherly advice, not as an order—to abandon spousal shunning because it often did more harm than good. The divine institution of marriage is of greater significance than shunning.[45]

The wish expressed in a postscript asked "the beloved brother Menno and all the ministers and elders in the Netherlands" not to push the ban to the extreme, but to seek peace, love, and unity in the great church of God.

The brotherly admonition was not heeded. On the contrary, Dirk and Menno felt obliged to justify their position to the brotherhood, to unfold their ideas about the ban, and to warn against a lax conception of the treasure that was entrusted to the church.

Dirk's booklet first appeared dated February 5, 1558.[46] The piece is calmly admonishing and shows an almost academic objectivity.[47] As in most of Dirk Philips' writing, the texts in the title, 2 Thess. 3:6 and I Cor. 5:11, point to the booklet's contents. The title, "A Gentle Warning," clearly shows that he did not want to deal with the tricky problems of the ban or shunning—he avoided the issue of "spousal shunning" altogether–but would deal only with the question of how a strict Christian congregation should deal with those who were accepted by baptism into the congregation of saints, and later fell into public, mortal, or carnal sin.[48] This subject was clearly and exhaustively discussed. However, about half of the booklet is devoted to a general admonition directed to members who were suffering persecution. Dirk comforted them with God's promises, and with the hope of future glory.[49] Because the readers belonged to the elect, he urged them to seek true Christian peace, and to avoid quarrels and divisions. There is a warning against "the rash and popular souls who call attention to themselves with pompous words, and slander the church of the Lord." They compare the ministers of Christ to foolish shepherds who forsake their duty to the flock because they separate public sinners from the rest of the congregation.[50] The last pages are also a loving admonition to the brothers to persist faithfully in their calling.[51] If some take offence at the strict application of the ban and choose to defect, it will not harm the church of God which remains strong and unshakable in the doctrine of Christ Jesus.[52]

Dirk continued: From the beginning, God's plan was to punish the wicked, namely the sinners whose misdeeds are public. This was proven by quotations from the Old and New Testaments. The following texts from the New Testament were cited: I Cor. 6:9-10; Galatians 5:19-21; Ephesians 5:5; Rev. 22:15. The guilty must be removed from the congregation. They must bear punishment until they have paid for their mistakes, and have repented.[53] However, this does not apply to weaknesses and offenses which cleave to all persons. Whoever sins out of human weakness and slips (Gal. 6:1), to him or her the sin is not accounted, and he or she is forgiven because of Christ's righteousness.[54] The text in Matt. 18:15 is only applicable to secret sins, to evidences and faults which occur because of human weakness, but not to public works of the flesh.[55] Wanton sinners should experience the full strength of the ban, and for them no exception is to be made. No delay should be considered, and the threefold admonition also does not apply. Banning must be followed by shunning, for three reasons. First, the congregation must not share in the sins of the others, for a little leaven sours the whole dough (I Cor. 5:6). Second, the member who has committed a public sin must be publically shamed. The flesh must be punished so that the spirit will be saved in the day of the Lord (I Cor. 5:5). Third, God's church must not be slandered because of the sinner, nor appear guilty before the Lord on account of the sinner.[56]

The church may not tolerate any evil and carnal persons in its midst;[57] it must be pure and holy.[58] Only holy brothers and sisters belong to it, namely those who greet each other with the peace of Jesus Christ and the kiss of love. In brief, the church should be a credit to her name, "the bride of Christ." Therefore, fornicators, adulterers, idolaters and other evildoers must be separated by the ban. It is impossible for them to be members of the body of Christ and to be accounted to the temple of God. It would be an ungrateful and terrible sin if the bride should forsake her bridegroom and start living according to the flesh.[59]

At the end of his argument, Dirk felt compelled to respond to some real or possible objections. He mainly defended his conviction that a sinner must be punished with actual separation and shunning, even if the sinner had repented and promised to change. True repentance must be demonstrated outside of the church, not with words but with deeds.[60] The genuine penitent will agree to a strong, but well-deserved, punishment imposed in the name of the Lord and his church.[61] In the end, Menno's former view of the ban, proposed in 1541, was expressed.[62] Whoever commits fornication, adultery, and such sins is already separated from the congregation of God and, to indicate this, is cut off from them. But whoever truly repents is accepted by God in grace and, as proof, is welcomed back with joy by the congregation.[63]

Following the example of Pijper,[64] I will quote from other treatises where Dirk Philips wrote about the church and the mandate it received to maintain the ban. Dirk characteristically preferred to describe the church as the new or heavenly Jerusalem that descended from heaven adorned as a bride (Rev. 21:2 and 9 ff.). Christ is the Lord and bridegroom of the church which is bound to him by the apostle who will be presented to him as a pure virgin upon his return (2 Cor. 11:2).[65] If I am correct, Dirk spoke only three times about having a church without spot or wrinkle (Eph. 5:27).[66] After he established that a Christian church could not exist without exclusion or shunning, he gave the church the power to bind and loose, to forgive and to keep sins.[67]

In "Concerning Spiritual Restitution" Dirk went through the Old Testament and showed how figurative portrayals there came to be literally and spiritually fulfilled later through Jesus Christ. When he recorded the apostasy and sins of the Israelites, he took the opportunity to mention the need to punish disobedient trouble makers with the ban.[68] He regretted that many teachers had became deserters.[69] Dirk said more about the ban in the treatise "(Concerning) The Congregation of God," in which he declared the fourth church ordinance to be evangelical separation.[70]

> *The unfruitful branches must be pruned from the vine, otherwise they damage the good and fruitful branches. The offending members have to be separated, otherwise the entire body will be destroyed. If one does not exclude public sinners and those who lead immoral lives, then the entire congregation is polluted. And if one keeps false members in the church, one participates in their sins.*[71]

As in the booklet ("Concerning the Ban") Dirk mentions three reasons for the ban and emphasizes one.[72] On theological grounds, the church has decisive power.[73] In the pages that follow, he repeatedly comes back to the congregation's duty to ban evildoers.[74] Following the condemnation of the godless from Revelation (21:8), he breaks out in a complaint:

> *Oh Lord, what will happen to those who now boast with brave and haughty words that they are the church of the*

Lord, they who are entirely steeped in carnal desires, are idolaters and liars and commit scandalous deeds before the Lord![75]

However, Dirk expressed sharpest criticism for apostates by citing Hebrews 6:4-6 and 10:26-29. Those who have once been enlightened, accepted into the God's church by baptism, and received by the Holy Spirit, and who then depart from the known and accepted truth, and wilfully sin, cannot regain by repentance the salvation lost by their own doing. Only the prospect of a terrible judgment remains for such wanton sinners, "for our God is a consuming fire" (Heb. 12:29).[76]

Menno's article, "Instruction on Excommunication," was first printed four months later, June 11, 1558[77] and, as far as I can judge, was printed with the same type used in Dirk's booklet about the ban. From this evidence, and because Menno used Dirk's arguments and further developed some of his thoughts—for example, David's sin and Peter's denial of Jesus—I conclude that in 1558 Dirk resided near Menno in Wüstenfeld.

Reading Menno's work one gets the impression that the debate in Harlingen was long and intense. They must have analysed the biblical texts carefully, and then established firm guidelines for the church. They also discussed the practical effects of a lax application of the ban, as well as deeper causes of the quarrels. Menno listened attentively to the arguments of Dirk and Leenaert, weighed everything on the scale of the divine Word, and became convinced that one must exclude scandalous, carnal sinners without any preceding warning,[78] for they had been already judged by the Word of God.[79]

Menno also accepted complete shunning in marriage, although that was more difficult for him.[80] In the fourth chapter of his booklet he defended shunning: "The true apostolic ban should not make exceptions for anyone."[81] The spiritual must not give way before the carnal, but the carnal before the spiritual. A Christian is bound to Christ in a spiritual marriage and the heavenly wedding has precedence over the earthly.[82]

I would like to add a few comments. Menno got agreement at Harlingen regarding secret sins.[83] This was considered a matter between the omniscient God and the person who had sinned and come to repentance through Christ's Spirit.[84]

Menno based his explanation of Matt. 18:15-17 on the words which are found in the official translation: "If your brother has sinned *against you*, etc."[85] This made it possible for him to preserve the three warnings for the daily transgressions of one brother against another. According to his exegesis, this admonition was meant as a guideline for the church which was mindful of a sinner's eternal salvation. Such a church would therefore also enforce shunning. The sin which gives occasion to call a brother to account is not described in detail, but it may be of a serious nature.[86] Menno did not want to use the three warnings for public sinners because that would lead to hypocrisy and would dishonour the church, which is the bride of Christ. For so long as evil doers are not banned they belong to the congregation and take part in all gatherings, including the Lord's Supper.[87]

One cannot blame Menno for thinking that the incestuous person of Corinth (I Cor. 5) was received back again a year or so later (2 Cor. 2:5-11). After all, this position is still with us today.[88]

"Heresy or sectarianism" were special cases. In such cases, Menno felt that only two warnings should be given. After that, the person causing disagreement must be shunned (Titus 3:9-11).[89]

It is striking that Menno did not mention the texts in 2 Thess. 3:3 and 14 ff. in his "Instruction on Excommunication," while Dirk quoted them not only in the title of his ban booklet, but also in the text.[90] Indeed, they are of importance to the institution of the ban. Instead, Menno gave a less clear reflection on James 5:19, 20 and 2 Cor. 12:20-13:4.

In the "Conclusion of the Book,"[91] Menno emphasized that he had clarified the holy ordinance of the apostolic ban according to Holy Scripture. He had added nothing new, and had not changed anything concerning the basic principle. As a consequence of discussions with the brothers, through the study of certain biblical texts, and because of recent experiences, Menno took a more rigid position regarding public sinners.[92]

Still, he regretted that the bride of Christ, God's church, had been split due to quarrelsome people, and that she must be dressed in ugly rags instead of in white, shining garments which celebrate the beauty of her virtues. This was why the church was ridiculed and slandered by many people. Menno complained, "My soul is often more afraid than I can write. May the God of power strengthen me."[93]

Menno certainly could have used power from above. Although according to his own admission he had chosen a firm position on the issue of the ban, he was nevertheless torn between his earlier opinion regarding spousal shunning and the opinions expressed in the "Instruction on Excommunication." In a letter to several brothers, dated December 15, 1558, he indeed supported spousal shunning, but would still permit exceptions for all kinds of reasons.[94]

It is not certain when the attack from Zylis and Lemke came into the hands of the Dutch elders, but I suspect it was early in 1559. From this writing, it is clear that the Upper German teachers supported the moderates and rejected Menno and his followers. They were not gracious in their rejection. Zylis called Menno a wavering reed, a weathercock that turns with any gust of wind.[95] He accused those who supported the strict ban of being heretics and marriage breakers, and called Menno's treatise on the ban "a book of fables."[96] Lemke boasted that he differed from Menno on three or four articles, including the doctrine about spousal shunning,[97] and that he could happily throw out more than half of Menno's book.[98] Furthermore, he bragged that he would rather be banned by the Dutch elders than accept their point of view.[99]

This pamphlet must have irritated the Dutch. It was discussed in detail in the congregations, and they decided that the elders must travel to Germany and deal with the Upper Germans again. If they could not win them over to the Dutch position, the delegates were charged to pronounce the ban on the Upper Germans.[100] Because Menno was no longer able to travel,[101] Dirk and Leenaert were assigned as leaders of the delegation (1559).

The debate at Cologne was long and furious. The Upper Germans believed that on the basis of the Holy Scriptures they could not agree with the Dutch position, and thus they were banned. Their baptism and church ordinances were nullified and declared useless, and they were no longer recognized as evangelical brothers.

This division between the Dutch (of course, only the adherents of Menno) and the Upper Germans had far-reaching consequences. Even the Upper Germans who had lived in the Netherlands for a long time and had been treated as brothers were now required to be baptized anew. Those who objected were viewed as "worldly people." The ban was also pronounced on Dutch members who had located in Germany and did not want to separate from the Upper Germans.[102]

Two writings resulted from the meeting with the Upper Germans at Cologne in 1559: A short piece, probably a sketch of a letter after "Reply (and Refutation) to (Two Epistles of) Sebastian Frank,"[103] and the "Epistle to the Wife of J. den S."[104]

As far as I know, the rough draft of the first writing was found among old papers early in the seventeenth century when the publisher P. van Wesbusch[105] prepared a second printing of "About the Marriage of Christians." He added the "Posthumous Work concerning the Ban," translated from French by his fellow believer Carel van Mander, as well as "Justification and Refutation" which had never been printed. Dirk was held in high esteem by the Old Flemish, and therefore everything he wrote was printed.

Dirk's letter is not easy to understand. It begins with the refutation of slander from certain Swiss brethren.[106] They called the order for shunning as instituted by Menno and Dirk, an inhuman, vengeful and tyrannical ban. Their argument was that on the basis of Galatians 6:8 ("the one who sows to please his sinful nature, from that nature will reap destruction," etc.), the Dutch elders felt themselves to be more enlightened and did not regard their Swiss brothers as equal "building partners" (Ezra 4:1-3). Dirk replied that he had in his possession a summary written in High German about a discussion of the Swiss brothers who had settled in Moravia eighteen years previously. Anyone with good intentions would be able to judge on the basis of this discussion whether or not banning and shunning was actually inhuman and tyrannical.[107] Finally, Dirk warned his opponents about God's judgment; they had to acknowledge that God gave David the kingdom, which will be the Lord's.[108] Whosoever does not honour the ban and, like Heliodorus, violates the Holy Sanctuary, will not escape divine punishment.[109]

The letter "To the wife of J[ochem] the S[ugarbaker] who lies in prison in Antwerp" was probably written in Cologne in 1559. K. Vos thinks that Dirk heard of her imprisonment when he was in Cologne through an elder of Antwerp who attended the conference, and who then took the letter with him.[110] At the end of the letter, Dirk greets several church members who perhaps had stayed in Cologne as refugees.[111]

The woman's name is not mentioned in the letter; we only learn it from van Braght. Laurens van der Leyen brings greetings in his third (undated) letter from Adriaentgen, Jochem's wife.[112] She was taken prisoner in May, 1559 and escaped from Het Steen, the Antwerp prison, on November 10th of the same year with four other imprisoned Anabaptists.[113] On the title page of the letter it says further, "and lost her life there afterward as a witness to the truth. Now published for the first time. Anno, 1579."[114] How is this to be explained? Either the publisher concluded from the contents[115] that she had been executed, or she was later incarcerated again and the death sentence was carried out without our knowing about the hearings.

Dirk called her husband "my dearly beloved brother whom I have loved from the bottom of my heart."[116] He must have been an elder, one of the principal leaders of the Flemish Anabaptists. Without a doubt J. den S. meant Joachim the Sugarbaker, elder in Antwerp.[117] He baptized many–according to one report more than three hundred–and in a letter from the Inquisitor Pieter Titelman to the Duchess of Parma (November 14, 1561) Joachim was called "the sovereign prince of the Anabaptists."[118] A proclamation of December 20, 1558 placed a price of 300 Carolus guilders on both his head and that of Leenaert Bouwens.[119]

Until now it has been assumed, on the basis of a letter which Matthias Servaes wrote to Heinrich Krufft,[120] that Joachim was only converted in Cologne in 1565 by Georgius Cassander, but in fact this had already happened in August 1562, in Cleve. In "Von dem Kindertauff" (*Concerning Infant Baptism*), at the end of the second preface it says:

> *Dated in the year 1562 on the 30th day of August, it was reported by godfearing and pious men that a man named Joachim Zuckerbecker, a pious minister among the Anabaptist brothers, a very intelligent and diligent man, who may have baptized over three hundred persons, willingly departed from his sect and publicly recanted their errors in the church in Cleve in the Land of Cleve.*[121]

Georgius Cassander talks extensively about the conversion of Joachim, although he does not report his name. He suggests that he was an extraordinary man among the ministers and preachers of this erroneous doctrine.[122] In a letter written after the appearance of his book *Concerning Infant Baptism*, and addressed to Gerard Velsius who was an evangelical court preacher for the dukedom of Cleve (ca. January, 1563), Cassander wrote: "I have made some comments in passing about our Joachim, on account of whom these testimonies were gathered; however, I have left out his name."[123] After the year 1565 Joachim apparently baptized again, probably disappointed that Matthias Servaes had been executed at Cologne at the end of July.[124]

The reason the letter from Dirk to the wife of J. den S. was not printed during Dirk Philip's lifetime must have been because this well-known elder became an apostate. The letter was not printed until 1579, when it was published along with the Confession of Thomas van Imbroich.

The years 1558 and 1559 were busy times for Dirk. He participated in various meetings of elders and, in addition, prepared several treatises for publication.[125]

Dirk probably left Cologne for North Holland. In Hoorn he ordained a second elder, Lubbert Gerritsz. Gerritsz was born in Amersfoort in 1534. He was a linen weaver by trade, and was accepted into the congregation by baptism in 1556. In 1559, summoned on account of his faith, he fled to Hoorn where he was immediately chosen by the congregation to be an elder. Dirk must have gladly added him as a colleague to Jan Willems to strengthen the influence of the conservative wing against the Waterlanders.[126]

It is speculated that during this year Dirk further extended his travels and went east, possibly even to the Prussian congregations to inform them about the struggle over the ban and to win them over to his and Menno's conviction.[127] He could confidently leave the organization in Friesland and East Friesland to Leenaert Bouwens and his faithful follower Hoyte Renix. Menno completed the "Reply to Zylis and Lemke" on January 23, 1560, and added the ban pronounced against the Upper Germans at the end.[128]

The Flemish Anabaptist deacon, Herman de Timmerman,[129] responded to Dirk and Menno's writings about the ban in his booklet "An Explanation of how and in what way the Lord Jesus gave His disciples power concerning separation, etc."[130] Taking the side of the moderates, the booklet distinguished itself by its dignified tone, and radiated a pastoral care for the congregation. The author tried to sway Dirk and Menno by pointing to Christ's love for sinners, to the gospel as good news, and to God, who with forgiving grace accepts the repentant sinner. He repeatedly called Dirk and Menno "dear Dirk Philips," and "dear Menno Simons." Although he respected and thanked these ministers for their faithful service, and defended them against slander, for the sake of his conscience he had to oppose their books.[131]

Timmerman was most bothered by the fact that Dirk wanted to exclude repentant sinners from the church, and view them as apostates until they brought forth fruits of repentance.[132] He also disagreed with Dirk's suggestion that repentant sinners would be at peace with the deserved punishment imposed on them by the congregation.[133]

Already in the Preface[134] he noted three points in which Dirk departed from evangelical doctrine, and he repeated these points in the argument directed against Dirk.[135]

1. One interferes in God's judgment when a repentant sinner is banned, for one judges a person who has been acquitted by God.

2. One proclaims a different gospel to a repentant sinner than Christ does, who grants forgiveness to repentant sinners.

3. Apostolic separation was given to us to assist in the conversion of sinners, not their destruction. For when repentant sinners are excluded, they are also robbed of association with the church and its communal prayer, and easily fall into depression.[136]

After Timmerman pleaded with the two Dutch elders to give fallen members time for repentance, he addressed himself particularly to Dirk Philips with the following admonitions: "Let God judge the heart of the repentant, and be obedient to the teaching of the holy apostle."[137] "Confess your sin, that is, your reckless writing, with a humble heart before God and your neighbour, and be reconciled with us again."[138]

One can give full credit to Timmerman for his plea on behalf of the repentant sinner, but he misunderstood that for Menno and Dirk the ban had to do with the pure church, the bride of Christ. Dirk attached little value to the testimonies of regret and promises for improvement offered by someone who had committed a public sin. After all, the kingdom of God is not a matter of talk, but of power (I Cor. 4:20). Therefore, the remorseful sinner must bring forth fruits of repentance while outside the congregation.[139] Furthermore, God certainly forgives the guilt, but does not relieve the sinner of deserved punishment, and the ban is the punishment commanded by God. If the sinning members are truly repentant they will accept punishment willingly.

In brief, Dirk and Menno focussed more on the basic principle, while Timmerman gave consideration to the individual and to that person's disposition. Timmerman's writings–though well intended–did not have the power to bridge the gap between the moderate and the strict persuasions.

X

Dirk Philips as Elder in Danzig and Visitor to the Netherlands

Sources do not reveal where Dirk stayed at the end of 1559 and into 1560, although earlier[1] I speculated that he went to the Prussian congregations. Perhaps there he found the tranquility to translate two treatises into Dutch: "Concerning Spiritual Restitution" and "The Congregation of God," and to prepare them for first printing.[2] Both treatises were originally written in Lower Saxon.[3] It is uncertain where the first printing appeared.

Dirk took the view that the concept of restitution[4] was one which could easily be misinterpreted because each person explained it according to his own discretion and understood it "carnally."[5] Here Dirk was referring less to Campanus than to Rothmann, whose *A Restitution or a Reconstitution of the True and Wholesome Christian Doctrine, Belief and Life*[6] had been published in Münster in October 1534. Dirk wanted to prevent simple people from being deceived by false prophets who supported their false doctrines with Old Testament symbols and gave literal reading to the stories. Indeed, many sects had originated from the unjust use of the Old Testament, above all the "lamentable misunderstandings of rebellious sects"[7] which had caused much damage and vexation at the beginning of the Anabaptist movement.

The same applies to Dirk's "Concerning Spiritual Restitution" as I noted earlier regarding "The Tabernacle of Moses"[8]: Bernhard Rothmann's ideas were not hinted at in the "Restitution," except in the introduction and perhaps at the end.[9] This is generally true when the contents of Rothmann's writings are compared with the writings of Dirk Philips.[10] "Concerning Spiritual Restitution" remained of current interest. It appears that Rothmann's booklet was still being distributed, and that it found readers and was seriously discussed in Anabaptist circles.

Dirk wanted to treat Old Testament figures just as he had in the "Tabernacle of Moses,"[11] and to reveal how all things were reconstituted and fulfilled in Jesus Christ. Typology ran rampant in his exegesis. In forty-five sections he went through the historical books of the Old Testament and did not omit the Song of Solomon. He set out to demonstrate that all events in the history of Israel, and the conduct and adventures of biblical persons, had been fulfilled through Christ.

Sometimes Dirk made strange comparisons,[12] but this should not surprise us considering to what absurdities the typological biblical exegesis of Melchior Hoffman had led. However, some parts still resonate with us, such as his portrayal of the spiritual temple and the city of God that is God's church which is to be built upon the foundation of prophets and apostles after the second deliverance from Babylon.[13] Found here already was a summary of the divine ordinance[14] later developed further in "The Congregation of God."[15] There was also an objection to the Münsterites who wanted to set up an earthly kingdom with carnal weapons.[16] He, on the other hand, described the character of God's people who fight with spiritual weapons and trust in God's help. "For the Lord is with his people and helps his servants faithfully. Amen."

As I have shown above,[17] "The Congregation of God"[18] was written shortly after "The Spiritual Restitution."[19] Dirk quoted the following articles in it: "(Concerning) Rebirth and the New Creature,"[20] "The Sending of Preachers"[21] and "(Concerning) the Ban."[22] These quotations prove that "The Spiritual Restitution" as well as "The Congregation of God" were published around 1560.

In the first part "The Congregation of God" Dirk gave a biblical view concerning what the church of God is, how it began, and how one can join.[23] This was followed by the seven ordinances which characterize the church of God.[24] Finally, God's church was described as the holy city, the New Jerusalem that already exists, in principle, on earth.[25]

The church of God originated in heaven where the angels praised and served God. On earth there was also a beginning. The first people, created in the image of God, lived in paradise, in purity and obedience. Therefore it followed that God's church was a fellowship of saints and—with a leap of logic—it was made up of the angels in heaven and of those reborn on earth who were renewed in God's image. But then came the Fall: First the angels fell, followed by Adam and Eve. However, God's promise of salvation came to the rescue (Genesis 3:15).[26] The apostate church was resurrected by God's promise, and fallen people were raised up to receive the image of God anew because they accepted, in faith, the preaching of the gospel, meaning the promise of the seed of a woman (Christ).

I must not go further into the development of Dirk's train of thought. He talked about the history of the patriarchs and showed how everything had happened with a view to the coming of Christ. Further, he expanded on the rebirth which takes place through the law and the gospel, and he directed the interested reader to the treatise "Concerning (the New Birth and) the New Creature."

With rebirth came a clear doctrine of one God, Father, Son and Holy Spirit. What Dirk wrote about the Holy Spirit was conventional:[27] He was the third name, person, power and action of the Godhead, of one divine being with the Father and the Son. He proceeded from the Father, through the Son, and was also there at the creation. This doctrine was undoubtedly orthodox, and Hoekstra's criticism[28]—that Menno and Dirk never taught about the Holy Spirit—is hereby shown not to apply to Dirk.[29]

The second part of the "The Church of God" contained the seven ordinances[30] instituted by Christ, to be observed by the congregation:

1. *The pure doctrine of the Word of God and the true ministers who are called by the Lord and the congregation.* Here Dirk said nothing about doctrine—he had already done that in earlier pages—but concerning ministers who had been called he gave a short summary with reference to his treatise "The Sending of Preachers."[31]

2. *The scriptural use of baptism and the Lord's Supper.* By these signs the church of God was distinguished from all the sects (churches) which do not practice these ordinances.

3. *Footwashing of the saints.* This was a new doctrine. Dirk first mentioned this ordinance in "(Concerning) the Rebirth and the New

Creature"[32] and now he offered a biblical motivation for it. Proceeding from John 13:1-20, he argued that footwashing was a symbol. Even after our sins have been washed away by the blood of Christ, still our lusts and carnal desires must be conquered and killed by the Spirit. We must be cleansed from all sinful stains. Furthermore, footwashing teaches us humility. We follow Christ's example by humbling ourselves and showing honour to our fellow believers.[33]

We do not know what influenced Dirk to give footwashing a place among the ordinances of the Lord. Menno commended it in an early writing as "a custom of the saints."[34] In the foreword to *The Ban* ("Instruction on Excommunication")[35] he portrayed Satan as one who presented himself as a pious Christian. As a hypocrite, "[he] gave alms, received the suffering, washed the saints' feet, etc."[36] Footwashing, then, was customary in the [Dutch Anabatist] church around 1558.[37] H. S. Bender pointed out[38] that footwashing happened only sporadically among the Swiss brothers. It was reported as a Christian ordinance only by Pilgram Marpeck.[39] Had Dirk been compelled to reflect more deeply on this matter, it might have been another proof for direct or indirect relations with the Overlanders or Swiss brothers.

4. *Evangelical Excommunication.* I have dealt with this subject in the previous chapter.[40]

5. *Brotherly Love.* This was to be a clear result of faith and genuine Christianity. The members should serve one another, not just with spiritual gifts, but also with material ones. The poor must be looked after in every way. Menno gave practical advice in this regard,[41] and in the Amsterdam congregation, for example, the poor were cared for unstintingly.[42]

6. *Keeping all of the commandments of Christ.* Dirk also called this "following Christ." Properly understood, this did not relate to moral effort built on one's own strength, but rather to the communal effort of Christ's disciples, whom He gathered into a body of regenerated people and new creatures, and who received the power to follow Him, from fellowship with him through the Holy Spirit.[43] The new walk to which Christ called his own was the "discipleship" that H. S. Bender called the main and fundamental

article of the Anabaptist vision.[44] Dirk Philips casually mentioned that Christ required that his disciples never swear (Matt. 5:34). This is the only place I know of where Dirk touched on the issue of the oath.[45]

7. *All true Christians must suffer and be persecuted*, but they themselves may persecute no one on account of faith. Christ gave the ban to his church as a tool to separate false members from the congregation, namely the quarrelsome and heretical, and indeed, all sinners. The church should not dominate consciences by using external force, nor should it compel unbelievers to faith. The church must judge and exclude guided only by the Word of the Lord.

Should someone object and say that the authorities did not receive the sword in vain, Dirk agreed. The authorities had received the sword not to condemn in spiritual matters, but to maintain order and peace among their subjects, to protect the pious, and to punish the wicked. God's order to Moses to kill the false prophets is found in the Old Testament, not in the New. Strictly speaking, Dirk did not advise nonresistance in this case. He also did not speak about fighting wars and the death penalty, but examined the demand for endurance under persecution.[46]

Most of Dirk Philips' treatises showed how the pressure of persecution and chicanery of the government weighed heavily on the Anabaptist congregations.[47] The leaders had to suffer most of all. Dirk wrote that true leaders must be tested by the cross.[48] During the time the three letters were written, the church apparently suffered exceptional persecution.[49] Still Dirk admonished the church to pray for the government, and for all people, that God might have mercy on them and enlighten them so that they might come to the knowledge of the truth and be saved.[50]

After another summary,[51] Dirk went on to an enthusiastic description of the church as the New Jerusalem and the Bride of Christ[52] on the basis of Revelation 21 and 22. He did not claim that the visible church could already *now* be considered equal to the New Jerusalem. That was only present in principle, in the spirit. The culmination would only take place at the end of time. However, Dirk's distinction between allegory and reality was sometimes confused, which makes this part of his writing less accessible for today's reader. I believe that I can be brief about this,[53] whereas Schijn-Maatschoen cannot praise it enough.[54]

I have wondered why the concept of the kingdom of God is scarcely to be found in Dirk's writings. The reason might be that he made relatively little use of the first three gospels and much more of John's gospel, and the letters of the apostles. This is just a thought. Another observation seems more relevant to me. What Jesus meant by the Kingdom of God–that is the Lordship of God which begins with the Son and comes through him here on earth, and yet is also in the future–Dirk called the church of God, the New Jerusalem, as described in the last part of "The Congregation of God." I find the connection between these two concepts in the following sentences: With the coming of Christ on earth the church expanded, and the Kingdom of God has increased over the whole earth through missionaries of the Lord. So the church has become a glorious house of the living God. No one may enter the Kingdom of God, this heavenly Jerusalem, unless one has converted, repented truly, and believed the gospel.[55] As a short definition we might say: The church is the Kingdom of the Almighty.[56]

Having discussed "The Spiritual Restitution" and "The Congregation of God" fairly extensively, I return now to the point of departure: Dirk Philips' stay in Prussia.[57] Dirk probably traveled there from Emden on a sailing ship, as many of his fellow believers had before him. The sea route to Prussia, and mainly to Danzig, was well known because of busy trade.[58] The difficult economic situation in the thirties, and the persecution of faith, forced many Dutch people to seek a refuge in Prussia. However, because they were not allowed in the city of Danzig, they settled in the suburbs called *"Garten."* They were chiefly tradesmen who were serious competition for the guilds in the city. There must have been Anabaptist refugees among them, and this was used as a pretext to make it difficult for all the Dutch. The refugees did well because they were accepted in the area of Danzig, the land of the bishop of Lesslau or Cujavie, in Schottland, and there found a peaceful existence. The Danzig guilds persisted in stirring up trouble against these "interlopers" and charged them with rebaptizing, but the bishop was more interested in keeping these industrious people in his territory. "Besides he derived a certain pleasure, as a Catholic, in protecting the Anabaptists, unlike the Lutheran Danzigers."[59] Dutch farmers were allowed to settle on city-owned land, in the so called Little or Danziger Werder (polder). Because they could not obtain the right of citizenship from Danzig they could not rent the land directly, but this took place through the mediation of citizens of Danzig. Between the years 1547-1552, Dutch colonists settled in this manner in five villages, among others in Reichenberg.[60]

It is difficult to say what religion the Dutch immigrants represented. Among them were Sacramentarians, also called Zwinglians, Anabaptists who had participated in the journey to Münster or in the riots in Amsterdam, and peaceful Melchiorites. Fear and disgust with the events in Münster—combined with economic motives—led to all the Dutch being called Anabaptists. One can speak of Mennonites only after 1547.[61] In that year, several pieces of land in the "Werder" were leased to Herman van Bommel and Theunis Florisz. Theunis Florisz almost certainly belonged to the Anabaptists, for he had fled from the Prussian dukedom because of his faith.[62]

In 1549 Menno Simons visited the congregations in Prussia.[63] According to his letter dated October 7, he mediated among various groups and temporarily restored peace. But he feared that peace would be fleeting, for not everyone was prepared to accept the brotherly discipline and instruction administered by Menno.[64] We do not know whether Dirk Philips accompanied Menno and remained there as elder of the Prussian church in Danzig.[65] As noted earlier, there is no proof supporting that conclusion.[66]

The statement by Jan van Sol on December 22 and 23, 1550 needs further explanation. The statement was made to members of the Secret Council in Brussels, and it has been cited as evidence.[67] Jan van Sol gives the impression of being an adventurer. He fled from Dordrecht to Danzig in 1530 because his business went bankrupt. If this is correct he was a Sacramentarian and not a Melchiorite.[68] Apparently he later joined the Anabaptists. At least he knew enough to be able to talk about their leaders, churches, and customs. He returned to the Netherlands to play the role of a traitor. He made various proposals about how to oppose the Anabaptists in the hope that he himself might benefit. But there he made a mistake. The council learned all his secrets, but did not follow his recommendations. They did not want to jeopardize business with Prussia on account of such a person.[69]

The following reports from the hearings of Jan van Sol are important to us: The leaders of the Melchiorites are said to be Dirk Philips, Menno Simons, and Jan de Verwer.[70] He mentions two "bearers of the purse" (deacons) in Danzig: Thonis Barbier from Emden and Michiel Janszoon from Oosterhout in Brabant, who had died shortly before in Elbing. Herman van Bommel, former chaplain of nobleman Karel van Gelre, governor of Groningen, and Huyghe Mathyszoon were mentioned together because they openly accused Jan van Sol of being a spy. Huyghe Mathyszoon is said to have held the office of minister (admonisher).[71] It is uncertain whether this Hughe Mathyszoon is the same person as the Dutchman Hugo Mattheisen, to whom the magistrate of Danzig leased a piece of land in 1562. If so, he must have changed vocation and become a successful farmer.[72]

I will not go into detail about the other Dutch colonies in West Prussia because that falls outside the scope of my study. However, I do want to mention that Dr. Greta Grosheide's dissertation demonstrates that there was much traffic between the Amsterdam Anabaptists and Danzig.[73]

We now leave the Danzig congregation and ask whether there is evidence that Dirk Philips lived and worked in Danzig in the sixties.[74] In the first place, there is the following report from the Danzig "Congregational Register."[75]

> *In the year 1567, here in Danzig, Dirk Philips was the elder sent from Friesland during the time of the division,*

> and he died there the following year, 1568. Then an elder called Steven Vader stayed here in Danzig, just as appears from the letter which Hans Sieke, the travelling companion of D.P., wrote to us, ending with: hearty greetings from us all to our elder by the name of Steven Vader.[76]

I have found more evidence in a book by Georg Hansen, minister of the Flemish congregation in Danzig: "A Foundation Book of Christian Doctrine, which was taught among the Mennonites in Prussia, etc. (called Danzig clergy)," Amsterdam, Barent Visser, Book seller, 1696.[77] In the debate, the writer quotes Dirk Philips' booklet about the ban from the *Enchiridion* of 1627. He then writes, "For we say with our beloved brother and elder Dirk Philips, who was an elder in God's church in Danzig..."[78] and he concludes the argument,[79] "so says Dirk Philips. Our dear elder wrote this warning one hundred and twenty-one years ago." That would have been in 1558. Therefore, in 1678 (the year of the debate) someone in Danzig still knew that Dirk Philips had been an elder there, and his writings were still held in honour by the Flemish Mennonites. As H. G. Mannhardt wrote to me [in 1914],[80] in Danzig they have always known that Dirk served the congregation as an elder from 1561 to 1567. In the chapter that follows we will see that Dirk travelled twice to Emden from Danzig.[81]

In 1561, after tidings of Menno's death had come to Prussia,[82] Dirk decided to travel and visit congregations in his homeland. He may have begun his journey by sailing to Emden to confer with Leenaert Bouwens, who had the leadership in the west. Dirk's friend was in a difficult predicament. Around 1561 he had been accused by some people in the congregation.[83] We do not know precisely what the accusation was. The quarrel was settled, peace was restored, and forgiveness granted. Leenaert was allowed to take communion again, but from 1561 to 1563 he was not permitted to make any missionary trips to other regions. We have no proof that Dirk was involved in this disciplinary action; rather, he would have admonished them to make peace.

I think that on his way to Friesland Dirk stayed with his old congregation in Appingedam, and ministered there with teaching and the Lord's Supper. In Friesland he met Hoyte Renix, the elder in Bolsward, whom he had already met in Harlingen in 1557, and who had been baptized and ordained by Leenaert Bouwens.[84] Dirk probably discussed the whole situation of the brotherhood in Friesland with him and, now that Menno was no longer with them, admonished him to be a faithful shepherd and servant of the church. They agreed to follow the same guidelines and separated in friendship. How different their relationship would be six years later![85]

After crossing the Zuiderzee [South See, now the Ijsselmeer] Dirk probably visited Hoorn. Jan Willems and Lubbert Gerrits lived there, both ordained as elders by Dirk. They discussed important issues. Perhaps here Dirk arranged that they should confer with the other leaders in North Holland concerning important matters.[86]

A few traces remain of Dirk's trip through North Holland. In Waterland, 1561, he baptized Willem Janszn.[87] I conclude that Dirk administered the baptism because during a later quarrel between Dirk Philips and another person—probably Jan Willems—Willem Janszn took the side of the first party. Janszn was banned from the congregation for his stance. I believe that Janszn was moved to do this out of loyalty to his baptizer. It is a fact that Dirk baptized Clara Jansd van Ransdorp, who lived in Edam in 1575. She states that she was rebaptized 12 or 13 years earlier by Dirk Philip who, according to her, later "departed from his faith."[88] Therefore, she belonged to the party of the Frisians. Either Clara had forgotten the date, or else Dirk conducted the baptism on his return trip from Utrecht. The same goes for a baptismal service that was held around 1562 in Amsterdam. Jan Quirynszn was baptized, along with 10 or 12 other persons.[89]

Who was the baptizer? It could not have been Leenaert, and Joos Verbeek, who had been baptizing in Amsterdam in 1560, was burned in Antwerp on June 21, 1561.[90] Jan Willems only preached in Amsterdam in 1566 or 1567, at the time of the Frisian-Flemish quarrels, or after the break with Dirk Philips.[91] Other elders cannot be considered. Therefore it seems reasonable to conclude that Dirk led the baptismal service. Perhaps he had already made contact with the novices on his way to Utrecht, had examined them, and investigated each case separately.[92] Then, a few weeks later, on the return trip, the candidates could have received the desired baptism. This must have been in the beginning of 1562.

Fortunately, we are better informed about Dirk's doings in Utrecht.[93] Here a group of Anabaptists had formed a growing circle, with fluid boundaries. During Lent (February or March) 1561, the elder from Antwerp, Joos Verbeek, visited the congregation and baptized ten people. Among them were Willem Willemsz., a tailor and colleague, Henrick Emken, born in Loquard in East Friesland, and Emken's wife.[94] After the baptism they celebrated the Lord's Supper.

Around Christmas of the same year, a second meeting took place in the Cranesteyn house by the Cow Bridge, which belonged to Cornelis van Voordt, a well-to-do man. Once again, several people were baptized, among whom were the wife and two sons of van Voordt, and his maid Beatris Jansdr., originally from Nessen, near Wezel. About twenty people participated in the next Lord's Supper.[95] For reasons of security they gathered together before dawn, around four in the morning, and only went home in the evening around seven o'clock.[96] The elder who administered the baptism and the Lord's Supper was Dirk Philips. This came to light later, at the hearings.

In the spring of 1562, another gathering of believers was held in the Cranesteyn house. This meeting was raided on orders from the court. A number of those present escaped, but most were taken to jail. We learn several things about Dirk Philips from the testimonies of the captives. Anna, the wife of Henrick Emken, described him as an old man of medium height with a gray beard and white hair,[97] and Beatris said that the baptizer was clothed in black and wore a plain round cap.[98] They knew nothing about his place of residence.

Dirk's dialect gave people the impression that he came from a foreign country. Willem Willemsz declared that the baptizer was called Dirk, but claimed that he did not know his surname,[99] while Anna testified that "the baptizer, according to her understanding, was named Dirk Phillips."[100] It seemed to Willem that Dirk came from the East,[101] and Beatris thought that he spoke Brabants.[102] However, Beatris was a simple woman who could neither read nor write, and whose statements were less than clear;[103] one cannot rely on her testimony. Two of the captive Anabaptists were sentenced by the sheriff's court. Willem Willemsz was banned for six years and sent to His Majesty's galleys. On June 10, 1562, the Burgomasters and sheriffs sentenced Hendrick Emken to be burned at the stake, according to the decree of his Royal Majesty. The sentence was carried out the same day.[104]

By that time Dirk Philips had undertaken the return trip and, as we assumed earlier, travelled via Amsterdam to Emden. In the spring of 1562 he must have prepared reprints of "The Spiritual Restitution" and "The Church of God" for they appeared in the same year and were printed by Nicolaes Biestkens of Diest.[105] Biestkens was originally from Brabant and, according to popular opinion, ran a print shop at Emden from 1560 on. He became known through his publication of the whole Bible (1560) and of the New Testament (1562), both of which were highly valued by the Anabaptists.[106] Dirk returned to Danzig as soon as the shipping season opened.

At this point, I must insert an account of the "Three (Basic) Admonitions (or Epistles)"[107] because they have received little attention in the literature. They were not mentioned in the first edition of the *Enchiridion*,[108] but were added in the second edition with separate pagination. They were included in the register with the comment that they were sent to God's church "at diverse times."[109] I will briefly describe them and indicate the place they held in the story of Dirk's life.

Dirk Philips wrote as a father of the church: he liked to use language and admonitions from the apostles, and placed himself on a level with them, as it were.

The first letter.[110] Dirk learned that the church was threatened by persecution. He warned and comforted the members. The wording in this letter is similar to that found in the "Letter to the wife of J. der S."[111] The church was in danger of being influenced by the Davidjorists.[112] On top of that, some people were unwilling to apply strict shunning.[113] At the end of the letter, Dirk gave assurances that he felt united in brotherly love with those who received the letter, as they all had one common home in heaven and on earth.

All of this makes one think of Leeuwarden in Friesland, where Jacques d'Auchy, Hendrik Euwesz. and Claeske Gaeledr. had just been executed in March, 1559.[114] The fact that Dirk mentioned a "home in heaven" points in the same direction, as does the hesitation of those addressed regarding the ban and shunning, certainly understandable after the recent assembly in Harlingen in 1557, and the publication of ban booklets by Dirk and Menno (1558). The letter spoke about going to hear godless preachers who stand in the pulpit and falsify the Lord's Word,[115] and this is the only reason I hesitate to suggest absolutely that the letter's recipients were in Friesland. Perhaps here one must think of evangelical Christians who, although in name still Roman Catholic, proclaimed reformed ideas.

The third letter.[116] In my opinion, this letter was written before the letter that was printed second. Dirk had visited the congregation, and the letter was sent shortly after he had taken his leave.[117] He rejoiced that many had joined the church and that he was able to partake of the Lord's Supper with them in unity of spirit.

For the benefit of new members, Dirk wrote a sort of catechism. First he spoke about the basis of faith: Belief in God, the almighty Father, and in Jesus Christ, the only begotten Son of God (here he includes a short exposition of the doctrine of incarnation). This was followed by the doctrine of God's covenant with humanity, the first time such a doctrine was expressed in Dirk Philips' writings.[118] Baptism and the Lord's Supper were signs of the covenant, but His followers also must walk according to the gospel. Dirk warned against braggarts, wavering people, and frivolous souls who boasted about themselves and recommended the broad way. This admonition apparently alluded to his opponents in the struggle about the ban and shunning.[119] After his departure, he had heard that in some places persecution had begun, and he felt compelled to urge the congregation to persevere.

Then Dirk took leave of his readers; he had sent the letter to them as a farewell [*Valete*] or Christian Adieu.

Because more details are lacking, one can only speculate for whom the letter was intended. I suspect that it was meant for a congregation that Dirk had visited in 1561/1562, and probably was written before his departure for Danzig, perhaps from Emden. The mention of the "soft banners" suggests it may have been directed to a congregation in North Holland or Friesland. It is possible that this letter was directed to the congregation in Harlingen which was named at the end of the second letter.[120] The concluding words of both letters are almost identical.

The second letter.[121] This is the most important letter, for its tone is more personal than the others. In it Dirk opened his heart. He had visited his homeland, and had seen and heard with joy that God's church was blossoming and that the ordinances of the Lord were being maintained. With lyrical words Dirk, at other times so sober, described how the blessings of God were poured out, not only over his homeland, but also over the neighbouring lands (East Friesland, the Lower Rhine, Flanders).

Still, he was not blind to the dangers which threatened the church, particularly the threat from the promoters of the soft ban. As in the third letter, these people were sketched as braggarts, waverers, and flighty souls who boasted about themselves and were lax about shunning. These people accused true Christians, who had been instructed by God, of being enslaved by the letter, and Dirk had learned that they had found a following among some.[122] Therefore he warned his readers[123] to walk in a manner worthy of their calling. True Christians do good; they are born of God and do not sin. It is not sufficient to have an inner Christian inclination, one must show oneself to be a Christian outwardly as well.[124] Although apparently this particular congregation was not directly persecuted, still it suffered with the Church universal, robbed of her true servants, and with the members and fellow believers who were imprisoned and martyred in other places.[125]

They were to ask God for strength and patience. Then followed a reminder to be thoughtful: The readers should thank God that they had found faith and had become members of the body of Christ. Finally, there was a call to peace and unity. If they had been reborn through faith, then quarreling and partisanship could not exist among them.[126]

From the concluding words it would appear that Dirk wrote this letter from outside the country, probably after he had returned to Danzig. He would gladly have written to several members of the congregation separately but he had much work to do after his return. He spoke in veiled terms of difficulties in the congregation and outside of it. Therefore he asked his readers for prayer. He concluded the letter in the same manner as the third, which I think was directed to the Harlingen congregation:[127] "All the elders of our congregations greet you with the peace of God; greetings also from my travelling companion, who is well known to you."[128]

All things considered, I believe that the second letter was written from Danzig to a Frisian congregation, perhaps to the one in Franeker, where a fairly large minority did not agree with the strict application of the ban. Dirk's repetition of thoughts and arguments he had already used in the treatise on the ban (1558) and in other writings, is noteworthy.[129] Of course, it is possible that he kept a series of texts and examples so that he would not have to consult earlier booklets; it is also possible that he used the same basic arguments for the same topics.

The three letters are important for another reason. From them we learn about the Anabaptist congregations in Friesland, particularly about stricter congregations which other sources do not discuss. If, as de Hoop Scheffer suspects,[130] the pact between the four cities was concluded around 1560, it seems strange that Dirk was ignorant of this during his visit to Friesland.

At the end of the second letter Dirk hinted that he had struggled after his return to Danzig. He was worried by personal cares, and the church faced strife and persecution from the government and other churches. Dirk himself faced persecution from personal enemies.[131] Indeed, there were disagreements in Dirk's church, although the details are unknown to us.

We only know that Hoyte Renix and Leenaert Bouwens were asked to come over to settle the quarrel. They investigated the matter and banned several members.[132] During his stay in Danzig Leenaert baptized three people. He also baptized in Wüstenfelde, either on his trip to Danzig, or on his return home. Leenaert re-accepted the office of elder on January 1, 1563,[133] about a year and a half after he had been suspended from the service. Both Hoyte and Leenaert probably visited Danzig during the summer of 1563.

I suspect that Dirk sent Leenaert back to East Friesland with an important assignment, namely to bind together the treatises which, up to this point had appeared separately, and to have them printed by one of the Emden publishers. This effort resulted in the first publication of the *Enchiridion*.[134] The printing was fairly careless–it had many typographical errors and germanisms–and Dirk was not satisfied with the order of the writings, which were arbitrarily placed. He was even less satisfied with the title page, which was better suited to a work about Greek mythology than to a book about Christianity. Perhaps the printer chose the title page with the intention of misleading authorities about the book's content.

In any case, Dirk was unhappy with the effort, and when he came to Emden in 1565 he oversaw the production of a new edition, putting the treatises in order according to content, and adding the three letters as well as an extensive register. The quotations of biblical texts were placed on the side with the main sections not only given with letters–as was done in the first printing–but also divided into verses.[135] The title page read "now newly corrected and enlarged.," and at the end of the register it explicitly said, "we have annotated the different verses and have used symbols to indicate specific subjects."[136]

The first printing was probably deliberately destroyed, and it is miraculous that two copies still exist today. Because the first printing was annulled, Dirk gave the second the original year of publication: 1564. De Hoop Scheffer thought that the *Enchiridion* was printed at Emden (see the old catalogue in the Amsterdam Anabaptist Library). That assumption is in error, but the compiler printed the error in the new catalogue.[137]

XI

The Great Schism

During the years 1561 and 1562, Dirk Philips made several visits to his homeland. He spoke highly of the prosperity of the churches, of their perseverance in the faith, their burning love for God and His Word, their unity and peace, and the orderliness of their congregational life.[1] This tiny country had been blessed by God with grace and glory on behalf of the elect.[2] But Dirk could not rejoice for long about this happy state of affairs in the Frisian congregations. A few years later the great schism occurred, dividing the Frisians and the Flemish, and inflicting much damage on the Anabaptist fellowship.

Expert historians have written books about the controversy,[3] so I will not attempt to give another complete description of it. I will give a brief overview and try to explain Dirk Philips' position using several sources which have remained unknown until now.

I agree with Kühler[4] and blame Leenaert Bouwens for the difficulties which arose in Emden. Leenaert acted high-handedly in 1556 when he placed Swaan Rutgers under the ban, and his behaviour was similar in 1565. He travelled tirelessly, preaching and bringing many people to the church in Friesland,[5] but the people in Emden objected to the constant travelling of their elder. Many accusations surfaced which later appeared to be untrue, but which were still damaging to Leenaert.[6] He was charged with "grave matters" [*sware stukken*] which were already four or five years old and had not previously hindered his congregation from celebrating the Lord's Supper with him.[7] But the main problem was still "the matter of L. B. serving everywhere."[8] When criticisms were raised against him, he stated plainly that "a minister may live where he chooses, and further, a minister is no one's property, but is free."[9]

That statement certainly went too far. Were this attitude to prevail, the elder would have unlimited power without being subject to anyone.

The disagreement between Leenaert and his congregation became so heated that they resorted to a proven means and called seven outside ministers to investigate the case and settle the conflict.[10] Among these ministers were Hoyte Renix from Bolsward,[11] Ebbe Pieters[12] from Harlingen, and Dirk Philips who was called from Danzig. Dirk was the most appropriate person to assume leadership of the investigation, not only because of his age, but also because of his service to the fellowship. The other judges "entirely submitted [to him] and entrusted [him with] the judgment of the quarrelsome matter between the C[ongregation] at E[mden] and L. B., with the exception of E.P."[13]

Dirk Philips made short work of his fellow elder, who had once persuaded him to accept the strict application of the ban, and who now disappointed him with his worldly life style. Leenaert was suspended from the position of elder in 1565.[14]

In connection with the proceedings in Emden, a regulation was instituted about the calling and election of bishops and ministers.[15] Dirk supported this regulation with an article which he had published in 1559,[16] "On the Sending of Ministers or Teachers."[17] As in the article, the regulation required that a minister be doubly called, both by God and by the congregation. Whoever was unanimously chosen was ordained after fasting and prayer, according to the example of Apostolic times. A true servant must have both callings. According to the first he was a minister of the entire fellowship, and according to the second he served the congregation which had chosen him. If he wanted to serve the entire fellowship, he might do so only with the permission of the congregation in which he resided.

While Dirk Philips was still in Emden[18] an urgent request came from Friesland asking him to intervene again as an arbitrator. The judgment given by the seven elders had aroused unrest; Ebbe Pieters was guilty of inciting some of this dissatisfaction.[19] Furthermore, Leenaert had taken refuge in Friesland. Little remained of the submissiveness he had shown the elders in Emden. He claimed that he had been sentenced for trivialities for which a child would hardly be chastised.[20] This prompted the Frisian congregations to seek information about the reasons for Leenaert's suspension. They sent messengers to the arbitrators who apparently remained in Emden. However, the judges had agreed among themselves to keep the reasons for the suspension secret from church members.[21] This secrecy did not help to promote trust in their judgement. The Frisian congregations grew increasingly suspicious and demonstrated their attachment to Leenaert by inviting him to stay with them during the winters of 1565 and 1566. Invitations came from the congregations in Franeker and Harlingen.[22]

Secondly, a conflict arose between part of the Franeker congregation and Ebbe Pieters, pastor in Harlingen. The Flemish–who as a consequence of persecution in the Southern Netherlands had fled to Friesland in large numbers, where they were warmly accepted–deviated from the Frisians in character, clothing and customs.[23] They also had different views on the position of individual members in the church. They referred matters to church council sooner than was the custom in the Dutch Brotherhood.[24] Furthermore, many of the refugees had been robbed of everything and were dependent on assistance from the Frisian brothers.[25]

Gradually, friction developed. The spokesperson for the Flemish in Harlingen was a fairly young man, Pierken Pierson;[26] in Franeker, the leader was Jeroen Tinnegieter from Henegouwen. It was reasonable–if only because of the language problem–that the large groups of Flemish should get their own ministers in both congregations.

Jeroen Tinnegieter was legitimately elected by the congregation in Franeker. However, the elders in Harlingen objected to this choice without giving any specific reason. The disagreement became so severe that they called four outside ministers to help solve the conflict. Among these were the two Frisian elders, Hoyte Renix from Bolsward and Nette Lipkes from Dokkum.[27] Hans Busschaert from Cologne (earlier from Antwerp),[28] and Dirk Philips (who, as far as I know, was still in Emden) were also called.[29] They succeeded in settling the dispute,[30] although Jeroen never forgot that his appointment had been challenged by the people in Harlingen, and in particular by Ebbe Pieters.

During the investigation by the four ministers it was revealed that the people in Harlingen had appealed to a covenant which had been drawn up by congregations in four cities—Harlingen, Franeker, Leeuwarden, and Dokkum—"many years earlier."[31] Their mutual agreement had been established in nineteen articles. Unfortunately, the original document has been lost,[32] but it is certain that they agreed on this much: If a conflict arose in any church, the congregation would not get involved. Rather, the church council of that congregation would present the problem to the elders in the other churches and should they fail to reach an agreement, the conflict would be submitted to one or more "outside" ministers. Further, whoever was called as minister in one of the congregations would also serve the other congregations. In all four congregations, the matter of discipline was placed in the hands of Ebbe Pieters of Harlingen, who already had been chosen as elder, but had not yet taken office.[33] When he was fully installed, he would administer baptism and the Lord's Supper in all four congregations. Finally, because the large number of refugees burdened one congregation more than the others, they agreed that two deacons should be appointed from the four congregations who would administer assistance from a common fund.[34]

This "Covenant"—or, as they later preferred to call it,[35] "Ordinance of the four cities"—became a stumbling block in the struggle between the Frisians and the Flemish. "It appears that the Ordinance was adopted with good intentions," wrote Syvaert Pieters.[36] He continued, "the Ordinance was well known to the most important outside ministers and elders, and was more praised than censured." On the other hand, Outerman declared,

> The existence of such an ordinance was revealed to many only through the quarrel between Harlingen and Franeker; indeed, even certain ministers did not know of its existence, namely D. P., Hoyte R., Nette L. and Hans B.[37]

It seems likely that the Frisian congregations were relatively familiar with the Covenant, or at least with the practical application of the ordinance. They probably realized that the service of the ministers and the care of the poor was organized by some sort of agreement.[38] But the Flemish, who had not known about this ordinance, were upset when its existence was revealed because such secrecy was not in keeping with their beliefs on the rights of church members.

How was the Covenant viewed by outside leaders? Outerman noted that the leaders did not offer any objections to the ordinance based on Holy Scripture, and there were no documents accusing the proponents of the Covenant. Dirk Philips considered the Ordinance of the four cities to be "scriptural," an ordinance "by which God's church was built."[39] Clearly, at that time the outside ministers did not blame the conflict on the Covenant. However, Dirk Philips later changed his mind, for reasons I will soon discuss. Outwardly peace was restored, although the deeper cause of the dispute remained, and Dirk left for Danzig.

The struggle went on, and grew over time. Jeroen and his followers obstinately denounced the Covenant, and each party began to meet separately. This was the beginning of the schism.[40]

I will not discuss the details of these complicated disagreements.[41] In the heat of the conflict, the Frisians attributed an exaggerated value to the Covenant and the Flemish rejected it as a man-made commandment.[42] I agree with Kühler's remark:[43] "The Flemish were originally in the right, but sinned the worst in the struggle. The Frisians were less extreme, but defended an unjust cause."

It is hard to argue who was right, because there was no written "right," only a common "right." In contrast to the large churches which had a confession of faith and a church order, the Anabaptists wanted to settle all differences according to the Word of God, as it was interpreted by the elders or by the believers. In principle, all points of dispute were to be brought before the congregation, discussed there and, if possible, solved. If this were not possible, the congregation could invite one or more outside ministers to mediate. In the Frisian-Flemish dispute it now appeared that the parties could not agree on "which judges they should use to settle this dispute."[44] The Covenant's stipulation, that the church councils of the four congregations should regulate everything amongst themselves, violated the congregational principle. It was also customary that an outside minister could only accept the office of judge with authorization from his own congregation. But in violation of the congregational principle, [according to the Covenant] a powerful elder might accept the office of arbitrator without asking for permission from his own congregation. This was the case with Hoyte Renix in the conflict between Jeroen Tinnegieter and Ebbe Pieters concerning the denunciation of the Covenant by the Flemish.

At the invitation of the Frisians, and "against the will and warning" of the Flemish, Renix came to Franeker to act as an arbitrator. He came without permission from his congregation and against the advice of several fellow ministers, "saying that he intended to intervene at Franeker even though all the brothers of his church had decided not to."[45] Those who acted as judges were sometimes called "judges without congregations."

According to Kühler,[46] this expression was wrongly interpreted by de Hoop Scheffer. The phrase did not imply that judges intervened without permission from their own congregations–though that did happen, particularly in the last phase of the struggle–but that they pronounced a sentence without hearing from the particular congregation in trouble. Thus Outerman accused the Dutch judges, Jan Willems and Lubbert Gerrits, of approving the acquittal of Ebbe Pieters without consulting his congregation: "and they let themselves be used as judges without a congregation in the controversial affair."[47]

In August, 1566 there was a complete break between the Frisians and the Flemish. Ebbe Pieters was banned by a small gathering of Flemish and Flemish sympathizers in Harlingen. Of the 400 members of the Harlingen congregation only 40 were present. "With this ban the die was cast; the schism was irrevocable."[48] What followed was a consequence of this unjust decision. In Harlingen, and later in Franeker, all those who had been involved in sentencing Ebbe Pieters were banned by Hoyte Renix, in cooperation with the church councils of both congregations.[49]

Shortly thereafter a letter from Dirk Philips arrived, dated September 19, 1566.[50] The letter was addressed to the Harlingen congregation, but

Dirk wanted the letter passed on to the three other congregations in the Covenant–Franeker, Leeuwarden, and Dokkum–immediately after being read.

Reports about the dispute in Friesland had reached Danzig. The gist of these rumors cannot be determined from the content of Dirk's letter. Dirk did not take sides nor make judgments. He only expressed his sadness and anxiety, and pleaded with the two parties to make peace.[51] He had reflected on how the dispute could be settled. He had thought of writing to the churches and asking them to make peace with each other. "If, by God's grace, we could do something that would lead to peace, we would be more than willing to do so."[52] He had put the matter before the Lord in prayer, and had discussed it with several brothers. Then at last he had dared to send this letter to the congregations of the four cities,[53] "out of pure brotherly love," to encourage them to seek Christian peace and a godly life.[54]

It was a noble letter, free from partisanship, a gentle pastoral admonition, which "was, without any doubt, sincerely meant."[55]

But the letter had no effect. The flames of discord were too hot to be extinguished by a friendly admonition from Dirk Philips. The Flemish went ahead with separation, and they held a wedding ceremony in their own church in Harlingen to show that they were the only true congregation of God and all others were "but apostate or worldly people."[56] The Frisians reacted to the letter with stubborn silence,[57] although perhaps some of the more tolerant were influenced by it.

The elders from Brabant, Hans Busschaert and Hendrik van Arnhem, were among the more tolerant.[58] They directed the attention of both parties to the ministers from Hoorn, Jan Willems and Lubbert Gerrits,[59] and they named Gillis Schriver[60] as a mediator. Jan and [Lubbert] were prepared to accept the appointment, but stipulated that Hoyte Renix and Nette Lipkes would first have to consent to it. They also wished to consult with the other elders of North Holland,[61] and with their own congregation, before accepting the office.

A meeting took place in Amsterdam and among those present were both ministers from Hoorn [Jan Willems and Lubbert Gerrits], Hendrik van Arnhem, Gillis Schrijver, and Nette [Lipkes].[62] Hoyt Renix was absent, but he sent a threatening letter to Jan Willems and Lubbert Gerrits[63] in which he tried to persuade them to agree with him. During the meeting, it was announced that the elders from North Holland had approved the appointment of Jan and Lubbert. The congregation in Hoorn was prepared to delegate them, providing an invitation came from the Frisian side. Shortly thereafter a boat arrived from Friesland with two delegates who would accompany the new judges. After that, the group could depart for Friesland.[64]

The judges, however, would accept their task only on one condition: Both parties would have to commit themselves to accept the outcome, and forego any possibility of higher appeal. Both parties were to "compromise[65] and submit themselves to our dear brothers and servants, Jan Willems and Lubbert Gerrits, and to those accompanying them."[66]

The letter is dated 19 December 1566 and is signed by the principal Frisian and Flemish elders. However, before they could begin their investigation, the men from Holland had to address certain reservations of the Flemish., who wanted everything to be judged according to God's Word. Although this was promised to them, it was not noted in the text of the Compromise.[67]

The examination began in Harlingen, and the parties were heard separately. I draw attention to this because Dirk Philips later demanded that the dispute be handled in the presence of both parties.[68] The Flemish were given four days in which to express their grievances and defend themselves against the Frisians' accusations, "and, in addition, they could submit anything further in writing."[69] Jan Willems and Lubbert Gerrits realized that the ban on Ebbe Pieters was unjust, a realization which points to their discerning insight. Their diplomatic capabilities were equally strong. They induced the Flemish to make peace with Ebbe Pieters and Hoyte Renix, a peace which was recognized by the Brabant ministers.[70] However, as Frisians they lacked a certain sensitivity toward the principles of the Flemish church, and did not thoroughly appreciate their significance.[71]

Before the final verdict, the judges were adjured by Hans Busschaert, in the names of Hendrik van Arnhem and Gillis Schrijver, to split the blame equally between both parties and to leave the highest judgment up to God. But they did not want to promise that; they could only promise a mild judgment which would also correspond to the truth.[72]

The assembly during which the sentence would be announced was held in Harlingen on Saturday evening, February 1, 1567.[73] It opened with a solemn address by the chairperson, Jan Willems.[74] The judges did not wish to reveal details because it was "a general dispute." They wished to give "a general verdict." Should insincere and unrepentant persons be among the parties, God would judge them.[75] Therefore, the sentence read: "Both the Frisians and the Flemish should fall on their knees, acknowledge their transgressions and guilt, and ask each other for forgiveness, and from then on they should live and walk in peace and brotherly love."[76]

The Frisians were first.[77] They knelt down, acknowledged their guilt, and asked forgiveness, after which they stood up. The Flemish followed their example. But when they wanted to stand up "a very strange, divisive, and destructive thing happened." The chairperson let it be known that the verdict was different for them. They, the Flemish brethren, "being in the wrong, should not stand up by themselves, but should be helped up by hand."[78]

It is understandable that the Flemish had no desire to submit to this pronouncement. The judges had failed to notify them beforehand, and thus it was no administration of justice. The pronouncement appeared to be a secret arrangement between the judges and the opposition, intended to bewilder and humiliate the Flemish. Most of them jumped up indignantly, recanted their confessions of guilt and their compliance with the Compromise, and reclaimed their freedom of action, "and thus the last error on both sides was worse than the first."[79]

To justify Jan Willems and Lubbert Gerrits, one can only posit that they were influenced by a man of stronger will, namely Hoyte Renix. Before the judges met in Amsterdam, Hoyte had already "changed their minds" by sending them a threatening letter.[80] He objected to taking responsibility for banning the Flemish in Harlingen and Franeker, particularly in the presence of the opposing party. Hoyte, and perhaps other Frisians, almost certainly forced the Dutch judges to keep secret this peculiar punishment, meant only for the Flemish.[81] I agree with Kühler[82] that the Flemish sins were greater, due to their impulsive nature, but the judges should have been sensitive to this characteristic and warned them in advance. It is no surprise that the writer of "A Brief Demonstration," who researched the Frisian-Flemish conflict accurately and impartially, called "Hoyte Renix the main culprit in the dispute, on the Frisian side."[83]

Because of the Harlingen sentence, the Frisians felt superior, "helped onto a horse and put on top."[84] Jan Willems and Lubbert Gerrits flattered themselves with the hope that the first furor over their judgment would fade. Before departing from Friesland they even administered communion in some congregations, which really should not have occured when there was disunity between some of the brothers.[85] But soon a storm of criticism broke loose in the brotherhood, and many congregations sided with the Flemish. Reports from outside ministers, who had attended the affair at Harlingen as observers,[86] contributed to the criticism.[87]

Although the Frisians tried to defend the judges' verdict,[88] they knew the brotherhood was in danger of destruction if the sentence passed in Harlingen were not repealed by someone who possessed experience and authority. Who could better to fill this role than Dirk Phillips, who had already served the brotherhood for more than 40 years, and had participated in many elders' conferences as a friend and co-worker of Menno Simons? He was known everywhere because of his clear and edifying booklets, and in the previous year he had offered to mediate the conflict.

It appears that the Flemish were the first to propose this plan. Early on they had considered inviting Dirk Philips to act as arbitrator.[89] Before the Brabant ministers Hans Busschaert and Hendrik van Arnhem went home at the end of July, 1566 leaving the business unfinished, they warned Hoyte Renix "that he should use no sharpness" and tried to persuade him to write to Dirk Philips and ask him to come. They wanted to do so themselves, "but he rejected that and spoke as was told above."[90] According to Dirk Philips, Hoyte clothed the rejection in threatening language. Hoyte had no desire whatsoever to invite Dirk to arbitrate the conflict. He wanted to prevent Dirk from getting involved in the affair. Should Dirk come despite all the warnings, then he would be treated as the other elders, the Brabanders, and Nette Lipke had been.[91]

But the conviction was growing among the more dispassionate Frisians, that the only way to save the brotherhood was to put Dirk Philips in charge. Hoyte Renix–willingly or unwillingly–had to accede to the pressure, and invited Dirk in writing (April 17, 1567).[92] The letter began with a friendly invitation: Dirk and his whole family would be welcome in Friesland. He was promised that as a dear, old father he could spend his last years in the homeland, with care and assistance, surrounded by the churches. But then the tone became threatening: In order for Dirk to be welcome, Hoyte stipulated that he must accept the Harlingen sentence unconditionally. Should Dirk reject the stipulation, great misery would result, greater than he had ever experienced.

Thus Hoyte, in a most inappropriate manner, tried to win Dirk over to his side in advance. Anyone who knew anything about Dirk Philips' character would have known that threats would have a negative affect on him. Dirk himself said:

This is like the saying–thus you show me bread in one hand and lure me with it, and in the other hand you have a stone to strike me, should I not follow you or agree with you.[93]

Since the invitation had come from the Frisians as well as from the Flemish, Dirk Philips was prepared "in his old age, to perform a special service to help the church of God."[94] The church in Danzig gave its permission and delegated Dirk Philips along with two respected elders, Hans Sikken[95] and Geert Harms.[96]

Dirk had already been informed about the course of the dispute from the Flemish side.[97] Letters and petitions had come from the Netherlands which told Dirk and the Prussian congregation of the miserable situation in which the Dutch churches found themselves.[98] In his "Letter to the Four Cities" (Sept., 19, 1566) Dirk had suspended judgment about the Covenant, pleading only for peace. But he was now convinced that God's covenant–which alone deserved the name–had been obscured by a human covenant. In time he hoped to get a clearer picture.[99] In Danzig he had struggled with the question of allowing a compromise and, if it were allowed, how far it should go. He had concluded that God's Word suffered great damage through such human interference.[100]

It seems that Dirk Philips' opinion on this matter had changed. In 1565 he had called the Covenant scriptural and viewed it as an ordinance which could contribute to building up the church.[101] Some historians have accused Dirk harshly for changing his mind.[102] In my opinion, these historians accuse him wrongly.

In the first place, in 1565 during the controversy involving Jeroen Tinnegieter and Ebbe Pieters, and when the dispute with the Frisian elders about the judging of Leenaert Bouwens had scarcely been settled,[103] Dirk had little desire to argue anew with them. Further, he knew that Hoyte Renix was strongly in favour of the Covenant[104] and did not want to irritate him at that time.

Secondly, Dirk saw the issue differently later, whether or not he was fully convinced by the arguments of his Flemish friends. And is one not allowed to change one's mind? Is it not possible for a theologian to come to a different conclusion by further studying the Bible? A person like Dirk Philips, who wanted to be a true, devout Christian, and who wanted to direct church life according to Holy Scripture, can indeed be influenced temporarily by human factors, but will again and again orient himself according to the Word of God.

Kühler wanted to explain the entire course of the four-city struggle with his theory that it was a struggle about hegemony between Dirk Philips and Leenaert Bouwens.[105] It is possible that Leenaert worked behind the scenes against Dirk. After all, Leenaert had trusted followers among the Frisians,[106] such as Ebbe Pieters. Yet not he, but Hoyte Renix, kept Dirk Philips "at a safe distance."[107] Hoyte was Dirk's greatest rival.

Before I discuss the doings of the Danziger group in Emden, I must give attention to the Frisians' attitude toward the elder whom they had so respected. "By numerous actions they showed that the earlier veneration for him [Dirk] had been lost,"[108] and Dirk was grieved by it. Thus even before the journey began a certain tension existed.

Apart from the fact that the Frisians and the Flemish had both requested that the two Hoorn ministers mediate,[109] Jan Willems and Lubbert Gerrits were free to choose their fellow judges. By rights they should have asked for Dirk Philips, who already had offered his service as a mediator,[110] but they preferred Hoyte Renix.

Besides, Dirk felt wronged because the congregation in Harlingen had chosen their teacher, Egbert Kuiper, as elder, and had asked Hoyte Renix to ordain him. Hoyte and Dirk corresponded at first, and Dirk advised against the appointment for various reasons.[111] But Hoyte did not heed Dirk's warning. In a letter written April 17, he told Dirk that he would uphold his decision and ordain Egbert Kuiper.[112] Dirk was understandably angry about such stubbornness.

Thirdly, the Frisian side had insulted Dirk when the Hoorn congregation accepted into their church a certain Jasper van Coomen who had been banned in Danzig because of immorality, and who later moved to Hoorn. This could not have happened without the collaboration of Jan Willems and Lubbert Gerrits. The congregation in Hoorn had written to Danzig about the matter, requesting information. But before the reply came–which of course was negative–they had decided to accept him. The reason given was "that he was a man who spoke well and had much to say about Dirk Philips that pleased us."[113] Dirk Philips blamed Jan Willems and Lubbert Gerrits for this "unscriptural action,"[114] and later wrote about it to both elders and also to the congregation in Hoorn.[115]

Concerning the charge which the three Danzig delegates received from the congregation, Dirk Philips wrote: The church in Prussia was moved by the terrible need of the churches in the Netherlands to send us "to hear both parties, and to examine and learn the truth. We should support those who were in the right. We should accept and maintain all that stands for what is right."[116] It was clearly stated that Dirk Philips must hear *both parties*, establish where the truth lay only after careful investigation, and then support the conclusion. He also spoke about his task in two other places using similar wording.[117] Again, we know the instructions given to Dirk Philips only from "A Short but Basic Account." The fact that he wrote so openly about it either shows his naivete or his clear conscience. He felt that he had received a well defined task and was obligated to act accordingly. His duty included giving equal attention to both parties.[118]

The group came to Emden, as far as I know, at the end of May 1567 and received a friendly reception. After all, Dirk was well known in Emden, had many friends there, and most of his writings had been printed there. Shortly after his arrival he had the "Epistle to Four Cities" printed, with an appendix about calling and choosing ministers. He wanted to deal with the entire controversy in Emden, first in writing and then orally.

Why did Dirk not travel with his company to Friesland or even to North Holland, the area in which the quarrel was centred? De Hoop Scheffer believes that "he preferred not to risk being in congregations which had increasingly withdrawn from his influence."[119] K. Vos and Kühler accused Dirk of timidity because he had learned at Emden that Alva was approaching with his army and his bloody council.[120]

But these historians missed the simple explanation: Dirk Philips was an old man, struggling with sickness and weakness, and facing death.[121] The trip from Danzig to Emden was on a seaworthy ship,[122] but to get to Friesland one had to travel by tow-boat or by a coastal vessel. This way of traveling was too strenuous for Dirk, who was already 63 years old–a respectable age for that time–and in frail health. When his opponents later pressured him to come, he was prepared to go "over the Ems" as close as possible to the border.[123]

Before Dirk Philips came to Emden there was an episode with Leenaert Bouwens.[124] Leenaert, who had been suspended as elder in 1565 and had stayed in Harlingen for a short time,[125] had returned to Emden and withdrawn from all activities. But new complaints against him were surfacing in the congregation.[126] Leenaert, who anticipated that this time he would be banned, hastily departed for Friesland leaving a message that "if anyone wanted anything, he or she should follow him to Friesland."[127] Leenaert settled outside of Harlingen and joined the Frisian party.[128] After he was warned again, by a message, to appear before the congregation in Emden, the ban was pronounced on him.[129] All of this happened "around the time that Dirk came from Prussia to Emden."[130] This is not to say that what happened can be blamed on Dirk, but it is understandable that Leenaert fled before Dirk became involved in the process.

After the Danzig delegates were informed of the situation in the brotherhood in Emdem—they probably were briefed by Flemish who had fled across the border[131]—they began the proceedings. Dirk Philips tried first to listen to both parties.[132] He took the view that the procedure must be in accordance with the Word of God,[133] and in agreement with his congregation's charge. Both parties involved in the disagreement had to come to an agreement. The arbitrators who had been found wanting in their decision of February 1 must give an account before their accusers, and everything must be explained in an open session. After that, Dirk and his companions would give their pronouncement.[134]

To this end, Dirk wrote a letter to both elders from Hoorn, Jan Willems and Lubbert Gerrits, and invited them to come to Emden, "for he found he needed to speak with them about divine matters."[135] When a favourable answer was not received, this invitation was repeated in three consecutive follow-up letters, each one with a sharper tone.[136]

Pijper has correctly observed that these letters from Dirk Philips were preserved only in part. If we could consult the complete text, we would probably draw different conclusions.[137] Indeed, this applies to Dirk's letter to Hoyte Renix in response to the latter's epistle of April 17.[138] The introduction showed that Dirk cherished his friendship with Hoyte, but that he was saddened by the Frisian party's fanaticism. This sorrow was increased by Hoyte's letter in which he forewarned that Dirk would regret not agreeing with the decision of the Harlingen assembly of February 1st.

Dirk testified before God that he always sought peace and was innocent of the dispute between the Frisians and Flemish. Then, point by point, he dealt with the threats using the words known to us.[139] He did not let the threat frighten him, but was only saddened that Hoyte wrote so rashly. "I want to accept and support whatever is right and has been shown to me to be right, so help me God." After quoting several scriptural passages Dirk wrote about the case of Egbert Kuiper, at which point he pulled out all the stops.[140]

He poured his wrath over the recalcitrant elder [Hoyte], accusing him of having unjustly banned many people. Then Dirk pleaded with him in a friendly way, asking him "to suspend his service," and refrain from exercising his office. If Hoyte would not bow before this friendly and brotherly request, then Dirk commanded him "in the name of the Lord Jesus and by the power which He has given to His church and to us, to suspend [his] ministry" until he had given an account before his accusers. The time and occasion for this action Dirk would share with him later. As a last measure, Hoyte was notified that Dirk withdrew the "brotherhood" from him, thus placing him under the ban, although conditionally. That is, if Hoyte would not heed the request or the command, he would be banned. Dirk hoped, however, that Hoyte would think it over and not be contrary. Egbert Kuiper's ordination was not recognized by Dirk, and finally, anyone who might advise Hoyte not to heed Dirk's commands, whoever he might be and wherever he might live, was threatened with the ban.

The letter ended with several friendly words. Dirk had compassion for the poor souls who were redeemed through the blood of Jesus Christ, and whose interests in the struggle had been disregarded. If Hoyte were grieved by this letter, then might it be a sadness according to God's will. Dirk had written out of "great necessity" as Hoyte's letter of April 17th had unnecessarily saddened him. Might the Lord give him wisdom and work in him as pleased God, for the salvation of his soul.

Many questions arise. There is no doubt that Dirk could invite both parties according to his congregation's charge. It was inexcusable that the

Frisians should vacillate about appearing before an arbitrator of their own choosing.[141] Hoyte Renix's letter, which threatened Dirk and urged him to accept the Harlingen sentence, also deserves no praise. Every independent judge would reject such an inappropriate request.[142] On the other hand, one must admit that Dirk's letters to Hoyte and the Dutch judges failed to create a favorable atmosphere for the negotiations.[143]

Did Dirk Philips have the authority and the right to suspend Hoyte and the other judges from their offices and to threaten them "conditionally" with the ban?

Opinions differ. Dirk had been an elder from the earliest days of the Anabaptist movement. At that time most issues of discipline were decided during meetings of elders. Therefore, he now felt justified in his independent action. He appealed to the authority which the Lord Jesus had given to his church and to him.

In "A Short Account" he named three things which gave him this authority: The mission he had received from God, the call to office which he had received from the church, and the charge from the Danzig congregation.[144] But did this task also include banning and suspending those who did not satisfy his requests? Perhaps one could use the ban as a threat.[145] Suspension might also be necessary for the sake of investigation and could then be imposed by the arbitrator. But in pronouncing the ban, even conditionally, Dirk exceeded his power. The congregations to which these individuals belonged should have been consulted, and they themselves should have been heard.[146]

Hoyte Renix, who certainly felt that Dirk had gone too far, was obedient for a short time and discontinued his ministry, but demanded–an astute move–that Dirk should come to Bolsward to substantiate his charges before Hoyte's congregation. When Dirk twice refused to come, only referring to his letter, the congregation left Hoyte free to resume his work as an elder.[147] Apparently, Dirk resigned himself to the decision of the Bolsward congregation, but a few weeks later he still had various accusations against his opponent.

Meanwhile negotiations with the Hoorn ministers were not making headway. The congregation in Hoorn declared–it is not clear whether orally or in writing–that they would not permit their ministers to travel to Emden for various reasons which they would explain later.[148] Dirk responded to this with letters to Jan Willems and Lubbert Gerrits and to the Hoorn congregation.[149] In these letters he was more severe. He requested that they suspend their ministry, and if necessary he would command them to do so. He had ordained them many years earlier in the name of Christ Jesus, and that same power was still at work in him and gave him the authority to command them to suspend the office.[150] He reported the suspension to the congregation in Hoorn and requested–indeed, ordered–that they inform all the congregations of North Holland of the letter "through the Lord Jesus Chirst."

The North Holland congregations sent four messengers to Emden with a letter. They repeated that they could not comply with Dirk Philips' request and would not permit their ministers to appear before his court. On the contrary, they asked Dirk to come to Hoorn to plead the matter against their ministers before the congregation.[151]

At the same time, a delegation from Friesland came to Emden[152] numbering five brothers, and probably sent by the congregations at Bolsward and Harlingen. Dirk met with these nine people as many as six times.[153] Again and again he repeated the demand that "according to the Word of God and in agreement with His will," both parties needed to respond in each others' presence. Finally, when Dirk realized that the Hollanders and the Frisians were completely unwilling to travel to Emden, he accomodated them to the point of agreeing to negotiate with Jan Willems and Lubbert Gerrits as close to the border as possible.[154] Although Dirk conceded a little in this regard, he remained unmoved on his requirement: The judges must account for their pronouncement in the presence of the Flemish.

The negotiations with the two deputations may have lasted several days, up to a week. After receiving the letter from the Hoorn congregation, which messengers delivered by hand,[155] Dirk immediately sent a sixth letter to Jan Willems and Lubbert Gerrits on June 30.[156] In the letter he confirmed the suspension of both ministers and threatened them with the ban if they did not obey. In a postscript, all elders, ministers, and deacons in North Holland were ordered "to stop," and put no one under the ban nor accept anyone into the congregation.

The fifth letter to the ministers from Hoorn, and the letter to the Hoorn congregation, the date of which is unknown, compelled the Hoorn church council to call a general assembly to which delegates from various North Holland congregations were invited. This general assembly took place in Hoorn at the beginning of July.[157]

It must have been a tumultuous gathering because, in addition to the aforementioned letters, the sixth letter from Dirk Philips (June 30) had arrived and was also attended to.[158] There was widespread indignation about the actions of the Danziger elder. Some delegates vented their anger with scoffing remarks: "Although Jan Willems and Lubbert Gerrits might get a scratch on the nose, they must not therefore give in." Then another said, "someone may give Dirk Philips a scratch on the nose," and a third exclaimed, "that is a fight!" Jan Willems himself observed, "I fear Dirk Philips has gone the way of old Tobias who lost his eyes because an angry swallow shat in them"[159]

Thijs Joriaensz. was disheartened that Dirk Philips' messages and letters had been misinterpreted so badly. Never in his life had he heard anyone's words and letters interpreted in a more ugly way.[160] After Dirk's letter had been read, he reminded Jan Willems that no elder could command another to stop serving unless the matter was first dealt with before the accused's congregation, and then only if his congregation approved.[161] Thijs later applied this rule to the Hoorn ministers' position regarding Dirk Philips.

After emotions had settled down, the assembly decided to make one last attempt to arrange a meeting with Dirk Philips. Several respected elders were delegated to go to Emden to speak "to Dirk P. with love and in peace, but also with truth and righteousness."[162] Both ministers from Hoorn belonged to the delegation, as well as Pieter Willems Bogaert, a teacher in Monnikendam. Others must have gone along as well, such as Thijs Joriaensz., who had directed a stern warning to Jan Willems and Lubbert Gerrits immediately after Dirk was banned.[163]

When the deputation arrived in Appingedam, they met the nine delegates who were on a return trip from Emden. The deputation was informed of the lengths to which Dirk Philips was prepared to go. Dirk was prepared to come halfway for a meeting–this was no longer necessary due to the decision by the Hoorn assembly–but he still firmly demanded that the judges from Holland account for their judgment in the presence of their accusers.

The delegation from Hoorn considered their options. It seemed improbable that they could negotiate with the unyielding elder on an equal footing. But perhaps intermediaries could change his mind. Should this attempt fail, then they would remove him from the brotherhood. They drew up a proposal–in the sources it is called a statement [*sententie*] or an instrument[164]–in which the course of the dispute was sketched, beginning with the judgment in Harlingen and then describing Dirk Philips' actions. This was followed by a statement which read: As teachers and servants who have come here on behalf of the congregations in North Holland and Friesland, we disassociate the aforementioned Dirk Philips from his followers, in the name "of the Lord and the divine truth."[165]

Jan Willems and Lubbert Gerrits made it appear that they had been authorized to do this according to a charge given by the North Holland congregations, but this was refuted by Thijs Joriaensz.[166] They had to admit later on that they had not received congregational authorization for their action.[167] Therefore, not only did those who drafted the statement exceed their powers, but they also pretended to act by proxy for their congregations.[168] Their actions cannot be praised.

The entire company crossed over the Ems, and negotiations began immediately in Emden.[169] The Dutch-Frisian deputation told Dirk Philips that they "had a message for him." Dirk held his ground and insisted that he would receive Jan Willems and Lubert Gerrits only in the presence of the Flemish. However, Dirk did try to find out where the delegation was staying. In spite of all their searching, Hans Sikken and Geert Harms were unsuccessful in locating the delegation's inn,[170] as they deliberately kept themselves hidden. The delegation demanded that Dirk withdraw his requirement before they would agree to meet with him.

After Dirk had intensified his demand with the warning that "if they would not respond to their accusers, they could pack it in,"[171] there was one final meeting on July 8. The Dutch sent four messengers, among whom was Egbert Kuiper, and gave them the statement to take along. The messengers must speak one more time with Dirk Philips and his followers and request that he withdraw his requirement. If he refused, they must pronounce the ban over Dirk Philips and his two delegates.[172] Hans Sikken and Geert Harms came as Dirk's representatives. The brothers shook hands and gave each other the brotherly kiss.[173] Each side explained their position once again. But when Hans Sikken repeated the threat of the ban, Egbert Kuiper got angry. He more than anyone else felt disgraced by Dirk Philips. He shouted furiously: Because you act in such an unchristian way, and because Dirk Philips has aroused so much unrest in Friesland with his letters, "we cannot be at peace with his brotherhood and cannot have any fellowship with him or his group."[174]

After this outburst, the table cloth between the parties was cut in two. Hans Sikken understood the meaning of this and immediately told them that he refused to recognize the message as legitimate. When they refused absolutely to appear before the arbitrator, as requested in the letter and the last report from Dirk Philips, they were considered apostate.

> *You have no power because you separate yourself from the church of God: you take your leave because you are unwilling to do that which all the pious saints in the church are obligated to do according to God's Word, that is, answer your accusers.*

We do not know who first pronounced the ban on the other party, as opinions have differed about it. De Hoop Scheffer and Kühler claimed that the Flemish were the first to ban.[175] K. Vos wrote, "The end [of the negotiations] came when the Frisians pronounced the ban on Dirk and the Flemish did the same to them."[176] And likewise, "The Frisians, in their anger, pronounced the sentence of the ban on Dirk, which is to say that they cast him out of the church."[177] I agree with Vos' account. Earlier we noted that the Frisians had prepared the banning letter in advance, and that they sent it with their messengers to use if necessary. Furthermore, the expression "not to be able to have fellowship with someone" undoubtedly meant to ban him.[178]

It is not of great importance whether the banning letter was transmitted to Dirk Philips immediately or at some later date.[179] Hans Sikken's reply testified to a certain cleverness and judicial subtlety. It implied that the conditional ban, which had been announced in Dirk Philips' letters and in his last message, would be applied automatically when the Frisians explicitly rejected the elder's requirement.[180] Thus while Dirk had pronounced the ban on Hoyte Renix, Jan Willems, and Lubbert Gerrits only conditionally, the Frisians were actually the first to pronounce the ban, not only against Dirk and his fellow delegates, but also against all his followers.[181] I will relate the course of events further only to show how Dirk Philips reacted to the Frisians' banning sentence.

Before Dirk had knowledge of the "epistle to Groningen" he probably published "A Short but Basic Account."[182] The ban against Dirk and his followers had occurred, and the conditional ban against the Frisians had been implemented.[183] Dirk wrote this booklet "in haste,"[184] but I doubt that he could have completed it in a few days. It must have been based on notes and details written about, for example, the judgment in Harlingen, God's covenant, and the Compromise. Some parts create the impression that it was originally a journal, and that only the preface and the last pages, in which he calls the Frisians apostate,[185] were added to the manuscript after July 8.

Dirk began by discussing the judicial statement of February 1, 1567. He could not approve of it, for it had been made by unworthy judges and did not accord with God's truth.[186] Later he intimated that the judges had failed to correspond to the apostolic example, but he spared them and did not go into detail. In any case, the judges had excluded many innocent people from the church, and had caused offence.[187] Dirk would have accepted their judgment if they could have substantiated it with God's Word but, as it stood, he saw it as an unfair verdict, given by "unwise, biased, and corrupt judges" who, when compared to scriptural examples, ought not to have been judges.[188]

In the second part Dirk discussed God's Covenant. He had already done this in earlier writings,[189] but the treatment here was more fundamental in character.[190] God made a covenant with man and promised to be his God and Father. Man responded by leading a godly walk as a covenant companion and child of God. Faith worked through love, and the believer was a person reborn from God. But now, in place of God's covenant with its promises and obligations, a human covenant had been presented, with the appearance of having been instituted under God's Word. Dirk compared this human covenant to the golden calf which Aaron erected in the wilderness, and Jeroboam later erected in Bethel. They gave this covenant a new name—"the ordinance of the four cities"—but that did not make it a good ordinance, for it was not grounded in Scripture, and did not agree with God's Word and with faith.[191]

Jereboam erected a second golden calf in Dan. The Compromise, which the parties were allowed to sign before the judges' verdict, was the second golden calf.[192] Only God should be the judge, but in Harlingen the judges placed the Compromise before God's Word and it influenced their decision. By doing this they raised a human command above God's commands. When the Flemish objected to signing the Compromise, they were assured that all would be handled according to the Word of God, but this promise had been broken.[193] Therefore Dirk felt compelled to call the Covenant and the Compromise the two golden calves. The Word of God was truth and must be the foundation of justice. It needed no Compromise. That a Compromise had been drafted was a sure proof that God's Word had not been followed.[194]

In the following chapter, Dirk rendered an account of his letters to Hoyte Renix and the judges in Holland.[195] This chapter also could have been prepared in advance. However, the last part, in which he defended himself against the accusation that he had refused to receive the Frisian and Hollander delegates, appears to have been written in part just before the break, and in part immediately after July 8.[196] The booklet concluded with an admonition to godfearing people, and Dirk testified to his own innocence and clear conscience.[197]

The Frisians did not stop after banning Dirk Philips. They announced the banning to various congregations, and specifically wrote an "epistle to those in Groningen and Appingedam."[198] Dirk had originally been ordained as elder in Appingedam and during his first years of work had lived near the city of Groningen. Presumably he had friends there who remained true to him. The letter of July 12 is lost. We know the contents mainly from the argument in Hoorn in 1622, because the letter was read there and an extract included in the minutes.[199] Although this letter was signed by Lubbert Gerrits, Jan Willems, Pieter Willems (Bogaert), and Hoyte Renix jointly, it seems probable that Hoyte Renix initiated it.[200]

And now to discuss "the horrible letter." Firstly, the Flemish were rebuked for not submitting to the decision of the judges from Hoorn. Hoyte Renix had acquitted [the judges] of guilt on the issue of banning the Flemish Anabaptists in Harlingen and Franeker. They maintained that this ban could not exist according to either heathen or evangelical truth.

The second accusation was directed toward the Flemish teachers who signed the Compromise, but recanted after the sentence.[201] They were scolded for being dishonorable, rebellious people who had broken their promise and upset the peace because they had withdrawn from the Compromise and did not shun the banned persons. This was an offence against the ministers, the holy institution of the ban, and customary practice.[202]

The accusations in the banning letter were repeated against Dirk Philips.[203] He had caused unrest and tumult, slandered and disgraced the ministers, tried to oppress them, etc. Finally, he was accused of rejecting God's holy sacraments and practices, without any critical examination, and of offending the divine statutes. This last accusation related to the course he had followed against the banned Flemish.[204]

The letter to Groningen soon became known to Dirk Philips and created a stir among his followers. Although he would have preferred to remain silent, many people wanted him to clarify his position in this unhappy dispute.[205] Furthermore, Dirk's opponents, who were probably still staying in Emden, urged him to come to a meeting where they intended to prove that his description of events in "A Short Account" was unfair and that he had been justifiably banned.[206]

In response Dirk published a new booklet: "An appendix to our Booklet written about the controversial case in Fr. between the Fr. and Fl. (as the two parties are called)."[207] Once again he repeated briefly that in accordance with his mandate, he had tried to bring both parties together in order to judge which party was in the right. But the Frisians had refused to comply with this "little request and scriptural requirement."[208] On the basis of God's Word he had to reject the Covenant of the Four Cities and the Compromise, both human creations, because these had caused divisions and difficulties in God's church.[209] The judges were unworthy and gave their verdict according to their own opinion, [and so] their judgment was worthless before God.[210]

Dirk could not, therefore, enter into negotiations with the Frisians, and he considered them to be apostate.[211] Nevertheless he left the door open slightly. He would give them an opportunity for a meeting if they met with two conditions. First, the Frisians must repeal the ban sentence and do penance. Furthermore, they must satisfy the requirement he had always firmly held: Both parties must meet and give their account of everything that had occured since the dispute began.[212]

Dirk replied incidentally to the accusation that he had mentioned his opponents' names in "A Short Account" and had thereby endangered them. After all, that could bring them to the attention of the government.[213] Dirk had written his own name in full,[214] but had only indicated the names of the Frisians with the first letters to avoid misunderstanding. Those who wrote the letter to the congregations in Groningen and district of Groningen cannot be so easily defended. They named several pious members by both first and last name, and gave partial addresses. That might have been a great handicap for them.[215]

Much space was taken up in the "Appendix" with personal complaints, mainly directed against Hoyte Renix.[216] In "A Short Account"[217] Dirk claimed that Nette Lipke had already charged Hoyte with misbehaviours which deserved the ban, but that Hoyte had not replied to the charges. The

Appendix only mentions that "many complainants, accusers, and witnesses were against H.R."[218]

Hoyte Renix did recall the sentence that he and six other judges had pronounced against Leenaert Bouwens in Emden, and he acknowledged his guilt in the decision. Dirk thought ill of the acknowledgement and accused him of hypocrisy.[219]

Hoyte had a "false basis of doctrine," and departed from the teachings of Jesus Christ as they were accepted in God's church. Dirk would have asked him for an explanation had the Frisian-Flemish dispute not intervened. This was another reason Dirk could not assent to the ordination of Egbert Kuiper.[220]

Finally, Dirk suspected Hoyte of obtaining information about him, either directly or indirectly, from the Mennonites in Prussia who, at the time, had been excluded from the church by Hoyte and Leenaert.[221] Hoyte must have asked whether or not there was information about the Danzig elder which could be used against him. Dirk said that the rumour had reached him from Prussia. He knew more about it but did not wish to dwell on it.[222]

All in all, with these accusations Dirk Philips showed that he considered Hoyte Renix to be his most important opponent in this last phase of the struggle.

The mission of the three delegates from Danzig went completely awry. It would be unreasonable to blame this entirely on Dirk Philips' attitude. Certainly when the accused Frisians finally came to Emden he could have been more accommodating. I do not believe that his position sprang entirely from the obstinacy of old age. Dirk had always held rigidly to an acknowledged truth, particularly when based on Holy Scripture. He would not surrender his requirement, at any cost, that the Frisians must respond in the presence of the Flemish.

The Frisians continuously objected to this, although it was a justified requirement.[223] It is true that the Frisians had heard both parties separately before the Harlingen sentence[224] and, based on a comment from Dirk Philips,[225] we can conclude that this was the reason they acted as they did.

But such a method of investigation would have been entirely new, and not in agreement with God's Word. It also would have made it impossible for Dirk to carry out his congregation's charge.

Remarkably, Dirk was fully convinced that he was right.[226] He claimed to be innocent in the dispute. He had sought nothing but the honor of God, the salvation of souls, and the well-being of the church.[227] He was not aware of having curtailed anyone's rights.[228] His conscience was pure before God, and that was sufficient for him.[229] By the grace of God, he had done everything possible to seek peace.[230] It was unacceptable to him that the church now suffered endless quarrel and bickering, and he had tried more than once to restore the peace by letters and warnings.[231]

One can only be amazed at this self-assurance, this lack of self knowledge and realization of sin. He was not indifferent to the fact that his mediation attempt had failed. He regretted that it had come to this division,[232] and declared that he would have given his life should such a sacrifice have prevented the schism.[233]

According to Dirk, the whole issue concerned the honour of God and the purity of the church, the honourable institution of the ban, and obedience to biblical precepts. He wanted to hold to these commands and stand firmly on the teaching of the Gospel and the true faith.[234]

I do not think one may lay blame entirely on Dirk Philips. Seventeenth century authors who wrote about the Frisian-Flemish disputes tried to split the blame equally.[235]

Had Dirk been successful in bringing the parties together and reaching an agreement, it would have been the crowning achievement of his life's work. Instead, however, his attempts failed, and it was a sad ending. In the eyes of the Flemish Dirk remained the honoured elder. His writings were even translated into French for the sake of those among them who spoke that language. But Dirk no longer mattered to any Dutch Anabaptists who did not belong to the Flemish group.

Any trace of order was missing throughout the entire dispute—not an order imposed from above, but arrived at by mutual consent. There should have been a rule included to solve differences. The Covenant of the four cities certainly pointed in that direction, but this covenant failed to involve the congregations. The Compromise, in theory, was a useful means, but the judges were not impartial. A few clear regulations could have prevented disaster.[236]

It is the "tragedy of history" that such regulations were lacking, and that Dirk Philips "in the last days of his life, was the victim of a clash which was unavoidable" because elders on both sides were unconcerned about their congregations' charge.[237]

I will pass over the consequences of the great schism because these did not personally involve Dirk.[238] I will only point out that the Flemish proceeded to pronounce a general ban on all the Frisian congregations. The Frisians had taken the trouble, as was their custom, to pronounce the ban separately on Dirk and his traveling companions, and later on the Flemish teachers and their adherents, but it proved impractical to do so against the Frisian leaders and their congregations who were rich in numbers and had many members. For this reason, four respected Flemish elders decided to make a virtue of necessity, and introduced "a general and universal ban and separation" on all the Frisian Anabaptists, regardless of which nationality they belonged to, with all the attendant consequences such as shunning and avoidance. With this act the great division became an accomplished fact.[239]

XII

The Last Writings and the End

In "A Short but Basic Account" Dirk announced that he hoped to return to his congregation in Danzig as soon as possible. He had lived there, at peace with the church, before he left for Emden and had kept out of the dispute in Friesland.[1] Now he longed to go back to Danzig, to spend his last days in peace and unity of faith.[2] But man proposes and God disposes. First the Frisian side requested that he participate in a debate with them, which he had to refuse on principle.[3] After that, many "godfearing" persons urged him to justify his position, and he was pressed to write what became the "Appendix" and to have it published. Finally, when all that was over it was autumn and shipping to the Baltic Sea had stopped.

It is possible that Dirk was not very sorry about that, for it appears that he was not in the best of health,[4] and had hoped to recover in a comfortable environment, or at least to find medical care. He probably lived in Falder, close to Emden. He must have had the opportunity to associate with educated people and to consult a private library. The many Latin quotations and expressions in his last writings point to this.[5] On four occasions he cited the Vulgate Bible and the translation of Erasmus.[6] Occasionally Dirk also used Latin sayings.[7] The proverb from Jerome ("The truth is bitter and whoever proclaims it will be filled with bitterness"[8]) he probably borrowed from Menno. One Latin quotation requires some explanation. Dirk quoted a verse from Horatius[9] and then wrote:

> *Please excuse us that we cite so much from the aforementioned poet. For the Apostle Paul also quoted Menander and Epimenides whenever there was occasion for doing so. (I Cor. 15:33; Titus 1:12.)*

Vos thinks[10] that Dirk found this explanation in the *Annotationes* of Erasmus, but it is quite possible that Dirk found these names reported in the Bible translation of Bugenhagen.[11]

Blesdijk reported that Dirk also knew Greek.[12] In fact he used and explained several Greek words in his writings.[13] With regard to his knowledge of Hebrew, we find only two expressions which he might have remembered from his reading or from debates.[14] The peculiar translation of the name *Achitophel*–"the apostate brother"–is more difficult to explain.[15] However, he could have read even that translation somewhere without having studied Hebrew.

In September 1567, Dirk was allowed to baptize seven or eight people. I suspect that the ceremony took place in Emden in the Flemish congregation.[16] One of those baptized was Pieter Verlongen from Kortrijk who, like so many others, had fled to Emden on account of his faith. Shortly thereafter Pieter, still a young man, returned to Flanders and established himself as a weaver in Borgerhout near Antwerp. He married in the congregation, and the wedding ceremony was performed by Herman de Timmerman. In February 1569, however, he was imprisoned, and on March 30 was burned at the stake with two fellow believers.[17] We know from an old chronicle that this martyrdom marked the first time that the prisoners' mouths were clamped shut by means of iron tongs to prevent them from singing or speaking, as had happened at earlier executions.[18]

Over the course of the year 1567 and the beginning of 1568, Dirk wrote several treatises in addition to "A Short Account" and the "Appendix," as follows:

a) The (new) Ban Book

b) "Posthumous Writing on the Ban and Shunning"

c) "An Account and Refutation of Two Epistles by Sebastian Franck," and

d) "On Christian Marriage."

I will discuss these booklets in order.

a) The (new) Ban Book.[19]

The French title was: *Claire et manifeste remonstrance de l'excommunication euangelique et institution d'icelle... par Théodore Philippe* [Clear and Manifest Demonstration of Evangelical Excommunication and its Institution...by Theodore Philips].

This treatise bore clear traces of the Frisian-Flemish quarrel which preceded it.[20] Dirk stated with sadness that the "world" and those who wandered from the truth had blasphemed the most holy faith, and the article of the ban in particular. They said that this doctrine of the Lord and the apostles [the ban] was part of a new pharisaical rule. They made Dirk and his followers out to be "destroyers of the sacraments,"[21] narrow-minded agents of the ban, judges without compassion, and marriage wreckers."

Dirk stated that he had already concerned himself with the ban, to a degree, twenty-four years earlier, and then sixteen years after that;[22] and he had dealt with it often in his writings.[23] Now, at the end of his life,[24] he wanted to focus on this important issue once more, looking at all sides. Perhaps he felt that this had not been done satisfactorily in his previous treatise "(Concerning) The Ban."[25] At the end of his discussion, he requested that this confession on the ban be added as an appendix to the *Enchiridion* before his death.[26]

This wish could not be granted immediately and for this reason the treatise was first published separately. Virgile de Las, who translated the *Enchiridion* into French and about whom I unfortunately could find no other details, omitted the earlier treatise "(Concerning) The Ban" (1558) in 1626, and replaced it with "The (new) Ban Book."

Dirk began with the statement that Christ had wanted to establish a pure church without spot or wrinkle. True believers were described as people who had left Satan and the world, and had been baptized on the basis of their faith. They were participants in all the blessings: They were children of God, their sins were forgiven, and they were filled with the Holy Spirit who would show them the way to all truth and would comfort them during oppression and persecution.[27] But anyone who had confessed the truth and become a backslider must be cut off. For that reason Christ instituted the ban and gave his church the power to cut off false members who disobeyed and persisted in sin. Thus the evangelical ban was Christ's ordinance and the teaching of the apostles.

Dirk enlarged upon this subject in some detail. He cited examples from the Old Testament and also quoted the word of James (2:10): "For whoever keeps the whole law, and yet stumbles at just one point, is guilty of breaking all the commandments."[28] According to Hebrews 2:2, every trespass and disobedience must receive rightful retribution, and this must happen without regard to the individual. If God required such purity in the symbolic Israel, how much more must He demand it in the spiritual Israel, which is God's church. Still, there was a difference between the Old Testament and the New Testament. While the Law applied the death penalty, the Gospel instituted the ban as the means for keeping the church pure.[29]

It appears that Dirk Philips once more studied the subject of the ban in detail, for he supplied new proof texts from the Old Testament.[30] He repeatedly encouraged teachers to instruct their congregations in the right doctrine of the ban.[31] Then he gave a summary of sins worthy of the ban:

a) The sin of one brother against another, if the former will not let himself be reprimanded (Matt. 18:15-17.).

b) False doctrine (Rom 16:17; 2 Tim. 3:5; Titus 3:10; 2 John 10 ff.).

c) Disorder and misconduct (I Cor. 5:11; 2 Thess. 3:6.).

d) Disobedience and disdain for the teachings of the apostles (2 Thess. 3:14.).

As in earlier treatises,[32] Dirk listed the purposes of the ban: To protect the congregation from contamination, to make the sinner ashamed and to bring him to repentance, and to ensure that Christ's name would not be slandered on account of unworthy members who were tolerated by the congregation.[33]

Next followed a rather cumbersome exposition of why the commands of Christ must be obeyed. Chirst was the good shepherd who cared for the sheep, who sought those who had strayed, who healed the sick and bound up the wounded. But the sick ones who would not let themselves be healed by the oil of grace must be expelled to ensure that one mangy sheep would not infect the whole flock.

Then followed the article quoted by Nicolai[34] which compared Christ to a physician who applied healing medicine to the weak and, like a good Samaritan, treated the wounded man with oil and wine, but did not flinch at cutting away the bad member.[35] Therefore the ban must be called a work of love,[36] and the church of Christ is kept safe through wholesome teaching and unity of faith. Furthermore, trespassers are brought to conversion [by the ban]. No Christian church can exist without the evangelical ban. Christ himself gave the church the keys to the kingdom of heaven, and gave also his Spirit and Word so that the wicked ones could be recognized and expelled.[37]

The last six pages of the tract[38] contained a question and answer game. This was characteristic of Dirk Philips' last writings, although there is also some of this in earlier treatises, for example, in "Concerning Baptism" and in "(Concerning) The Ban."

The *first question:* To what extent must those who have wandered from the truth be shunned?

Dirk answered: According to Christ's rule, the banned brother or sister must be viewed as a heathen or tax collector. The Apostles also taught complete shunning.[39] But may one not associate with a fallen sinner or eat and drink with him or her out of love? Dirk admitted that one might speak with an apostate to admonish with the Word of God (2 Thess. 3:15). But to associate with an apostate out of love, or to eat and drink with an apostate, was nothing more than an apparent good, human and contrived wisdom. Dirk then added a verbose section about true love toward God and the neighbour. When a member stumbled and could not be corrected by any admonition, then nothing was as healing for the soul as the ban. This constituted genuine brotherly love.[40]

Second question: Was it permitted to give alms to a needy backslider?

Dirk took the view that the ban was in no way instituted by God for the destruction of persons, but for their improvement. Christians should not act like the Pharisees, but should give priority to love and compassion. Mercy for banned members would make an impression upon them and win them over for Christ.[41]

Third question: A husband and wife were both members of God's church and bound in marriage. If it happened that one of them deserted God and was expelled from the congregation, must the innocent spouse then break off all fellowship with the other?

The answer was: Jesus Christ gave shunning as a general rule, and it must be applied without respect of person. Therefore complete shunning in marriage is required.[42]

First objection: Spouses cannot divorce. According to Matt. 19:9, the only allowable reason for divorce is adultery.

Dirk gave an extensive explanation of this commandment. The Jews had abandoned their wives. To shun a banned spouse was not the same as abandoning her, and the husband may not take another woman in marriage. Thus spousal shunning was not the same as divorce. The Christian withdrew from the banned partner, asked God for the gift of chastity, and waited with prayer and sighing until the other repented and was reconciled with the Lord and with His congregation. Only then could the brother or sister receive the strayed spouse with joy, thanking God for His mercy.[43]

Second objection: A Christian can remain with the fallen partner and nevertheless remain a true Christian, for the evangelical ban would not be broken by that.

Dirk found this reasoning incomprehensible. Acting according to this rule transgressed the clear command of Christ and the apostles.[44]

Third objection: Spiritual separation is sufficient, for the marriage bond does not allow for external separation.

Dirk's answer was extensive, but it was summed up in essence in the first few sentences. Natural marriage and mutual love could in no way disengage the need for the evangelical ban. Faith and love toward God must be placed first, before which any other love must give way, including married love. As proof, Dirk quoted Old Testament texts (Deut. 33:9, 10 and 13:6-9), and the example of Phinehas (Num. 25).

Dirk certainly felt that he was on a slippery slope and defended himself with the counter-question: Was the faith of the patriarchs who lived in the fear of God not the true faith? He tried to defend the discrepancy that exists between the Old and New Testaments. In his argument he referred to Hebrews 11 where the patriarchs, especially Abraham, were praised for their faith. Just as there was one God in both the Old and the New Testaments, so there was also one faith and one love. The love owed to God was the first and greatest commandment, and love of God ensured that his commandments were kept.

Dirk used a second argument to show the insufficiency of mere spiritual separation from the banned spouse. The fifth commandment undoubtedly applied. Nevertheless it had to give way before another commandment: A man will leave his father and mother and be united to his wife and the two shall become one flesh (Matt. 19:5). Certainly marriage must give way to God out of faith and love, because of the Word and the commandment of the Lord. One must strive for the spiritual marriage that exists between Christ and believing souls.[45]

Dirk closed his argument with several kind words to his readers. He invited them to measure his deliberations against the true standard, the Word of God, and spoke humbly of his simple mind, of the one talent granted him that he had used to the honour of God, and of the widow's mite which he had contributed for the building and maintenance of the Christian temple. He wished that someone else would treat this subject better and more completely. I have discussed the postscript earlier. It was an attack against false charges and a witness to his faith that the Lord would protect him. Dirk ended with a salutation for the dear members.

I have given an extensive overview of this treatise because its existence was previously unknown, and because reading the original text may prove difficult for some. If we compare this writing about the ban with the "Friendly Admonition" of 1558, we observe that Dirk dealt with the problem in more detail here. He acknowledged the objections of his opponents and attempted to refute them. In 1558 he had limited himself to a discussion of the shunning of public sinners, but here he sums up all sins worthy of banning.[46]

On the other hand, he did not touch the issue of whether repentant sinners should be excluded or, if they were truly repentant, whether they should be at peace with it.[47] Dirk did not discuss which position to take when facing human weakness and offense, nor did he treat the threefold admonition according to Matt. 18:15-17. However, the separation between husband and wife, which was not mentioned in the "Friendly Admonition,"[48] was discussed in detail here. In fact, the principle of spousal shunning was strictly maintained. With regard to helping a sinner who was in need, Dirk was more positive than in the "Confession Concerning Shunning."[49] However, friendly association with a backsliding member was strictly forbidden.[50] By way of exception, association was permitted when one admonished the banned member with biblical texts.[51]

From a passage in the *Spiritual Restitution,* Pijper concluded that Dirk demanded divorce in a marriage with a Roman Catholic,[52] but that was a misunderstanding. Dirk taught that divorce was allowed exclusively on account of adultery (Matt. 19:9). The passage in question dealt with *shunning* in marriage.[53]

Even leaving aside the strongest statements in the booklet "Concerning the Ban" (1558), we must admit that Dirk was no more moderate in "The (new) Ban Book" than in earlier writings. He persisted in teaching the strict ban to the end.[54]

b) "Posthumous Writing about the Evangelical Ban and Shunning"[55]
The introduction to the French translation noted that this treatise was found separately in manuscript form written by Dirk Philips.[56] The manuscript was found after his death. It was read and preserved by his circle of faithful followers, the Flemish Anabaptists. Because many Flemish were not sufficiently fluent in the Dutch language, it was translated into French. Perhaps this translation had already been printed before 1602, but if it was that edition is lost to us now. It is also possible that Carel van Mander translated the written copy back into Dutch as commissioned by P. van Wesbusch, who published it in 1602 along with a second printing of "The Marriage of the Christian" and the "Refutation."[57] I cannot determine whether Virgile de Las included the aforementioned French translation in

his *Enchiridion*, or whether he translated the Dutch manuscript himself. As a working hypothesis, I have assumed that the "Posthumous Writing" was developed by Dirk in 1567. Footnotes in the summary of "The (new) Ban Book" already indicate where the same thoughts were found in "Posthumous Writing," sometimes word for word. The introduction and biblical teaching about the ban were shorter here, and answers to objections were more concise, for example in the section concerning loving God and the neighbour.

Some differences exist between the two treatises on the question of whether or not shunning in marriage is commanded. The "Posthumous Writing" was clearer on the spiritual marriage of the believer with Christ, which was considered of greater significance than the carnal marriage between husband and wife.[58] The answer to the third objection (spiritual separation) was shorter and therefore more powerful.[59]

One question and its answer were not found in "The (new) Ban Book": Should a husband abandon his wife in the name of God, out of love for Christ and the Gospel, when he had to flee because of persecution and being taken captive?[60] The "Posthumous Writing" ended with the first objection and its answer.

In rewriting, Dirk enriched the subject with many biblical texts and examples, as well as with extensive discussions. He provided the tract with a personal preface and postscript. Because both writings are available for our scrutiny, we get an insight into the author's working style. Dirk spared no effort in treating this subject, which was so close to his heart.

c) "A Reply and Refutation to the two Epistles of Sebastian Franck."[61]

The only opponent whom Dirk Philips mentioned by name was Sebastian Franck. Dirk's attack was directed at two particular letters from Franck,[62] which had been translated into Middle Dutch and given a preface by Pieter Anastasius Overd'haghe (Hyperphragmus)[63] of Zuttere. The letters had been published before 1564[64] (letter to Campanus,[65] the rhenish antitrinitarian, and letter to "Several people in the Eyfelt"). Both letters were originally written in Latin, but the Latin original of the first letter was lost,[66] while a copy of the Latin letter to Joannes à Bekensteyn was found and printed by Hegler in Koningsbergen.[67] Considering the controversy which later arose, it seems doubtful to me that de Suttere, in memory of Franck, did him a service.[68] But the publication has been useful for our knowledge.

These letters were first translated into High German and refuted by Joh. Ewich, a doctor in Duisburg and author of the "Counter Report" which appeared in 1563.[69] Dirk Philips argued against de Zuttere's Dutch publication. Dirk almost certainly read this booklet when he was living in Emden in 1567 and immediately replied to it.[70] The booklet was sent to him by several elders and brothers with the request that he write against it, on behalf of simple people whose faith might be tempted.[71] Dirk started this task immediately and completed the answer within a short time.[72]

I cannot admire his "Refutation." Dirk failed to consider Franck's deeper motives. He had not the faintest understanding of his opponent's spirituality, nor did he refrain from abusive language and ugly words, which were customary in the theological polemic of the sixteenth century.

Dirk began with an answer to the printer's preface,[73] and lifted out only one sentence which dealt with the gifts of the Holy Spirit (Isa. 11:2). Because de Zuttere[74] attributed these gifts to everyone who was born of God and the truth, Dirk felt compelled to point out emphatically that Isa. 11 referred to Jesus Christ, and that the same spirit which was in Him also became part of all true Christians: First to the ministers of the Word, and then to all who clung to Christ as members of the body of which He was the head. Further, Dirk gave a biblical exposition of the Holy Spirit's six gifts which sounded much like a sermon. Finally, he stated that whoever possessed these gifts was wholly spiritual and could judge all things by God's Word and with help from the Spirit, including that which was proclaimed by false teachers. Therefore, neither Sebastian Franck nor others could mislead the true Christian with their subtle arguments.

However, Dirk did not note that, in his preface, de Zuttere offered objections to Franck's views. De Zuttere condenmed Franck's sharp criticism of scholars and people who earnestly sought after God, as well as his rejection of all ceremonies and sacraments.[75]

After the elaborate preface, Dirk began to argue against the two letters.[76] He did not follow Franck's views step by step, but picked out a few ideas to be the target of his anger. His irritation was particularly aroused by Franck's claim that the sacraments, baptism and Lord's Supper, were given to the early Christians as "doll's play and children's games."

Before he started on the letters proper, he proposed that everything be judged according to God's Word, which was the only standard. According to God's Word, Jesus Christ was given to us as the foundation of faith, and his words were spirit and life. From this standpoint he emphatically denied Franck's rejection of the sacraments (*First Thesis*).[77]

Everything that God created in the beginning was good. Human beings were created by God as essentially good. Fallen humankind was restored and renewed by Christ and by rebirth, which must be brought about through the Spirit and faith. Circumcision, the sign of the covenant, was also spoiled by abuse, but it had kept its value until Christ came, ended the symbolism of the Old Testament, and instituted the new ordinances of baptism and the Lord's Supper: "Abuses do not nullify use."

But Franck had called the ordinances of the Lord "doll's play and children's games," and maintained that God baptized the believers with his Spirit and fed their souls (*Second thesis*).[78]

Dirk did not specifically dwell on it, but presented a long argument that Christ was the only begotten Son of the Father and described, quoting many biblical passages, the significance of Jesus Christ for humankind. By doing this he apparently felt he had proven that Sebastian Franck was unjust in giving the sacraments such a shameful name.

According to Franck the outward ceremonies, which had been spoiled by the Antichrist, had not been discontinued but still existed in debased form to be used according to the devil's will. God accomplished all that the sacraments represented by His Spirit, in His spiritual church (*Third thesis*).[79]

Dirk's answer was brief: His opponent had blasphemed the holy commandments of the Lord. Nowhere was it written that God turned over the outward sacraments to the devil, so that his wantonness could have free rein. Nor did God ever accede to a Christian participating in the abused sacraments. That would have been hypocrisy and idol worship. I will take up Dirk's other arguments later.

In the *fourth thesis* Dirk repeated his earlier accusations,[80] and replied to the following statement from Franck: "The doll is taken, not the child, when it has been played with long enough."[81]

The answer was that God certainly was Spirit and those who worship Him must do so in spirit and in truth. According to Scripture, Christ's words were spirit and life. Therefore Christ's teaching, and whatever was done in agreement with His Word, was spiritual and genuine. Christ and the apostles, in whom the Spirit truly lived, themselves received and used the sacraments, and bade the believers keep them. Sebastian Franck was offending God and His ordinances when he maintained that in the early youth of the apostolic church the sacraments had been given to the Christians as playthings, but that the church could dismiss them when it reached adulthood. Oh bold audacity, yes, foolishness of heart!

A new idea was introduced in the *fifth thesis*. Franck had written that the church of the Lord had fallen into apostasy immediately after the time of the apostles, and that the Antichrist had spoiled everything. No one would be able to resurrect the apostate religion, however, unless explicitly called to it by God. Because Franck thought that no one had received this calling, the abuse of the sacraments continued and the devil could carry on with his game.[82]

Dirk admitted that the Antichrist had devastated the early church, but in spite of this, each minister who was legitimately called by the church had to try to restore the New Testament church. With regard to divine calling, Dirk referred to his book "(Concerning) The Sending of Preachers."[83] Apparently in that treatise he alluded to Franck's adherents, or more generally stated, to spiritualists who proposed that no one could proclaim the Word nor resurrect the apostate religion unless called by God, and indeed called by a voice from heaven, as had happened to Elijah (I Kings 18) or Joshua (Joshua 5:2).[84] As a second requirement [Franck had argued that] ministers, even now, had to establish their mission by signs and wonders, just as the apostles had.[85]

Dirk answered that the example of Elijah,[86] used several times by Franck, was no proof at all. Elijah had warned disloyal Israel to worship only God with their sacrifices, and not Baal. He restored the Old Testament religion and thereby declared that his God was the only God. All those who followed Elijah's example with zeal and divine calling sought the honour of God.

In the *sixth and last thesis,* several of Franck's statements were quoted in which he said that the church of God existed invisibly among all peoples, namely among Christians, Jews, heathens and Turks. Those who feared God had to be considered brothers and sisters, even if they had never heard of baptism nor known anything of Christ.[87]

Dirk was indignant about such eccentric ideas. His answer was as follows: In the booklet already mentioned, "(Concerning) the Sending of Preachers," he had devoted several pages to the question of the church's visibility.[88] Although the church was founded in spirit and truth, still she was visible. Dirk derived this conclusion from the linguistic explanation of the words *ecclesia*, which means assembly, and *ecclesiastes*, which means someone who speaks to an assembly.[89]

There was no doubt that the visible church of God existed according to the example of the church founded by Christ and the apostles. In her midst, godly people and bad people were found next to each other. The ban existed to cleanse her and on the last day all unworthy souls would be excluded.[90] Salvation was impossible without faith and the knowledge of Jesus Christ. Therefore it was nonsense to regard heathens, Turks, and Jews as brothers to the extent that they feared and confessed God, as Franck wished to do.[91]

Dirk's opinion of Franck's two letters was not favorable. He considered them to be scandalous writings, opposed to the truth and the faith, full of lethal poison. In conclusion, Dirk gave a short summary of his own faith in five articles.[92]

I must also consider two parts which are so remarkable that I cannot leave them unreported.[93]

1. Dirk wrote[94] that many years before he had read a letter from Franck directed to "his particular and special friend," in which Franck permitted his friend to perform infant baptism, and engage in all kinds of hypocrisy with the world, on behalf of peace. Dirk accused Franck of allowing this only because he feared people. Possibly Dirk was referring here to a writing that has since been lost. But it is equally possible that he had read the letter to the brothers in Lower Germany twenty-five years earlier in East Friesland,[95] forgotten all about it, and only retained this statement in his memory. After all, there was a place in the Middle Dutch text from which such a teaching by Franck could be deduced, but the translation departs here from the original Latin text.[96]

2. Dirk blamed Sebastian Franck for teaching people the broad way and leading the way himself. The broad way pleased natural human nature, which explained why Franck had so many adherents, readers, and disciples.[97] Dirk was not alone in this accusation. It was expressed repeatedly by Anastasius Veluanus, as well as by Gerardus Nicolai in his insertions in Bullinger's "Against the Rebaptizers," and also by others.[98]

In fact, it was never Franck's intent to found a new sect.[99] He was a spiritualist who did not seek the fellowship of faith: "Religious individualism was the strongest motivation of his nature." Nevertheless, there were kindred spirits in Germany and the Netherlands who were inspired by his thoughts and eagerly read his books.[100] These people would pose—in time—a danger for the Anabaptist churches. For this reason, Dirk Philips vehemently attacked Sebastian Frank's two letters and did not hesitate to denigrate him personally.

His attitude however is understandable when we remember that he wrote in times of sickness and old age.[101] His attitude is also explainable by the opposing circumstances of Dirk Philip's ecclesiastical needs—much more strongly present for him than for Menno Simons—and Franck's extreme spiritualism.

[It has been said concerning this writing that] "The style was much more fragmentary than in the rest of the author's works, and his sentence structure, elsewhere so correct and clear, was often ugly and forced,"[102] all of which must be due to the haste in which the "Refutation" was apparently prepared. The inaccuracy of biblical citations also points to the fact that the author worked too hastily.

The first known printing of the "Refutation" was in 1602. We do not know whether an earlier printing was lost, or whether the brethren were not pleased with the article and did not want it published, or whether Dirk himself, after deliberation, did not want it printed.

The other booklets which Dirk wrote in the last months of his life were better designed and demonstrated the author's earlier qualities.

This would be the place to mention the motto–that is, I Thess. 5:19 ff., "Quench not the Spirit"–which Dirk Philips placed on the title pages of the separate editions of the "Book of Faith,"[103] as well as on the *Enchiridion* of 1564.[104] The motto seems strange, because that aphorism was a favourite of Sebastian Franck and other spiritualists of the sixteenth century.[105] It appeared on the title page of "A Letter from Sebastian Franck,"[106] and also on the title pages of other spiritualistic treatises which Pieter de Zuttere published about 1563[107] such as "The Key to the Secret of the Lord's Supper."[108] Is it possible that deep down Dirk had spiritualistic inclinations, in spite of the strong disdain for spiritualism contained in the "Refutation"?

I can provide another solution. Sebastian Franck provided a short biography of Martin Luther in the *Chronicle*.[109] At both beginning and end, the reader was advised to test all things and to keep that which was good. One may not quench the Spirit nor despise prophecies. Dirk, who had used the *Chronicle* diligently in the composition of the "Book of Faith,"[110] apparently found this motto fitting to serve as the fundamental confession of his faith. It was adopted automatically with the printing of the *Enchiridion,* which begins with the "Book of Faith."

d)"Concerning the Marriage of Christians."

I can be more brief about the contents of Dirk Philip's last treatise.[111] The contents are excellently reproduced in the oft-mentioned book by Dr. Wessel.[112] I will touch on a few points only.

1. The title was misleading. The booklet did not actually deal with Christian marriage, "how it was commanded by God, and how it should be maintained by believers."[113] Rather, it dealt with "outside" marriages, that is, the marriages of church members to unbelievers. An unbeliever was the same as a heathen, and could be not only Roman Catholic, but also anyone from a Protestant church, and later anyone from another Anabaptist group.

2. What led Dirk to write this treatise? The church was the scene of many quarrels. As a result of the Frisian-Flemish controversy there was much unrest, and decay was everywhere. Dirk was probably alluding here to the growing Calvinist church, which many who tired of the quarreling were joining. Voices were being raised in the church for more freedom in the choice of spouse. The strict regulations on outside marriages were being opposed.[114]

Dirk was not inclined to concede this point. He feared that if biblical decrees were not maintained, the church would collapse. In his opponents' demands he saw human beings giving way to the flesh to serve evil and immoral lusts. Such carnal unions could never be called marriages instituted by God.[115]

3. It was not the first time Dirk had confronted this problem. It had often kept him occupied, among other times, at the conference at Wismar.[116] Now he had to put his ideas in writing once again, although he was old and sick and facing death. Perhaps he was also driven to this by the decision of an assembly held by three teachers and many ministers and deacons of the Waterlanders, in January 1568 outside of Emden. According to the agreement drawn up there, outside marriage was strongly condemned in the twentieth article, and threatened with the ban. If the banned person wished to be accepted again, he or she first of all had to leave the unbelieving person married outside of the congregation.[117] Dirk wanted to follow the same line, and gave precise rules for the reacceptance of a repentant member.

4. What was a Christian marriage? Dirk had already written about it in "The Spiritual Restitution."[118] The example given was the union of Adam and Eve in paradise, created in the image of God. Christ had renewed this

marriage, and it could only be conducted by two believers who were reborn in the Spirit and joined by God himself. The purpose of the marriage was the growth of the human race by God's blessing.[119]

We are also told how a Christian marriage took place in the congregations led by Dirk. According to the custom of the time, a marriage was made legal by wedding vows. Dirk only partially agreed with the custom, for other obstacles might exist which must first be investigated by the congregation. Perhaps a time of testing needed to be arranged. As long as the congregation had not granted its permission, the engaged couple had to bide their time ("wait in Christian patience"). Dirk compared this situation with that of a candidate who had requested baptism. Although not yet a member of the congregation, such a person had to behave as if baptism had already taken place. Just as the candidate was first accepted into the congregation by baptism, and was recognized by the shaking of hands and the kiss of peace as a "covenanted companion," so also the marriage was solemnized by the engaged couple in the presence of the congregation with a handshake, and they were joined together by a minister with prayer for the presence of God in the marriage.[120]

5. Dirk also recognized a second kind of marriage as valid, namely a marriage which had been contracted between two people during their time of unbelief, according to the manner of the world, that is to say, by an ordinary promise of faithfulness. If one of the two became a believer and joined God's church, there was no need to divorce the other person. They could remain together on the condition that the unbeliever would not trouble the faithful partner. This was done on the basis of I Cor. 7. There was always the hope that the unbeliever would come to faith by God's grace.[121]

6. For the "third" marriage or, as Dirk called it, the outside marriage, the case was different. This was strictly forbidden and had to be disciplined with the ban. The entire article dealt with this case. There were conditions to be met if an apostate saw the light and sought reacceptance into the church. Attention had to be given to three things:[122] True repentance, public confession of the sin before God with a request for forgiveness, and the

abandonment of the sin. The last requirement was laid out in detail. Repentant sinners had to leave the spouse they had married outside the church, in opposition to God's Word, although they were to continue to provide for the spouse's care. However, such members could not remarry and had to abstain from sexual activity (Dirk calls this circumcising oneself on behalf of the kingdom of heaven). Finally, such a member had to pray without ceasing "that God might open [the spouse's] eyes to understanding and convert him or her."[123] Note that Dirk made a harsher judgment here than he and Menno had made in Wismar,[124] while at the conference of the Waterlanders they had wanted to present further regulations later, in writing.[125] Dirk emphasized that as long as he was a minister no one who married outside would be re-accepted into the congregation in any way other than this: In order to be admitted to the congregation, the unbelieving partner first had to repent.[126]

7. A congregation by itself could not decide to reaccept an outside married person. Teachers, elders, and servants from other congregations (as many as were available) must be called together and consulted, and their advice followed. When God's church followed this guideline, all proceeded smoothly and there was peace. But as soon as some congregations began making decisions on their own concerning "heavy" matters, without including elders and teachers from other congregations, quarrels and division occurred. It was obvious today![127]

If we understand Dirk Philips' position, and accept the biblical grounds on which his views were based, then we must acknowledge that he was correct. We cannot impose the standards of today on him, nor proceed according to our expectations of marriage, mutual love of the marriage partners, and intimacy. The difficulties that Dirk touched on sometimes still occur in "mixed" marriages nowadays. Also we must admit that Dirk had true insight when he wrote that the existence of the church was endangered by outside marriages. And although the requirements were severe, I think he showed real pastoral care, particularly when he spoke about Christian marriage. Pijper was right when he wrote: "The subject he discussed could have a radical effect on family life. The most tender relationships were at stake."[128] For that reason, the treatise was reprinted several times and also included in some German and American translations of his works.

Dirk completed his booklet "About the Marriage of Christians" on March 7, 1568.[129] Shortly thereafter he died. He truly had spent his energies serving the brotherhood. The year of death was firmly established by Malet's note in Nicolai's "Insertions," which were published by Nicolai.[130] Nicolai had written in the text, "This, then, is the earliest origin of the old Mennonites or Menno's congregation, whose main leaders and teachers now are Leenaert B. and Dirk P." Nicolai died in 1567 or 1568–probably in 1567[131]–so it was Malet, who lived in Emden and therefore would be up to date on Dirk's death, who added the note: "Dirk Philips died outside of Emden at the Valder in 1568."

We can figure out the date of death (in the second half of March) because we know that Leenaert Bouwens, who had been suspended as elder by Dirk in 1565 and lived in a village near Harlingen, resumed his office on April 10, 1568. Therefore, we can assume that the report of his critic's death had reached him shortly before that time, and he considered himself authorized to resume his work.[132]

Dirk was interred in the rest home cemetery of the Valder,[133] also known as the Franciscan cemetery. In 1561 it had been transferred, along with the cloister and the church of that order, to the Reformed Church of Emden.[134]

Ironically Dirk, the former Franciscan, was buried in the same cemetery where many of his Franciscan brothers had been buried before him.

Kühler wrote correctly:
> *We need not subscribe to the harsh judgment of Carel van Ghendt that "he [Dirk Philips] ended his days with a heart and mind filled with the bitter gall of controversy and disunity, as was abundantly clear from his last deeds."*[135]

Although it is unlikely that his thoughts had changed, we know nothing about his frame of mind in his last days.[136]

My remaining task is to evaluate the significance of Dirk Philips' contribution to the Anabaptist brotherhood. In the beginning, after he had broken the fetters of the Franciscan cloister and joined the Anabaptist movement by baptism, his role was modest. He stood in the shadow of his brother Obbe, and later of Menno Simons. His greatest credit was that he was a true friend and fellow worker of Menno. He stood in for Menno during Menno's trips to Friesland. He accompanied Menno on the flight from East Friesland to the Rhineland. He participated with Menno in various conferences and supported him in the leadership of the brotherhood.

Later Dirk became more prominent through his writings and his zeal for the purity of the church. He was undeniably a more competent writer than Menno. His books excelled due to a clear line of reasoning, in spite of his preference for allegorical exegesis. His style was clear and natural. He was the dogmatist among the Anabaptist writers. It was easy to build a dogmatic system from his writings. He confronted his opponents expertly, particularly the Davidjorists and the House of Love, but also the Roman Catholic Church and evangelical preachers.

Dirk did not lack self confidence, particularly when his books became influential and he realized that they were being noticed by Protestant and Catholic scholars. He often spoke of his small gift, saying that he was a poor and useless servant of the Lord,[137] but he was nevertheless convinced that his exposition of Holy Scripture was correct and irrefutable.[138] Likewise, he was fully confident that his position was right in the Frisian-Flemish controversy.[139] He hoped that in the day of judgment he would be able to stand, by God's grace.[140]

Although Dirk had a good mind and urged the purity of biblical doctrine, he was first and foremost a religious person. Faith was the dominating force of his spiritual life.

> *The knowledge of Jesus Christ, in whom God has revealed his love to us, is not historical knowing, but a living and powerful work of God in the person, by which he is changed, reborn out of God, and illuminated and*

gifted by the Holy Spirit, so that he is of a like mind with Jesus Christ.[141]

This faith should bear fruit in good works and be visible through a love for God and for the neighbour. Pure brotherly love was a sure sign of true faith, and love for God was shown by keeping His commandments.[142] Therefore Dirk encouraged his readers, again and again, to abandon the world, to die to sin, and to strive for sanctification.[143] But he did not preach moralism.[144] He knew that human beings could only be saved by grace, not by works,[145] even as he opposed the Lutherans' one-sided preaching of grace and justification.[146]

Dirk was sure that the founding of the Anabaptist fellowship had brought about the great turning point in the history of the Christian church. By God's grace the Gospel had been rediscovered and revealed to humankind.[147] He discussed this topic extensively in the booklet "Concerning Spiritual Restitution": "Now we are in the second liberation from Babylon (the Roman Catholic Church), now the second temple is being built, and the New Jerusalem erected." In "The Congregation of God" this thought was developed further to show that the true church of God was now visible on earth in the form of the Anabaptist fellowship.[148] The best proof of this was that the symbols of baptism and the Lord's Supper had been restored to their original form.[149] Dirk compared the church to Noah's ark. Christ, the spiritual Noah, built the Christian church as a refuge for all believing souls. Those who enter the ark will be kept unto eternal life, but those who despise the proffered grace will not escape punishment. God's wrath will be visited on them in the day of judgment.[150]

Walther Koehler noticed an "ecclesiasticism" in Dirk's writings, and implied that his concept of the church corresponded to Luther's.[151] Dirk wrote:

The heavenly Jerusalem exists everywhere that God's Word is correctly taught, and the sacraments are practiced rightly according to the Word.[152]

Dirk emphasized that he did not proclaim a new doctrine, but that his church was based on the true church of God which was founded by Christ and the apostles. Therefore he wanted to be led completely by the example of the early apostolic church.[153] He admitted that corruption of the church of Christ had entered quickly,[154] but some members who did not follow the Antichrist had always remained: A branch of the justified children of God.[155] These were the ones allowed entrance into the ark by God's grace. Dirk did not care that the true church was small and insignificant, and that only a few entered the narrow gate and found the path to eternal life.[156] Christ had predicted that.

The search for church order was especially obvious in the institution of the ban, which served as a kind of spiritual policing. Dirk had thought about the new image of the church. She resembled a city whose citizens were believers. The citizens of an earthly city had to be single-minded and live by the same rules and statutes, otherwise the city could not stand. Likewise the church could only exist if members were one in spirit and faith, if they walked according to the Word of God, and kept the divine laws.[157]

In previous chapters, I have written about the ban, about its maintenance, and the conflicts which it caused. I would like to repeat that Dirk, as a proponent of the strict ban, was rigid and harsh: "He lacked the tact and insight which could have prevented impending division."[158]

Nevertheless, "His love for the brotherhood was above suspicion."[159] For thirty-four years he gave his best efforts to the church, and tried to make her the pure bride of Christ. The conflicts of his final ten years threw a shadow over his life and have influenced our opinion of his character. Let us not forget, however, that he guided many with his literary works, and strengthened them in their faith. Although his writings do not translate easily into the twentieth century, they are still worth studying.

My hope is that this study will clear the way for a better understanding of Dirk's personality and his work.

Postscript

Originally I had intended to dedicate a separate chapter to the literary opponents of Dirk Philips. But because I feared that time and strength would not suffice, I have discussed Matthijs Wyer, Herman de Timmerman, Guy de Brès, and Jacobus Kimedoncius in the course of my book (see the Index). I will report about two other opponents here.

1. *Dirck Volckerzoon Coornhert* (1522-1590). He refers to Dirk Philips repeatedly in his works. The fictitious discussion between a West Frisian Mennonite and himself is well-known: "Concerning the Sending" (1575)[1] about which Kühler writes.[2] But he also mentions Dirk Philips in other works as in, for example, "The Consistory Treatment of not Handling the Lord's Supper" (the end of 1579 or the beginning of 1580),[3] "Concerning Adult Baptism" (1575),[4] and "The Pretended Goodness of the Sects" (1574).[5] The *Enchiridion* of Dirk Philips is also quoted in one of the letters.[6] A careful search of the writings of Coornhert will probably disclose still other places.

2. *Jean Tafflen* (1529/1602.)[7] In his book *Instructions Against the Errors of the Rebaptizers*[8] he contends against the Anabaptists, and probably also attached four unbound writings.[9] In the second chapter of his book he defended infant baptism in the form of an interview between Dierick (Philips) rejecting infant baptism and Jan (Tafflen) tolerating and maintaining it. This conflict with the Baptizers deserves a closer examination in connection with the teachings of Dirk Philips.

To my regret I could not consult the book by George Hunston Williams, *The Radical Reformation*, Philadelphia, 1962, because my manuscript was already finished when my attention was drawn to it.

Notes

Chapter I

[1] This year is mentioned by all later authors on the authority of Schijn Maatschoen. Still older is the portrait of Dirk Philips (Amsterdam's Mennonite Congregation Library, vol. II, no. 3142), with the description Dierck Philips, born at Leeuwarden in Friesland 1504. The engraver C. Koning lived in the beginning of the 17th century, D. B., 1890, p. 69 ff.

[2] That their father was a priest appears from the report of contemporaries: In his confession on Feb. 7, 1538, Jan Batenburg named as leaaders David Joris, Obbe, and Dirk his brother. In the Amsterdam copy the following is added: O. a priest's son born in West Friesland; see de Hullu, *Bescheiden betr. de Hervorming in Overijssel*, Dl. I, Deventer, 1899, p. 252. Nic. Blesdikius, *Historia vitae Davidis Georgii*, Daventriae, 1642, p. 135: "Ubbo et Theodoricus Philippi fratres, sacerdotis Lewardini fillii." The assertion of Guido de Bres, that Dirk was a "Costers Soon van Leeuwaerden" appears to me to be untrue. It stands, indeed, only in the index of *De Wortel, Den Oorsprong, Ende het Fundament der wederdooperen* of 1608, not in the editions of 1565 and 1570.

[3] In the notes of A. J. Bruinsma (Provincial Library of Leeuwarden) about the Diaconate Leeuwarden a vicar Philippus is mentioned several times, fol. 152, 155, 167. He was vicar of St. Catharina Church "op den Hoeck" [on the corner], and in addition a clergyman at Cammingabuur. See also, W. Eekhoff, *Geschiedkundige beschrijving van Leeuwarden*, dl. II, 1846, p. 398 ff.

[4] *Bibliotheca Reformatoria Neerlandica*, vol. X: "De geschriften van Dirk Philipsz." edited by F. Pijper, 's-Gravenhage, 1914, p. 5.

[5] J. Reitsma, *Honderd jaren uit de geschiedenis der Hervorming en der Hervormde kerk in Friesland*, Leeuwarden, 1876, p. 4 ff. and 11.

[6] J. S. Theissen, *Centraal gezag en friesche vrijheid*, Groningen, 1907, p. 452.

[7] K. Vos, *Menno Simons, 1496-1561, Zijn leven en werken en zijne reformatorische denkbeelden*, Leiden, 1914, p. 219 ff.

[8] In D. B., 1884, p. 1 ff.

[9] My article "Joachim Kükenbieter (Nossiophagus). Ein lutherischer Eiferer des Reformationszeitalters," N.A.K.G., vol. XLIV, 1961, pp. 157-176. The letter to Johannes Garcaeus, p. 219 ff.

[10] P. Beda Verbeek, O.F.M. "Oud en Nieuw Galilea. De Kloosters der minderbroeders in Leeuwarden," *Uitgave Frisia Catholica*, no. XIV, Joure, 1951.

[11] Op. cit., p. 23 ff.

[12] Op. cit., p. 36 ff.

[13] Op. cit., p. 42. What K. Vos "Een bisschop in Appingedam." *Gron. Volksalmanak*, (1916, reprint, p. 11) wrote about the lay brother Dirk, he based on Dirk's attitude after 1554.

[14] W. J. Kühler, *Geschiedenis der Nederlandsche Doopsgezinden in de zestiende eeuw*. Haarlem, 1932, p. 65. That Hoffman was in Friesland, Reitsma, op. cit, p. 41, reports without giving his source.

[15] K. Vos, *Menno Simons*, p. 24; Kühler, op. cit., p. 65

[16] K. Vos, D.B., 1917, p. 159 ff.; Kühler. op. cit., p. 68. The Moravian Brothers also suspended baptism in 1531, see J. Kiewiet, *Pilgram Marbeck*, Diss. Zürich, p. 53.

[17] B.R.N. VII, p. 124.

[18] *Ibid.*, p. 127.

[19] Kühler, op. cit., p. 70 ff.; B.R.N. VII, p. 127 ff.

[20] H. Detmer, *Bilder aus den religiösen und sozialen Unruhen in Münster*, Part II, 1904, p. 114. Fritz Blanke, "Das Reich der Wiedertäufer zu Münster 1534/35," in *Aus der Welt der Reformation*, Zürich, 1960, p. 52.

[21] B.R.N. VII, p. 129. The comment of A. F. Mellink, *De Wederdopers in de Noordelijke Nederlanden, 1531-1544*, Groningen, 1953, p. 353, that the name Dierick Cuyper by Obbe Philips must be an error, seems to me incorrect. See K. Vos, D. B., 1917, p. 100 ff. About Willem de Kuiper at that place, p. 100 ff., 103, 111.

[22] That Hans Scheerder was a colleague of Obbe appears to me doubtful. He was also mentioned in the articles as "wantscheerder" = cloth shearer, see M.E., vol. II, p. 651.

[23] "Confession of Obbe Philips" [*Bekentnisse van Obbe Philips*] op. cit., p. 129.

[24] *Ibid.*, p. 130. Peter Houtzager baptized on the way to Leeuwarden in Arum in December 1533 (D.B., 1875, p. 60 ff.) and his preaching at Workum was remembered (D. B., 1899, p. 31).

[25] Kempo Martena, *Landboek*, H. S. Foliant in the Provincial Library of Friesland, no. E. 359, fol. 213r° and v⁰.

[26] B. R. N. VII, p. 130 ff.

[27] B. R. N. X, p. 182 ff. (Translation from WDP, p. 176).

[28] G. F. thoe Schwartzenberg and Hohenlandsberg, *Groot Placcaat- en Charterboeck van Vriesland*, Leeuwarden, 1768-1793, vol. II, fol. 650 ff. Obbe baptized Jan Kanneghieter van Koesfeld outside of Dokkum either before his departure from Friesland or later in Groningen. See Mellink, op. cit., p. 250.

[29] Joseph Niesert. *Münsterische Urkundensammlung*, vol. I, Coesfeld, 1826. p. 296 ff; de Hullu, op. cit., p. 267 ff.; K. Vos, "Kleine bijdragen VII, Obbe Philipz.," D.B., 1917, pp. 124-127.

[30] "Die doiper aldair hett Obbo van Lewerden barbyrer." de Hullu, op. cit., p. 214.

[31] B.R.N. VII, p. 131; K. Vos, "Kleine bijdragen, op. cit., p. 125; Kühler, op. cit., p. 106; Mellink, op. cit., p. 367 ff.

[32] *Archief Zeeuwsch Genootschap*, vol. II, 1866-1869, 6th part. K. R. Pekelharing, *Bijdragen voor de geschiedenis der hervorming in Zeeland, 1524-1572*, pp. 240-243. Kühler makes a plausible case that the baptism of David Joris took place already "in wintertime," op. cit., p. 198, note 3.

[33] Kühler, op. cit., p.. 60, note 2 and p. 142; Mellink, op. cit., p. 118 ff.

[34] For the Münster revolt, see Kühler, op. cit., pp. 78-191; F. Blanke, op. cit., p. 48-71.

[35] B. R. N. VII, p. 132 ff.

[36] B.R.N. VII, p. 136; Cramer, op. cit., note 1 points out that between the ordination of Dirk Philips, David Joris, and Menno Simons some time must have elapsed. J. H. Hilmers, *Commentatio historico-ecclesiastica de Ubbone et Ubbonitis*, Diss. Rostock, 1733, p. 18 ff. thinks it is probable that Obbe baptized his brother not long after his own ordination. Both were always named together and strove together against the Münsterites.

[37] K. Vos, "Een bisschop in Appingedam," op. cit., p. 7 and "Kleine bijdragen VII," op. cit., p. 126. See also P. G. Bos, "De Groningsche Wederdooperswoelingen in 1534 en 1535," in N.A.K.G. vol. VI, 1908, pp. 1-47, p. 7 ff.

[38] K. Vos, *Een bisschop*, p. 7, and *Menno Simons*, p. 3.

[39] Kühler, op. cit, p. 420; B.R.N. X, p. 573.

Chapter II

[1] Concerning the Groningen Anabaptist disturbances, see P. G. Bos, op. cit. Use Nicolai as a supplement, B.R.N. VII, pp. 361-370. Further: Kühler, op. cit., p. 143 ff.; Mellink, op. cit., p. 254 ff.

[2] K. Vos, "Kleine bijdragen, V," op. cit., p. 105, M.E. vol. I, p. 614.

[3] K. W. Bouterwek, "Zur Literatur und Geschichte der Wiedertäufer," *Zeitschrift des Bergischen Geschichtsvereins*, vol. I, Bonn, 1864, pp. 345-359. Concerning the contents of Rothmann's booklet, see Kühler, op. cit., p. 129 ff.

[4] Joseph Niesert, op. cit., p. 297.

[5] This all happened in the middle of January, 1535, according to the letter of governor Schenck to Deventer, Jan. 18, 1535; de Hullu, op. cit., p. 183 ff.

[6] Reitsma, *Honderd jaren*, p. 46 ff.; Kühler, op. cit., p. 166 ff.

[7] P. B. Bos, op. cit., p. 34 ff.; Kühler, op. cit., p. 169 ff.; Mellink, op. cit., p. 262 ff.

[8] de Hullu, op. cit, p. 256.

[9] B.R.N. VII, p. 135.

[10] *Ibid.*

[11] *Historia Davidis Georgii*, p. 6.

[12] Op. cit., p. 51.

[13] B.R.N. X, p. 341 in the Foreword of the "Spiritual Restitution," translation from WDP, p. 317.

[14] See the word "Munsterschen," B.R.N. X, p. 110.

[15] B.R.N. X, p. 373, translation from WDP, p. 346. This reference makes one think of Menno Simons' "Tegen Jan van Leyden" ["Against Jan van Leyden"], 1627, C 3 v⁰. K. Vos made me aware of this reference.

[16] "Misuerstand" ["Misunderstanding"], B.R.N. X, pp. 284, 310 ff.

[17] "De vreemde leer van de Hutten Moysi" ["The strange teaching concerning the tabernacle of Moses"], *ibid.* p. 251; the figures, p. 290; eschatology, p. 310; the mistaken and the true restitution, p. 342 ff., and p. 375.

[18] B.R.N. VII, p. 361 ff., "de oproerighe wederdoopers Batenborch ende Obbo Philips met haren aenhanck."

[19] S. Cramer in B.R.N. VII, p. 93 ff.

[20] B.R.N. VII, p. 461.

[21] *Toetsteen van de versierde Apostolische Successie*, 1603, p. 15. See B.R.N. VII, p. 9, note 3.

[22] V. P., *Successio Anabaptistica* in B.R.N. VII, p. 61. "There is little with which to honour his brother Dirk Philipszoon, Bishop in the Dam, for he was one of the rebels who traveled to Oldeklooster." That the author of *Succession* knew the *Toetsteen* appears in B.R.N. VII, p. 17. See S. Cramer's comment, op. cit., p. 9, note 3.

[23] D.B., 1917, p. 126.

[24] N.A.K.G., vol. VI, 1908, p. 8.

[25] Op. cit., p. 128 ff.

[26] Joseph Niesert, op. cit., p. 297. The Mudder family was still supporting Eikelman with money in 1541.

[27] Mellink, op. cit., pp. 267 and 390.

[28] *Ibid.*, pp. 374 and 381: That Obbe explicitly named the rebellion "in the dam, at 't Zandt" in the *Bekentenisse* ["Confession"], B.R.N. VII, p. 136, is no proof of his presence there for he lists all the disturbances: Amsterdam, the Oldeklooster, Hazerswoude, Appingedam, at 't Zandt, and above all, Münster. One need not conclude from silence concerning the attack at Warfum that "fear made him silent."

[29] Obbe in the *Bekentenisse*, op. cit., p. 135: "The love of so many hearts also made us sad. This the most high King of glory knows, that my soul was often saddened unto death ... I may certainly say with truth that the love of the brothers in the zeal for the house of the Lord had just about done me in."

[30] J. C. Burgmann, *Dissertatio histor. eccl. de historiae mennoniticae fontibus et subsidiis.* [Def. J. H. Burgmann] Rostochii, 1732, fol. 25.

[31] See above, note 10.

[32] Blesdikius, *Historia Davidis Georgii*, p. 6 ff.

[33] According to Gerdt Eilkeman the name Obbites [or Obbenites] "signifies that he and all of those named Obbens were baptized, called Obbites, and were opposed to the Batenburger sects." Joseph Niesert, op. cit., p. 298. "Obbites, who are called Mennonites today," Blesdikius, loc. cit., p. 8; Kükenbieter in his letter to Garcaeus: N.A.K.G., vol. XLIV, p. 174 ff. See further, B.R.N. VII, pp. 46, 361 ff., 461 ff.

[34] For particulars see Kühler, op. cit., pp. 192-211.

[35] Blesdikius, loc. cit., pp. 8, 11.

[36] Blesdikius, loc. cit.; see W. J. Kühler, "De verkiezing tot oudste in de zestiende eeuw," *Zondagsbode*, 29 Nov., 1925, p. 47. J. H. Wessel, *De leerstellige strijd tusschen Nederlandsche Gereformeerden en Doopsgezinden in de zestiende eeuw*, Assen, 1945, p. 36.

[37] Blesdikius, loc. cit., p. 11.

[38] In his "A Clear Response to a writing of Gellius Faber," *Sommairie*, 1646, fol. 413-611; reference at fol. 474a.

[39] Date given by Ubbo Emmius, *Grondelicke Onderricthtinghe van ... David Joris*, Middleburg, 1599, p. 2. Concerning the convent where they met, see above all W. J. Kühler, vol. I, pp. 199-206.

[40] Loc. cit., p. 14.

[41] Kühler, op. cit., p. 199.

[42] *Ibid*. p. 205.

[43] The departure occurred on January 30, 1536, the baptism probably a bit later. See N. van der Zijpp, *Geschiedenis der Doopsgezinden in Nederland*, Arnhem, 1952, p. 40, above all note 10. B.R.N. VII, p. 362, note 3.

[44] *Sommarie*, 1646, fol. 474b.

[45] Blesdikius, loc. cit., p. 8.

[46] *Sommarie*, 1646, fol. 474b.

[47] *Ibid*.

[48] B.R.N. VII, p. 136, note 1.

[49] K. Vos, op. cit., p. 54.; Blesdikius, loc. cit., p. 135: Menno abiisdem [Obbe et Dirk] persuasus ... passus est se huius novae factionis episcopum creari.[Menno, of the same persuasion (as Obbe and Dirk), allowed himself to be elected bishop of this new group"].

[50] *Sommarie*, 1646, fol. 475b-476a. The careful reader will note that I have tried to give a reasonable portrayal of Obbe and Menno's baptism and ordination, based on the sources. Some of the reports about the chronology and the places where Menno stayed are ambiguous. I mainly agree with Cornelius Krahn, *Menno Simons*, Karlsruhe, 1936, p. 35 ff. and with N. van der Zijpp, op. cit., pp. 40 and 44. The baptism of Peter Janss van Blankenham at Oldersum (East Friesland) must have taken place after the ordination of Menno. See Kühler, op. cit., p. 194, note 3. This is also assumed by H. W. Meihuizen, *Menno Simons*, Haarlem, 1961, p. 22, but in my opinion he places the ordination of Menno incorrectly in 1536. "About four years" makes the time period uncertain. The phrase can just as well mean 3.5 as 4.5 years.

Chapter III

[1] Mellink, op. cit., p. 15 ff.

[2] J. S. Theissen, *De regering van Karel V in de noordelijke Nederlanden*, 1912, p. 116.

[3] S. Blaupot ten Cate, *Geschiedenis der Doopsgezinden in Groningen, Overijssel en Oost-Friesland*, Leeuwarden en Groningen, 1842, vol. II, p. 167 ff.

[4] Theissen, op. cit., p. 186.

[5] The draft of this letter is in the Gemeentearchief Groningen. According to a report from the archivist Dr. A. T. Schuitema Meijer, the letter from the governor to the city council dated March, 22, 1537, is not present in the city archives. G. E. Frerichs also made use of the letter from the council dated April 2. See D. B., 1906, p. 20. I have corrected some mistakes.

[6] On orders from the city on May 3, 1534 all Anabaptists who were not citizens had to leave the city within 12 hours. Blaupot ten Cate, op. cit., p. 167.

[7] The form to be followed is attached.

[8] K. Vos, "Kleine bijdragen" in D. B., 1917, p. 136.

[9] See my article, "De Anabaptisten in Oostfriesland ten tijde van Hermannus Aquilomontanus," N.A.K.G., vol. XLVI, pp. 87-99.

[10] K. Vos, *Menno Simons*, pp. 53, 71, 243.

[11] F. Ritter, "Henricus Ubbius' Beschreibung von Ostfriesland v. J. 1530," *Jahrbuch der Gesellschaft f.b. Kunst u. vaterl. Altertümer zu Emden*, vol. XVIII, 1913, p. 86 ff. note 39; Gerh. Ohling, *Junker Ulrich von Dornum*, Aurich, 1955. According to Ohling, pp. 17, 22, 25 Ulrich was no longer lord at Oldersum after 1527, but had a new manor "auf der Siewe," gem. Tergast.

[12] F. Ritter, *ibid.*, p. 91 ff., note 45.

[13] G. E. Frerichs, "Menno's verblijf in de eerste jaren na zijn uitgang," D. B., 1906, pp. 1-52, esp. p. 44 ff.

[14] K. Vos, op. cit., pp. 64-69, 71. Quirijn Pieters van Cruiningen (not Groningen) was baptized by Menno at Pygnum in 1539. See G. Grosheide, *Bijdrage tot de Geschiedenis der Anabaptisten in Amsterdam*, Hilversum, 1938, p. 151.

[15] See my article in N.A.K.G., vol. XLIV, pp. 157-176.

[16] *Ibid.*, p. 174 ff.

[17] K. Vos, "Een bisschop in Appingedam" in *Gron. Volksalmanak*. 1916, p. 6, places the debate at Norden. This is based on my report of July, 1916.

[18] Certainly in connection with the disputation of 1537.

[19] *Ibid.*, p. 174 ff.

[20] B.R.N. X, p. 13.

[21] Obbe later called himself Aelbrecht. D. B., 1917, p. 136. A Statement of Jan van Sol, Dec., 1550.

[22] B.R.N., X, p. 12.

[23] See Chapter I, note 2.

[24] B.R.N. VII, p. 130.

[25] B.R.N. VII, p. 136.

[26] B.R.N. VII, p. 47. Perhaps the author of the "Succession" concluded this from Obbe's report.

[27] B.R.N. VII, p. 136. Obbe's defection was explained in this way by earlier authors: De Hoop Scheffer, "De bevestiger van Menno Simons", D.B., 1884, pp. 20-22; S. Cramer, B.R.N. VII, pp. 96-99; K. Vos, *Menno Simons*, p. 60 ff.; above all W. J. Kühler, "De Successio Apostolica," *Zondagsbode*, May 30, 1926, p. 295a. More recently, Obbe's defection is justified by pointing to the dislike of the individualistic and spiritualistic Obbe by Menno's congregation, with its strict ordinances: N. van der Zijpp, op. cit., p. 45; H. W. Meihuizen, op. cit., pp. 30-34; J. A. Brandsma, *Menno Simons van Witmarsum*, Drachten, 1960, p. 50. The first line (B.R.N. VII, p. 122) in my opinion is aimed at the sacramentarian oriented circle in Leeuwarden. Concerning the second line the marginal note correctly says that Obbe here expresses the feelings

which he had after his "recantation." The place cited by Brandsma (B.R.N. VII, p. 137) refers to the division of Münsterities, David Jorists, Batenburgers, etc. See also K. Vos, *Menno Simons*, p. 61, note 2.

[28] B.R.N. VII, p. 133 ff.

[29] P. Kawerau, *Melchior Hoffman als religöser Denker*, Haarlem, 1954, p. 4.

[30] Published and clarified by K. Vos, N.A.K.G., vol. XI, 1914, pp. 342-350. See also by the same author, *Menno Simons*, p. 256 ff.

[31] Actually Io. Herm. Hilmers, *De Vbbone Philippi et Vbbonitis*, Rostock, 1733, p. 43, note X.

[32] B.R.N. VII, p. 520. Does this mean, as it does later, that he no longer held the office of elder?

[33] Menno Simons, *Sommarie*, 1646, fol. 587 b. See for the later fate of Obbe my: "Die Täufer in Mecklenburg," M.G.Bl., 1961, pp. 33 ff., 43 ff.

[34] B.R.N. X, pp. 199, 275.

[35] N.D.B., vol. I, p. 300 ff. "Anna von Oldenburg."

[36] *Evang. Kirchenlexikon*, vol. II, col. 1037 ff. For the biography of à Lasco, see the review of the book from Oskar Bartel in A.R.G., 1956, Year 47, p. 279 ff.

[37] See my "The Anabaptists in East Friesland", op. cit., p. 90.

[38] Claes Garbrantszn. visited Menno outside of Emden after 1542. G. Grosheide, op. cit., p. 165. The wife of the martyr Jan Claeszn., Aleid Barentsdr. gave birth at Oldersum before 1544 (not 1545). She had her child baptized at the time of the imprisonment of her husband. K. Vos, *Menno Simons*, p. 71, combined with G. Grosheide, op. cit., pp. 149, 151.

[39] F. Nippold, "David Joris von Delft," *Z. f. histor. Theol.*, 1863, pp.. 141-149; Kühler, *Gesch.*, I, pp. 239-241.

[40] Blesdikius, *Historia Davidis Georgii*, p. 133.

[41] For particulars, see J. P. Müller, *Die Mennoniten in Oostfriesland vom 16. bis 18. Jahrhundert,* Emden and Borkum, 1887, part I, p. 19 ff., above all the notes.

[42] Blesdikius, *Historia Davidis Georgii*, pp. 137-139, Nippold, op cit., p. 150 ff.

[43] K. Vos, *Menno Simons*, p. 72 ff.; Corn. Krahn, op. cit., p. 60 ff.

[44] J. P. Müller, op. cit., p. 21 ff.

[45] *Ibid.*, p. 23 ff.

[46] *Ibid.*, p. 24, note 39; Bl. ten Cate, *Groningen, etc.*, part II, p. 213 ff., gives a better text. In the police order the name of Menniten and Mennisten appears for the first time in print, correctly noted by H. W. Meihuizen, op. cit., p. 40.

Chapter IV

[1] "Menno in het Rijnland," K. Vos, *Menno Simons*, pp. 83-87; Corn. Krahn, op. cit., pp. 62-64; above all, J. F. G. Goeters, "Die Rolle des Täufertums in der Reformationsgeschichte des Niederrheins," *Rhein. Vierteljahrsblätter*, vol. 24, 1959, pp. 217-236.

[2] B.R.N. VII, p. 50.
[3] Kühler, *Geschiedenis*, I, p. 232.
[4] *Ibid.*, p. 289. I see the episode at Goch differently, as I will show in Chapter V.
[5] *Opera*, 1681, fol. 475
[6] J. A. Brandsma, "Warum hat Menno Simons nicht friesisch geschrieben?" M.G.Bl., Jhg. 18, p. 14 ff.
[7] J. F. G. Goeters, "H. von Wied," R.G.G.³, vol. 3, p. 240 ff.; idem., *Rhein. Vierteljahrsblätter*, op. cit., p. 229 ff.
[8] The peace treaty of Venlo, Sept. 7, 1543. H. Forsthoff. *Rhein. Kirchengeschichte*, vol. I. *Die Reformation am Niederrhein*. Essen, 1929, p. 246 ff.
[9] Forsthoff, op. cit., pp. 256-270.
[10] For example, Mörs, Forsthoff, op. cit., pp. 283-294; Schleiden, M.L., IV, p. 66 ff. (E. Crous).
[11] E. Crous, "Auf Mennos Spuren am Niederrhein," *Der Mennonit*, 1955, no. 10. p. 155; no. 12, p. 186.
[12] Hans H. Th. Stiasny, "Die strafrechtliche Verfolgung der Täufer in der freien Reichsstad Köln, 1529-1618," *Reformationsgesch. Studien und Texte*, Issue 88, Münster i. W., 1962, p. 22 ff.
[13] J. F. G. Goeters, "Das aelsteste rhein. Täuferbekenntnis" in *A Legacy of Faith*, ed. Corn. J. Dyck, Newton, Kansas, 1962, pp. 197-212.
[14] *Annalen des histor. Vereins für den Niederrhein*, VI, p. 62 in a composition of P. B. Bergrath, "Das Wüllenamt in Goch." This report was used by K. Rembert in *Die Wiedertäufer im Herzogtum Jülich*, Berlin, 1899, p. 495 ff. and M.L., I, p. 363. It was adopted by K. Vos, D. B., 1909, p. 116 and M.E., II, p. 533; see also Heinr. Kessel, "Reformation und Gegenreformation im Herzogtum Cleve (1517-1609)" in *Düsseldorfer Jahrb.*, 1918/19, vol. 30, p. 109.
[15] Op. cit., p. 485, M.L., I, p. 363.
[16] K. Vos, D. B., 1909, pp. 104-116; E. Crous, op. cit., no. 12, p. 187.
[17] Rembert, *Wiedertäufer in Jülich*, p. 488.
[18] See Chapter V.
[19] Published and clarified by me in N.A.K.G., vol. XLIII, pp. 15-21.
[20] Except for the places mentioned by me in note 9 above, I cite from Kessel, op. cit., p. 18, that the town of Wezel had accepted Walloon Protestants who had been driven out of the bishopric of Liege, and allowed them reformed preaching.
[21] B.R.N. X, p. 19, note 2, reprinted pp. 313-337. In my opinion it was printed about 1558.
[22] Concerning him, see Chr. Sepp, *Kerkhistorische Studiën*, 1885, p. 139 ff.; Ed. Simons in *Theol. Arbeiten aus dem Rhein*, wissenshaftl. Prediger-Verein, N.F., Issue 9, Tübingen, 1907, pp. 30-49; R.G.G.², vol. V, 1896.
[23] N.N.W.B., X, p. 1190; R.G.G.², vol. V, 1895 ff.
[24] *Grondelick Onderrichtinghe van veelen Hoochwichtighen Articulen enz.*, Frankfurt, 1579, pp. 49-51. Available in the Doopsg. Bibliotheek in Amsterdam.

[25] It seems to me that the booklet described by S. Cramer, B.R.N. V, p. 12, "Eyn kort Bericht um to kommen tot den waren Gehoor des ... Woirdts Gots" compiled by Pieter de Zuttere is composed from the writings of Matthijs Wijer. However in that case the date of death is given incorrectly as April 15, 1560 instead of April 25, 1560.

[26] B.R.N. VII, p. 50.

[27] M.L. I, p. 76. Not a brother of Gerh. Westerburg. He was called Arnt (Arnold), Münster. *Quellen*, II, p. 293. See about him: "Een onbekende brief van Dirk Philips," op. cit., p. 15 ff.

[28] K. Vos, *Menno Simons*, pp. 95-99 and *passim*. See new information about him in G. Grosheide, op. cit., pp. 252-256.

[29] Lemke was deacon at Illikhoven about 1545. Menno lodged at his place after the martyrdom of Theunis van Hastenrath, elder in Oppergelre. He baptized in 1559 in Waldfeucht, K. Vos, op. cit., p. 86 ff.; Otto R. Redlich, "Jüllich-Bergische Kirchenpolitik am Ausgange des Mittelalters und in der Reformationszeit," vol. II. *Visitationsprotokolle und Berichte,* first part, Jüllich (1533-1589), Bonn, 1911. p. 523; E. Crous, "Auf Mennos Spuren," op cit., p. 187; M.E. III, p. 320. Not the same as Kremer, a hatter from Venlo who preached in Bracht in 1533, Redlich, II, p. 146, note b; also not the same as the bag maker Lemke whom W. Bax names in "Het Protestantisme in het bisdom Luik enz.," The Hague, 1937, part I, pp. 136, 142, 302. According to K. Vos, "Martelaars uit Gelderland," N.A.K.G., vol. X, 1913, p. 264, Jater said at his hearing in Arnhem (1550) that in Illikhoven there lives a man "who goes with an iron stand." He is called Lemken and is a deacon.

[30] Zillis, a coal burner, was a minister in 1550 at Simmerath (Ambt Montjoie), and baptized many. Redlich, II, 1, p. 531, above all note 2; E. Crous "Auf Mennos Spuren," op cit., p. 187, 9. Jhg., p. 10 ff. and "Schleiden," M.L. IV, p. 66; M.E. IV, pp. 1022b/1023a.

[31] Redlich, II, 1, pp. 479, 497, 864; K. Vos, *Menno Simons*, pp. 85-87; E. Crous, "Auf Mennos Spuren," op. cit., p. 187. His wife was called Trijn; Petgen Pyntgens is another inhabitant of Hastenrath. The confession was printed by K. Vos in D.B., 1909, pp. 120-126; M.E. II, p. 67 ff.

[32] D. B., 1890, pp. 58-60.

[33] K. Vos, op. cit., p. 86. He ministered in Goch about 1546, but did not baptize, D. B., 1909, p. 124.

[34] Redlich, II, 1, p. 497, note 2.

Chapter V

[1] Nic. Meyn. van Blesdijck, *Billijcke Verantwoordinge ende Eenvoldighe wederlegginghe op eenen Scheltlasterighen Brief door Dr. Hier. Wilhelmi ... teghens die heylsame leere D. J. ... geschreven in 't Jaer 1544*. Bibl. der Verenigde Doopsg. Gemeente Amsterdam. Blesdijk's answer is dated March 13, 1547. This booklet was only known to Fr. Nippold by the title. *Z. f. Hist. Th.*, 1863, p. 9. K. Vos,

Menno Simons, p. 102, apparently knew it, note 3, but made no further use of it. For the quotations above, see fol. 12r° and v°, fol. 95v°, 96r°.

[2] Adam Pastor chose 25 articles because David Joris in his "Onschuldt, gedaen vnde gepresenteerd an ... Vrouw Anna, gheborene Grauinne van Oldenburch, etc. [Wtghegaen int Jaer 1540]" defended himself against 25 accusations. F. Nippold, op. cit., pp. 124-130.

[3] This is the so-called "Great Innocence," to which Roland Bainton, *David Joris, Wiedertäufer und Kämpfer für Toleranz*, Leipzig, 1937, (A.R.G. Ergänzungsband VI) p. 52 ff. drew attention, and which G. Nicolai quoted, B.R.N. VII, pp. 303 and 420.

[4] *Billijcke Verantwoordinge*, fol. 96r°, v°.

[5] B.R.N. VII, p. 463.

[6] See F. Pijper, B.R.N. X, pp. 20-26; K. Vos, D. B., 1909, pp. 104-116; K. Vos, *Menno Simons*, pp. 100-107; W. Kühler, I, pp. 284-290; Corn. Krahn, *Menno Simons*, p. 67 ff.; above all S. Cramer, B.R.N. V, pp. 315-581. The doctrine of Adam Pastor has been dealt with extensively by J. H. Wessel, op. cit., *passim*.

[7] *Billijcke Verantwoordinge*, fol. 12r°, 96r°; B.R.N. VII, p. 50.

[8] D. B., 1909, pp. 107-114: 1546-48 in Westfalen, 1548 in Zutfen, Deventer, Doetinchem.

[9] M.L., III, p. 292 ff.; D. B., 1909, pp. 109, 125. See also, E. Crous "Auf Mennos Spuren," op. cit., p. 187.

[10] D. B., 1909, p. 108.

[11] "De pennestrijd tussen David en Menno," Blesdikius, *Historia*, pp. 126-133; Nippold, op. cit., pp. 141-149; Kühler I, pp. 239-241; Menno's answer is reprinted by K. Vos, *Menno Simons*, p. 277 ff.

[12] Blesdikius, *Historia*, p. 133.

[13] Blesdikius, *Historia D.G.*, p. 134. He wrote 1546 explicitly.

[14] F. Nippold, *Z. f. hist. Th.*, 1864, p. 538.

[15] The three booklets of Blesdijk which deserve consideration are discussed extensively by Nippold, op. cit., pp. 539-553. See also K. Vos, *Menno Simons*, p. 89 ff.

[16] *Weder-antwoort op zekeren Brief by Gellium onderteeckent*, (1546), fol. 23b.

[17] *Ibid.*, fol. 24b.

[18] *Ibid.*, fol. 23b. The meeting in Lübeck became an occasion for the government to forbid once again the residence and sheltering of Anabaptists by three mandates (1546, 1547, and Oct. 29, 1547). R. Dollinger, *Gesch. der Mennoniten in Schleswig-Holstein etc.*, 1930, p. 194.

[19] B.R.N. V, pp. 509-515. See also p. 354. The hypothesis that opposition to Adam Pastor had already begun, as K. Vos, *Menno Simons*, p. 103, and Kühler I, p. 287 contend, is a misconception. It was proposed by S. Cramer, B.R.N. V, p. 320, but he himself dismissed it.

[20] *Hooft-Somma vnde Gront van 'tgene wij wt die Leere D.J. hebben connen verstaen ...*, 1547.

[21] Nippold, op. cit., p. 557.

[22] B.R.N. VII, p. 463

[23] I note this from the Hamburg manuscript: "Een vermaninghe, belijdinghe van der drie-eenighen, eeuwighen ende waren God," Sept. 9, 1550. Another manuscript at the Amsterdam Doopsg. Bibliotheek, Inv. Archief I, no. 619; see K. Vos, *Menno Simons*, p. 301 ff. The first printing of the treatise is now in the Gemeente Bibl. at Rotterdam.

[24] B.R.N. VII, p. 50.

[25] This is the first time that seven elders assembled; later at important conferences seven elders were always present. By the number seven the fullness of divine power was expressed on the basis of Isaiah 11:2. There is also the example of the seven deacons from Acts 6 and from the seven churches in Revelation 2 and 3. R.E.³, Bd. XVIII, p. 310 ff.; *Theol. Wörterbuch zum N.T.*, ed. by G. Kittel, Bd. II, p. 628 ff.

[26] J. G. de Hoop Scheffer, "Opmerkingen en mededelingen betreffende Menno Simons," in D. B., 1894, pp. 10-70, esp. pp. 13 and 17 ff.

[27] "Menno ... stont toe de Echtmijding," B.R.N. VII, p. 50.

[28] B.R.N. VII, p. 58. The whole letter, *ibid.*, p. 448 ff.

[29] J. G. de Hoop Scheffer, op. cit., p. 20, note 1, says correctly that the "Successio" contradicted itself by quoting the letter to Emden.

[30] B.R.N. X, p. 626 ff. Pijper translated this into modern Dutch, op. cit., p. 22.

[31] K. Vos, *Menno Simons*, p. 124, Art. 1.

[32] B.R.N. VII, p. 50.

[33] P. Kawerau, *Melchior Hoffman als religöser Denker*, Haarlem, 1954, pp. 31 ff., 46 ff.

[34] See J. H. Wessels, op. cit., p. 169 ff.; H. W. Meihuizen, op. cit., p. 43; above all J. A. Oosterbaan, "De theologie van Menno Simons," *Neder. Theol. Tijdschrift*, 1961.

[35] B.R.N. V, pp. 374-386.

[36] *Ibid.*, pp. 344 ff., 376, 377, 382.

[37] *Ibid.*, p. 385 ff.

[38] *Ibid.*, p. 517; see also, p. 319.

[39] *Ibid.*, p. 50.

[40] *Ibid.*

[41] *Ibid.*, pp. 50, 464, 470. It was a great risk to gather there with so many, therefore it had to happen in secret.

[42] K. Vos, *Menno Simons*, p. 104, also notes the place of assembly. Theunis had been in Cleve in 1546 and probably also in the same year in Goch. At Goch he alone had preached. D.B., 1909, p. 123 ff. Was the reason for this that Dirk participated in the meeting at Lübeck?

[43] See above, Chap. IV, note 14.

[44] B.R.N. V, p. 322, note 5. Nicolai quotes various expressions of Adam Pastor from the report and says that his adherents were very pleased with the booklet and usually carried it with them. B.R.N. VII, pp. 408 ff., 410 ff., 463 ff., 470 ff.

[45] B.R.N. VII, p. 408. The same indirectly, B.R.N. V, p. 542.

[46] *Ibid.*, p 409 ff.

[47] More precisely, Psalm 97:7 or Deuteron. 32:43 (LXX).
[48] B.R.N. VII, p. 411 ff.
[49] Adam Pastor always denied this "change." See above, note 36.
[50] B.R.N. VII, p. 470 ff.
[51] *Ibid.*, p. 464.
[52] *Ibid.*, p. 51.
[53] J. G. de Hoop Scheffer, D. B., 1894, p. 22 ff.; K. Vos, *Menno Simons*, pp. 104 and 331. The report from G. Brandt, *Historie der Reformatie*, vol. I, p. 185 ff., is no proof. It originated from the *Succession. Idem.*, "Een bischop te Appingedam," op. cit., p. 14; W. J. Kühler, "De macht der oudsten in de zestiende eeuw," *Zondagsbode*, Dec. 6, 1925; also in *Geschiedenis* I, p. 288; H. W. Meihuizen, op. cit., p. 44 ff.

Other opinions: S. Cramer, B.R.N. V, pp. 322, 341 ff.; F. Pijper, B.R.N. X, p. 21; John Horsch, *Menno Simons*, Scottdale, Pa., 1916, p. 197 ff.; K. Vos, M.L., vol. II, p. 130a; Corn. Krahn, op. cit., p.. 69 ff.; W. Keeney, "Dirk Philips Life," M.Q.R., vol. XXXII, 1958, p. 178 ff.; N. van der Zijpp, op. cit., p. 47; J. A. Brandsma, op. cit., p. 78 ff.

[54] K. Vos, *Menno Simons*, p. 331 and my essay: "Een onbekende brief van Dirk Philips," N.A.K.G., vol. XLIII, p. 17, note 8.
[55] See above, note 51.
[56] B.R.N. V, p. 322. According to note 6, Pastor attacked mainly Menno. See pp. 521 and 522: "Since you will not deal with me, I write my answer here to your opposition and that of your banning comrades." See also the explanation of S. Cramer, op. cit., p. 343, which I have used, with thanks.
[57] *Ibid.*, p. 537. A letter of ban had to be extended on the basis of 2 Thess. 3:14 (Luther's translation).
[58] *Ibid.*, p. 549 ff.
[59] *Ibid.*, p. 537.
[60] Rom. 8:3. See also J. H. Wessels, op. cit., pp. 139, 185..
[61] B.R.N. V, p. 528.
[62] *Ibid.*, p. 550.
[63] *Ibid.*, p. 549
[64] *Ibid.*, p. 521 ff. Pastor appeals here to statements by Menno in the *Fundamentboek* and in the preface to the 25th Psalm.
[65] *Ibid.*, p. 523.
[66] *Ibid.*, p. 519 ff.
[67] From the first edition, 1597, by Aert Hendricksz., Amsterdam, present in the Gem. Bibl. at Rotterdam, Aij^{vo}; likewise in *Opera*, 1681, fol. 385.
[68] D. B., 1894, p. 23. Vos and Kühler agreed. See above, note 53; even S. Cramer, B.R.N. V, p. 522, note 7 and B.R.N. VII, p. 51, note 1.
[69] The Hamburg and Amsterdam manuscripts, see above, note 23.
[70] The turn of the phrase "op de bane voeren" or "brengen" must be fairly unusual in the Dutch of the sixteenth century, as K. Vos wrote to me in a letter of April 9, 1914. But I found the following expressions "op de bane gebracht," (twice by Nicolai,

B.R.N. VII, pp. 424, 463) and "op de bane gekomen" (Carel van Ghendt, B.R.N. VII, p. 544). And although in Verwijs-Verdam, *Middelnederlandsch Woordenboek*, vol. I, 1885, col. 556 ff., one finds only the expression "Enen in sine bane bringhen" = to win someone to one's side, in Lasch-Borchlingen, *Mittel-Niederdeutsches Wörterbuch*, vol. I, Neumünster, 1956, col. 141, it says "bäne, bän, Weg: wat nîes up de bäne bringen" = "to bring something new onto the carpet [agenda]."

[71] D.B., 1894, p. 17.

[72] H. W. Meihuizen, op. cit., pp. 45, 136 ff.; C. Krahn, op. cit., p. 152, note 215. He reproduces a quotation from the "Lieffelijke Vermaninghe," 1541, A VIII^{vo}

[73] D. B., 1894, p. 22.

[74] *Sommarie*, 1646, fol. 549a and b.

[75] B.R.N. VII, p. 51. In the copy of the elders (K. Vos, *Menno Simons*, p. 256) his defection is not recorded as 1549 (the ban by Menno) but in 1554.

[76] B. R. N. VII, p. 51. K. Vos, *Menno Simons*, p. 105 assumed that they transferred to Adam Pastor's side, but I think rather that they withdrew because a delegation was arriving in Gulik. Concerning Antonius, see my article in N.A.K.G., vol. XLIII, p. 20.

[77] Pastor worked in 1547 and 1548 in Westphalia, after Dec. 1548, in Zutphen, Deventer, and Doetinchem. K. Vos, "Adam Pastor," in D. B., 1909, pp. 107-116.

[78] D.B., 1909, p. 125; E. Crous, "Auf Mennos Spuren am Niederrhein," *Der Mennonit*, Dec., 1955, p. 187.

[79] B.R.N. VII, p. 464. S. Cramer, B.R.N. V, p. 323 ff., provides all kinds of reports about the after effects of Pastor's doctrine.

[80] B. R. N. VII, p. 51.

[81] *Sommarie*, 1646, fol. 728, 737a

[82] See my article, op. cit., p. 21.

[83] This according to the inscription in S. Blaupot ten Cate, *Fesch. der Doopsg. in Friesland*, 1839, p. 263 ff.

[84] Printed in B.R.N. X, p. 693 ff, and illustrated by Pijper, p. 672.

Chapter VI

[1] Published by me in N.A.K.G., vol. XLIII, 1959, pp. 15-21.

[2] See Appendix I of J. ten Doornkaat Koolman, *Dirk Philips: Vriend en Medewerker van Menno Simons, 1504-1568.* (Haarlem, H.D. Tjeenk Willink & Zoon N.V., 1964) or the English translation in WDP, pp. 612-17.

[3] See above, chapter IV, note 20.

[4] Hrch. Forsthoff, op. cit., pp. 257, 265. Evangelical preaching ended in Wezel, however, in 1548.

[5] *Ibid.*, p. 18 v.

[6] For example, in the Athanasian Creed, "Our Lord Jesus Christ, the Son of God, is both God and Man. He is God, of the Substance of the Father, begotten before the worlds; and he is Man, of the Substance of his Mother, born in the world..." *Book of*

Common Prayer (Canada, 1962), p. 697. C. Mirbt, *Quellen zur Geschichte des Papstums*, 1924⁴, p. 84.

[7] John 1:1.

[8] See above, Chapter V, pp. 33-34.

[9] These Latin words were a mystery to me. I found the solution by consulting Menno's Confession of the Triune God in the Hamburg manuscript. There the following citations were given: Hebrew 1:6, John 1:14, 3:18, I John 4:9, Col. 1:15; only Rom. 8:32 is missing. Dirk quoted Christ's sayings following the Vulgate.

[10] Those expressions are also in Menno, *ibid*. On eternal wisdom, see Prov. 8:22 and Ecclesiasticus 24:5. See Menno's argument in H. W. Meihuizen, op. cit., p. 190.

[11] Hebr. 10:5.

[12] Col. 1:19.

[13] 2 Cor. 5:19.

[14] B.R.N. X, pp. 60-64

[15] B.R.N. X, pp. 135-153 and pp. 155-178.

[16] B.R.N. X, p. 25, note 4.

[17] See my article in N.A.K.G., vol. XLIII, p. 16 and G. E. Frerichs, "Menno's taal" in D.B., 1905, pp. 106-108.

[18] I do not share Pijper's ideas in this regard. He dates a few writings quite early, for example, in B.R.N. X, pp. 15-19. I agree with W. Keeney, "The Writings of Dirk Philips," M.Q.R., vol. XXXII, p. 300, who dated the printing of both booklets in 1557. See "About the Christology of Dirk Philips," Cornelius J. Dyck, M.Q.R., vol. XXXI, pp. 147-155, and W. Keeney, "The Incarnation, A Central Theological Concept," *A Legacy of Faith*, pp. 55-68.

[19] *Archief Doopsgez. Gemeente Amsterdam*, vol I, no. 620. De Hoop Scheffer described it, D.B., 1894, pp. 55, 61 ff.; K. Vos, *Menno Simons* quoted it, pp. 141, 330; likewise, W. Keeney, M.Q.R., vol. XXXII, p. 299 ff. See Appendix I in J. ten Doornkaat Koolman, op. cit., or in WDP, pp. 612-617.

[20] It is known that the two treatises by Menno, "A Clear Account of Excommunication" and "Some Questions" belong together, *Sommarie*, 1646, fol. 631-656 and fol. 894-904. According to Alenson both are directed to the churches in Groningen and in Groningen land, B.R.N. VII, pp. 206 and 232.

[21] *Sommarie*, 1646, fol. 898a, contains the oft-cited words: "Therefore I say with our faithful [and much beloved fellow] brother Dirk Philips that we should not [desire] to use the ban to the destruction of humankind." [Trans. from CWMS, p. 480. The words in parenthesis are added since they are in the Dutch original but not in the translation]. Dirk, in the treatise "A Confession about Separation" § 3, says: "...the ban is also ordained by God in order to shame the external person so that the internal person may be saved" and § 4 "there is in this matter [shunning] no better medicine ...to shame the external person ...for his own improvement." [The English translation does not summarize as neatly as does ten Doornkaat Koolman in the Dutch which he quotes. See WDP, pp. 613 and 614 for these statements].

[22] B.R.N. VII, p. 442, in the margin.

[23] *Sommarie*, 1646, fol. 368a. [In CWMS, p. 974 this is translated as "In the same vein I wrote a little book in 1549..."]. Thus the booklet was written in 1549 and copies distributed in 1550. On fol. 904 is written: "1550. Finis." De Hoop Scheffer, D.B., 1894, p. 25, without a reference; see also C. Krahn, op. cit., p. 75, note 265.

[24] See D. B., 1894, p. 23 ff., W. J. Kühler, *Geschiedenis*, I, p. 304 ff.

[25] *Sommarie*, 1646, fol. 633a, 901b, and 902a.

[26] § 3 and § 5.

[27] Menno allows it if no "commerce in companionship" follows. He takes into account barter among farmers. *Sommarie*, 1646, fol. 899b.

[28] 1 Cor. 9:19-23, Rom. 14:13-23. Menno finds it more polite to respond to the greeting of an apostate. If one stubbornly looks away, it does not help reform the other. *Sommarie*, 1646, fol. 897a.

[29] I would draw attention to the fact that women had a voice in the congregational meetings.

[30] Dirk makes mention of "the present business." Did he mean a case that would be dealt with during the conference, or did he only mean that each case was to be examined separately? Menno also wanted to spare weak consciences as much as possible. *Ibid.*, fol. 896b.

[31] Dirk presents here a striking picture of the sad social circumstances of his time.

[32] Menno, op. cit., fol. 897b-899a. "The ban is a work of God's saving love and not a bad, unmerciful, heathen cruelty." One must serve the apostate with temporal goods if the need requires it, but no regular association should follow.

[33] In the earliest books Menno still speaks about "Saint John." K. Vos, *Menno Simons*, p. 56, note 1.

[34] Martin Micron accuses Menno of this. See K. Vos, *ibid.*, p. 116, note 3. Later Vos corrected his statement in *Zondagsbode*, Aug. 13, 1916. Guy de Bres, *La Racine, Source et Fondement des Anabaptistes*, 1565, fol. 117, repeated this accusation. He probably copied it from the *Waerachtich verhael of M. Micron*, as well as the charge that the Mennonites would not put on a clean shirt on Sunday because the unbelievers do that. I found the following in Fr. Theophil Kettner's, *Dissertatio de historia Mennonis ejusque asseclarum*, Leipzig, 1696 (§ 17): "The Mennonites in Altona use a different calendar than ours and, refusing to use the heathen names of months, they call them by the ordinal words, so that for them, December 12 is the twelfth day of the twelfth month."

Chapter VII

[1] *Geschiedenis*, I, p. 310. W. Keeney has conclusively challenged this, M.Q.R., vol. XXXII, 1958, p. 185.

[2] H. G. Mannhardt, *Die Danziger Mennonitengemeinde 1569-1919*, Danzig, 1919, pp. 25, 42.

[3] Martin Micron, *Een waerachtigh verhaal*, Emden, 1556, p. 183 ff.

[4] See my article, "De Anabaptisten in Oostfriesland," N.A.K.G., vol. XLVI, pp. 87-99.

[5] J. P. Müller, op. cit., p. 26 ff.; S. Blaupot ten Cate, *Gesch. der Doopsg. in Groningen, Overijssel en Oostfriesland*, vol. I, 1842, p. 22 ff.

[6] B.R.N. VII, p. 51.

[7] Concerning Leenaert, see Vos, *Menno Simons*, p. 128 ff.; *idem.*, "De dooplijst van L. B." in *Bijdragen en Mededelingen van het Historisch Genootschap*, vol. XXXVI, pp. 39-70; G. Grosheide, *Bijdrage tot de Geschiedenis der Anabaptisten in Amsterdam*, Hilversum, 1938, p. 134 ff., esp. note 158, and p. 257 ff., and *passim*, where there is much new information about him.

[8] S. Blaupot ten Cate, op. cit., p. 111.

[9] This date is set by the memorial song of Jan Jacobs, Vos, *Menno Simons*, p. 131, and "De dooplijst van L. B.," op. cit., p. 42.

[10] This idea is from Brandsma, *Menno Simons*, p. 94 ff. Menno's letter is in *Opera*, 1681, fol. 455 ff.

[11] A. L. E. Verheyden, *Gesch. der Doopsgezinden in de Zuidelijke Nederlanden in de XVIe eeuw* (Verhandelingen van do Kon. Vlaamse Academie der Wetenschappen, Letteren en schone Kunsten van België. Klasse der Letteren). Verhandeling no. 36., Brussel, 1959, p. 73 ff.

[12] B.R.N. II, p. 112 ff.

[13] Verheyden, op. cit., p. 77 ff.

[14] B.R.N. II, p. 239 ff.

[15] B.R.N. V, p. 342, note 10; p. 549, note 6.

[16] *Ibid.*, p. 521 ff.

[17] *Ibid.*, p. 522 (on the basis of Isaiah 5:21 and 1 Cor., 14:29).

[18] *Ibid.*, p. 519.

[19] de Hoop Scheffer, D. B., 1894, p. 20, note 2 places the year when it appeared as 1553. S. Cramer, B.R.N. V, p. 320, note 1, believes that it was printed several years later. See also, *ibid.*, pp. 363 and 517.

[20] The title is in B.R.N. V, pp. 318 and 363.

[21] Friends, adherents, *ibid.*, p. 363, note 2.

[22] *Ibid.*, pp. 517-523.

[23] Heinrich Ebbink, also named Dr. Klumpe, worked together with Pastor in 1546 and according to the confession of Dyrich ten Bengevoirth whom he baptized agreed with Menno's doctrine of the incarnation. He was not the same person as Hendrik van Vreden since he left the movement in 1550. He lived in East Friesland in 1549. K. Vos, D. B., 1909, p. 107 ff.; *idem.*, *Menno Simons*, pp. 93 and 105.

[24] B.R.N. V., p. 347, note 1. It is strange that this B is missing for Bouwens, or has another letter dropped out after the B?

[25] Twenty-six times.

[26] *Ibid.*, pp. 526, 528, 540, 541.

[27] See Chapter V, pp. 35-37. S. Cramer gives an excellent overview of the ideas of Adam Pastor, B.R.N. V, pp. 348-353.

28 *Ibid.*, p. 526, cff. also p. 578 ff.
29 *Ibid.*, p. 572 ff.
30 *Ibid.*, p. 347. In my opinion Pastor avoided the word "Drieëenheid" [Trinity] because of the fact that at the time of the composition of the "Disputation" Michael Servet was burned as a heretic in Geneva (October, 1553).
31 Chap. VI, p. 42.
32 B.R.N. V, p. 323. [The introduction to Adam Pastor's "The Difference..."].
33 B.R.N. X, p. 137, cf. p. 27. [Italics added by the author; trans. from WDP, p. 134. ff.].
34 B.R.N. X, p. 152. [Trans. from WDP, p. 148].
35 *Ibid.*, p. 157. [Translation based on WDP, p. 152 ff.].
36 K. Vos, *Menno Simons*, p. 96 ff. The "Copia der Outsten" reports that Gillis deserted in 1552, op. cit., p. 256.
37 *Opera*, 1681, fol. 456a. [Trans. from CWMS, p. 1039].
38 In my opinion the letter of Menno must be dated earlier than 1553, the date given by Herrison, also in connection with the ordination of Leenaert in 1551.
39 K. Vos, *Menno Simons*, p. 108.
40 All information concerning these events is supported by H. Timmerman, *Een verklaringhe, hoe én in wat manieren de Heere Jesus zynen Jongeren in der afzonderinge macht gegeven heeft etc.*, first printing, Jan. 28, 1560, Haarlem, 1618, quat. Aij^{vo}; cf. Nicolai, B.R.N. VII, p. 458. The *Succession* copied it from him, B.R.N. VII, p. 59 ff.. See also, *Ibid.*, p. 233.
41 See my "Die Täufer in Mecklenburg," M.G.Bl., 1961, p. 34 ff.
42 D. B., 1894, p. 29, note 3.
43 K. Vos, *Menno Simons*, p. 127, note 1, and H. W. Meihuizen, op. cit., p. 51 guess that Hans Busschaert and Hoyte Renix were present in Wismar, but according to van der Zijpp, Hans Busschaert was only confirmed by Menno as elder in 1555, M.E., vol. I, p. 485a, and Hoyte Renix likewise in 1555 by Leenaert, M.E., vol. II, p. 824. Perhaps Herman van Tielt was the seventh, but he was only a teacher (admonisher), Vos, op. cit., p. 147. The naming of Herman de Timmerman is an error by Moded, for he was baptized only in 1556, Vos., op. cit., p. 147 ff.
44 For the text of the articles, see B.R.N. VII, p. 52 ff. K. Vos, op. cit., pp. 124-127, reprinted them with corrections.
45 S. Cramer, B.R.N. VII, p. 52, note 1.
46 B.R.N. X, p. 627. [Note that in the original text of ten Doornkaat-Koolman, a typographical error transposed two lines of text].
47 Pijper was only able to find one place in the *Enchiridion* where outside marriage was mentioned, op. cit., p. 370 ff.; scc also, *ibid.*, p. 346, concerning true marriage before God. Perhaps Dirk dealt with it in still other booklets that have since been lost.
48 *Ibid.*, p. 626 ff.; see also chapter V, p. 34. Dirk's setting of time periods in his last writings are not reliable.

[49] The treatise *Concerning the Marriage of Christians* was completed on March 7, 1568, *ibid.*, p. 649.

[50] *Geschiedenis*, I, p. 343.

[51] *De leerstellige strijd enz.*, p. 332, and also concerning Menno's position at a later time.

[52] Some guarantee was to be given that the unbelieving spouse would not make the believing spouse into an unbeliever. This was Menno's explanation. See B.R.N. VII, pp. 76 and 235.

[53] See Chapter VI, note 27.

[54] See Chapter V, p. 33. The letter to Emden, Nov. 12, 1556, B.R.N. VII, p. 448 ff. "Eerdaechs," p. 448, note 7 = earlier, before this. See Lasch-Borchling, op. cit., vol. I, col. 576; "eensdeels," p. 448, note 9 and "einsdeels" in the letter of Dec. 15, 1558 = in part, somewhat. See Lasch-Borchling, vol. I, col. 407.

[55] Published by De Hoop Scheffer in D. B., 1894, pp. 62-69. From this it is clear that Dirk was present in Wismar. The letter to Emden firmly lays down the law for the Emden conference, but leaves it open for Wismar.

[56] This writing was translated from French by Carel van Mander. Concerning him, see Kühler, *Geschiedenis*, II, pp. 117-124; M.E., vol. III, p. 453.

[57] B.R.N. X, p. 665 ff.

[58] I came to the same conclusiion about this article as did K. Vos, op. cit., p. 127, note 1.

[59] B.R.N. X, p. 533 ff.

[60] See my article, "Die Täufer in Mecklenburg," op. cit., p. 33 ff. Obbe was banned before 1554; his group did not have more than 6-10 members, *ibid.*, p. 44.

[61] See above, p. 52 for the title.

[62] C. Krahn, op. cit., p. 78.

[63] *Sommarie*, 1646, fol. 587 a and b. [Found with somewhat different phrasing in CWMS p. 761]. According to the insightful comment of Meihuizen, op. cit, p. 54 ff., "Gellius perhaps was able to detect a nuance in their leadership," especially after he had become acquainted with Dirk.

Chapter VIII

[1] *Geschiedenis*, I, p. 310.

[2] *Ibid.*, pp. 232, 289. Cf. Chapter IV, p. 23.

[3] See above, Chapter VII, pp. 47-48.

[4] Kühler, *Geschiedenis*, I, p. 280 places this change already in 1545 in connection with the conference in Goch.

[5] H. Reimers, "Eine Landesbeschreibung von Ostfriesland um 1600," *Emdener Jahrbuch*, vol. XVII (1910), p. 320, quoted by K. Vos, "Nieuwe berichten over Menno," *Zondagsbode*, June 7, 1925.

[6] K. Vos, *Menno Simons*, p. 2 ff., and J. A. Bradsma, *Menno Simons*, p. 101 ff.

[7] C. Krahn, op. cit., p. 85 ff.

[8] This is an assumption. I could only make superficial comparisons between the Fresenburger publications of Menno's writings and Dirk's earliest booklets. Research by an expert is called for.

[9] M. Schagen, *Naamlijst der Doopsgez. schrijveren en schriften*, Amsterdam, 1745, p. 78.

[10] *Gesch. der Doopsg. in Groningen enz.*, vol I, 1842, p. 246.

[11] Chr. Sepp, *Verboden lectuur*, Leiden, 1889, p. 260; *Geschiedkundige Nasporingen*, Leiden, 1872, vol. I, p. 88 ff.

[12] B.R.N. X, p. 55.

[13] The title is: *Een korte Bekentenisse ende Belydinge van den Eenigen/ Almachtigen / Leuendige Godt Vader / Soon ende heylige Geest etc. Mit noch sommige ander Leerachtige Boecxkes (in dat naestuolgende Blat angeteykent) by den Autoer desseluige gemaeckt / voertijts verscheide Gedruckt / ende nu om des Leesers geryffelicheit by een gevoeghet. D.P. Ghedruct int Jaer 1564.* For details, see my article in M.Q.R., vol. XXXVIII, October, 1964. [For a reproduction and translation of the title page, see WDP, p. 49].

[14] The earliest treatise that can be dated is *The Tabernacle of Moses,* B.R.N. X, p. 17, note 3.

[15] As was the case with Menno's writing, "A Clear Account of Excommunication and Confession of the Triune God." See above, chap. VI, note 23 and chap. V, note 23.

[16] Verwijs-Verdam, *Middelnederlandsch Woordenboek*, vol. IX, 1929, col. 865, vulder = voller, one who finishes wool, a cloth fuller.

[17] G. Grosheide, op. cit., p. 173 ff.

[18] Available in the Doopsg. Bibl. in Amsterdam, Catalogue 1919, p. 95. See also my article "Een onbekende brief van Dirk Philips," N.A.K.G., vol. XLIII, p. 15 ff. The signatures are "Het Geloofsboek" (without a title page), A2r°-P7v°; "Restitution" and "Gemeente Gods" have a continuous signature A1r°-O4v°.

[19] I mention as examples: "Geestelijke Restitution H.S., C2v°-C4r° in B.R.N. X, pp. 351-353 gives a different line of thought; "Van Gods Ghemeynte," H.S. H5r° is shorter in B.R.N. X, p. 382; *idem* H.S. K5r°, B.R.N. X, p. 392 ff. is missing "this holy divine threeness or threefoldness"; *idem*. H.S., L7r°, B.R.N. X, p. 400, is missing "Also no one should despise that judgment of the Church or think that it is human judgment." Of course there are also pieces of the *Enchiridion* that are missing in the manuscript.

[20] G. E. Frerichs, "Menno's Taal," D. B., 1905, pp. 106-108.

[21] B.R.N. X, p. 17, note 3.

[22] *Ibid.*, p. 25, note 4.

[23] *Ibid.*, p. 32, note 3. This piece makes me think of an expanded sermon. Nicolai calls it an "instruction booklet" [onderwijsingboecxken], B.R.N. VII, p. 471.

[24] B.R.N. X, p. 30, note 4.

[25] *Ibid.*, p. 32, note 5.

[26] *Ibid.*, p. 26, note 4.

[27] *Ibid.*, p. 27, note 1. The treatises are bound together, and have a continuous signature.
[28] See Chapter VI, note 18.
[29] See Chapter IV, pp. 25-26.
[30] B.R.N. X, p. 19 and note 2.
[31] *Ibid.*, p. 323; see also pp. 184, 397 ff., 407.
[32] *Ibid.*, p. 15. Those who thought that they could participate in Roman Catholic worship and imitate the world were, in my opinion, not adherents of Sebastian Franck, but Davidjorists and followers of Hendrik Niclaes.
[33] *Ibid.*, p. 15, note 4.
[34] *Ibid.*, p. 184. "The Church [Congregation] of God" quotes "The Sending of Preachers," *ibid.*, p. 394.
[35] *Ibid.*, pp. 181, 188, 202.
[36] *Ibid.*, p. 10, note 7, and p. 33, note 4.
[37] Also the manuscript copy in Amsterdam, see above, note 18. Only the Hamburg printing had a separate signature. See Chapter X, p. 110.
[38] B.R.N. X, p. 383, see also p. 379.
[39] *Ibid.*, pp. 400 and 394. "Concerning the New Creature" also was quoted, p. 388.
[40] See Chapter IV., p. 25. It is the 21st letter: "Onderscheedt tussen die boete ende wedergheboorte, aengaende dat boecxken by Dirick Philipsen, van de nieuwe creatuer. In *druck* wtghegeuen." ["The Difference Between Repentance and Rebirth, Regarding the Booklet by Dirk Philips, Concerning the New Creature. Published in *print*"].
[41] *Historia Davidis Georgii*, p. 188.
[42] *Ibid.*, p. 137, for "symmstiae" I found no other translation than leaders.
[43] K. Vos, *Menno Simons*, p. 252.
[44] Georgii Cassandri *Opera*, Parisiis, 1616, fol. 671; see also fol. 1151, Epistola LVI. Pijper printed the citation translated above, B.R.N. X, p. 7, note 1.
[45] B.R.N. II, pp. 393, ff., 407 ff.
[46] Chez Abel Clemence, MDLXV, s. l. 903 pp. Available in Geneva, Bibl. Cantonale; Amsterdam, Univ. Bibl.; Leiden, Univ. Bibl.; and Bibl. der Doopsg. Gemeente at Deventer. [Also available at Yale University Library].
[47] *Ibid.*, pp. 520, 529, 540, 576, 580, 666, 672, 678, 688, 696, 746, 785.
[48] *Ibid.*, p. 218.
[49] *Ibid.*, p. 149.
[50] *Ibid.*, p. 152.
[51] *Ibid.*, p. 515.
[52] Printed at Emden by Gellium Clematium, 1556, July 30. See Walter Hollweg, "Bernhard Buwo, ein ostfriesischer Theologe aus dem Reformationsjahrhundert" in *Emdener Jahrbuch*, vol. XXXIII, 1953, p. 71 ff. I first consulted this original print in the Stadtbibl. at Hamburg. It probably was destroyed in 1943.
[53] In the Preface, A4r°. Guy de Brès copied this story, op. cit., p. 506.

[54] The *Opera omnia* of Menno was already listed on the Index [of forbidden books] of Philip II in 1558, so the books of Dirk were not yet known.

[55] Chr. Sepp, *Verboden lectuur*, Leiden, 1889, p. 163.

[56] *Ibid.*, p. 260.

[57] S. Hoekstra, *Beginselen en leer der oude Doopsgezinden*, Amsterdam, 1863, p. 263 ff., esp. p. 264, note 1.

[58] This was a powerful argument in the polemic of the 17th and 18th century. Adr. van Eeghen, *Verhandlinge van de wet der nature*. Middelburg, 1701, p. 56 ff. Korn. van Huyzen, *Historische verhandeling van de opkomst en voortgang ... der Doopsgez. Christenen, Emden en Hamburg*, 1712, p. 24 ff. Schijn-Maatschoen, *Gesch. der Mennoniten*, Amsterdam, 1743-45, vol. I, pp. 375-378; vol. II, pp. 365, 373 ff. Even Chr. Sepp, *Geschiedkundige Nasporingen*, Leiden, 1872, vol. I, pp. 106 ff., 126 ff., thought that "(Concerning) Spiritual Restitution" and "The Tabernacle of Moses" were directed against Rothmann's "A Restitution" and "Concerning the Hiddeness of the Scriptures about Christ's Kingdom." He did point out that Dirk did not refute and did not mention the name of Rothmann, and that in the "The Tabernacle of Moses" the "Hiddeness" was not explicitly quoted.

[59] Cramer (B.R.N. X, p. 141): "It is understandable that Menno and his people did not report Hoffman and his works. They preferred to avoid mentioning a name which even distantly made one think of Münster."

[60] That is to say, the Anabaptist churches.

[61] The tabernacle described in Exodus 26 ff. and 35 ff.

[62] B.R.N. X, pp. 279-311.

[63] *Ibid.*, p. 284 ff., 290. The apostle does not speak about the courtyard.

[64] *Ibid.*, p. 290.

[65] *Ibid.*, pp. 291-294.

[66] *Ibid.*, pp. 296-303.

[67] *Ibid.*, pp. 303-310.

[68] John 6:35–Jesus Sirach 24:28 ff. (wrongly: vs. 25); Gen 22:30 (wrongly vs. 28)– John 1:18.

[69] *Ibid.*, p. 303. See A. Hegler, *Geist und Schrift*, Freiburg, 1892, p. 40 v. *passim*.

[70] *Ibid.*, pp. 307-310. He also quotes Isaiah 54:13; Jeremiah 31:31; Rev. 21:23.

[71] Published by K. W. H. Hochhuth, Gotha, 1857.

[72] op. cit., pp. 18-25. Another triad related to the tabernacle was faith, hope, and love, p. 34 ff. The tabernacle also served as a model for dividing world history into three periods, op. cit., pp. 47, 65 ff., 69.

[73] This classification according to Paul, op. cit., p. 36. Rothmann probably was thinking about Rom. 14, 1 Cor. 3:1 ff., 1 Cor. 11:30; Hebr. 5: 12 ff. See also B.R.N. X, p. 298.

[74] Chaps. V-XIII of "The Hiddeness of the Scriptures."

[75] B.R.N. X, p. 310.

[76] Obbe Philips: Hoffman began an exposition of Moses' tabernacle. B.R.N. VII. p. 123. For fragments, see P. Kawerau, *Melchior Hoffman als religiöser Denker*,

Haarlem, 1954, Literaturverzeichnis, no. 50, 55, 71; and further, an illustration, p. 68, and pieces from "Der Leuchter," p. 124 ff.

[77] Kawerau, op. cit., pp. 51-56 gives a systematic overview of Hoffman's ideas.

[78] B.R.N. V, p. 153 ff.

[79] *Ibid.*, p. 160.

[80] *Ibid.*, pp. 160 and 165.

[81] *Ibid.*, pp. 153 ff., 165, 197.

[82] *Ibid.*, p. 165. See further, Melch. Hoffmann, *Auszlegung der heimlichen Offenbarung Joannis*, 1530, quat Gvij^{vo} (Zentralbibliothek Zürich) and *Die eedele hoghe en troostlike sendebrief ... to den Romeren*, 1533, quat H4v° ad Rom 6:6 (Doopsg. Bibl., Amsterdam).

[83] B.R.N. V, pp. 195-197.

[84] *Ibid.*, p. 196.

[85] *Ibid.*, p. 186.

[86] *Ibid.*, p. 196; also true birth, p. 153.

[87] *Ibid.*, p. 154.

[88] *Ibid.*, p. 165.

[89] *Sendebrief to den Romeren*, quat. K8r°-L2° re: Rom. 8:14.

[90] *Ibid.*, quat. H 5r° re: Rom. 6:6 and quat. I 7v°-8r° re: Rom 7: 15 ff.

[91] *Ibid.*, quat. N 2r°-4v° re: Rom. 9:13, esp. N 3r°. See also W. J. Leendertz, *Melchior Hofmann*, Haarlem, 1883, pp. 201, 263, 265 ff.

[92] Fr. Nippold in *Z. f. histor. Theologie*, 1864, p. 629. I have not been able to discover in which writing David Joris gave this explanation.

[93] "Euangelium offte eine Frölicke Bodeschop" in a sheaf of treatises of H. N. as no. 6 (Doopsg. Bibl. Amsterdam), fol. 22v°-24r°. H. N. goes even further than the etymology of Gen. 25. He explains Edom = *rossig*, red as bloody and sees in the name Edom also the significance of earth. See V. Maag, "Jakob-Esau-Edom," *Theol. Zeitschrift*, Basel, 1957, pp. 418-429.

[94] H. de la Fontaine Verwey, *De geschriften van Hendrik Niclaes*, 's-Gravenhage, 1942 (Het Boek XXVI, 3), p. 192. In *de Spiegel der Gerechtigheid* H. N. gives "A figure of the true and spiritual tabernacle," *ibid.*, p. 191.

[95] Fr. Nippold, "Heinrich Niclaes und das Haus der Liebe" *Z. f. Hist. Theologie*, 1862, p. 355 ff.

[96] *Ibid.*, 358 ff.

[97] *Quellen und Forschungen zur Reformationsgeschichte*, vol. XXIV, 2, Hans Denck's writings = *Quellen zur Gesch. der Täufer*, vol VI, 2. Teil: Religiöse Schriften, ed. Walter Fellmann, Gütersloh, 1956, p. 118: Berichtigungen und Nachträge.

[98] *Ibid.*, p. 66 ff. A. Hegler, *Geist u. Schrift bei Seb. Franck*, Freibg. i.B., 1892, p. 30 ff.

[99] *Diallage, hoc est conciliatio locorum scripturae, qui prima facie inter se pugnare videntur*, Nürnburg, 1527. R.G.G.³ Sp. 293, Hegler, op. cit., pp. 28-48.

[100] Hegler, op. cit., p. 28 ff.

[101] *Quellen u. Forschungen*, vol. XXIV, ₂ = *Quellen zur Gesch. der Täufer*, VI, p. 71, lines 10-12. no. 22 and lines 13-16, no. 23. John 4:14 instead of John 6:35.

[102] Krebs-Rott, *Quellen zur Gesch. der Täufer*, vol VII, Elsasz. I, 1959, pp. 301-325 and H. Fast, *Der linke Flügel der Reformation* (Sammlung Dietrich, Bd. 269), Bremen, 1962, pp. 219-233.

[103] Krebs-Rott, p. 319 ff., B 4v°, 5r°; Fast, op. cit., p. 230.

[104] Krebs-Rott, p. 322 ff., B 6v°, 7 r°; Fast, op., cit., p. 232 ff.

[105] This explanation was supplied to me by Dr. Fast.

[106] Cf. B.R.N. X, p. 373.

[107] I cannot agree with Pijper's opinion, B.R.N. X, p. 44 ff., who thinks that Dirk's theology was characterized by a striking spiritualism. In the statements quoted Dirk opposes Roman Catholic and Lutheran ceremonies and external worship. He taught a faith that was grounded on the grace of Christ and he wanted to restore the church according to the example of the apostolic period.

[108] B.R.N. X, pp. 281, 310 ff.

[109] For the complete title, *ibid.*, p. 25, note 4.

[110] *Ibid.*, p. 460.

[111] B.R.N. VII, p. 224.

[112] *Bibliographie des martyrologes protestants neérlandais*, by F. Vander Haeghen, etc., La Haye, tom. I, 1890, no. 783; B.R.N. X, Preface, p. X.

[113] Printed in 1643, without place or name of the printer.

[114] Quoting B.R.N. X, p. 182.

[115] *Ibid.*, p. 15.

[116] *Ibid.*, p. 355.

[117] *Ibid.*, p. 383.

[118] *Ibid.*, pp. 60-64.

[119] *Ibid.*, pp. 61 and 63. Jesus Christ is born *of* Mary following the example of Melchizedek, without father and mother.

[120] *Ibid.*, pp. 65-68.

[121] *Ibid.*, pp. 69-111.

[122] *Ibid.*, p. 69.

[123] *Ibid.*, pp. 77 ff., 94 v.

[124] *Ibid.*, pp. 77, 97.

[125] *Ibid.*, p. 94, see also pp. 72, 77, 80 and *passim*.

[126] *Ibid.*, p. 102.

[127] *Ibid.*, pp. 81-106; cf. H. W. Meihuizen, op. cit., pp. 102-107.

[128] B.R.N. X, p. 90 ff.

[129] J. H. Wessel, op. cit., p. 220, see also pp. 147 ff., 203 ff., 206.

[130] See the summary by Meihuizen, op. cit., Chap. 5, p. 97 ff.

[131] The order: I. The essence of Baptism, the ordinance of Christ and the teaching of the Apostles are signs for the believers (B.R.N. X, pp. 69-80); II. The abuse of Baptism (infant baptism), op. cit, pp. 81-106; III. The disdain for Baptism as an external ceremony, op. cit., pp. 106-110.

[132] H. Fast in *Zwingliana*, vol. XI, Heft 7, 1962, no. 1. Likewise in: *A Legacy of Faith*, ed. C. J. Dyck, Newton, Kansas, 1962, pp. 213-231, see esp. note 67, p. 226.

[133] Concerning Thomas, see Hans H. Th. Stiasny, *Die strafrechtliche Verfolgung der Täufer in Köln*, Münster i.W., 1962, pp. 36-42.

[134] *Confessio/ Ein schöne be-//kantnusz eines frommen // und Gottliebenden Christen / Sampt // etlichen sendbriefen /vnd Christliche Er-//manungen ausz heyliger schrifft / sei-//ner hasuzfrawen vnnd brüdern // ausz der gefengnusz ge-// schrieben*, no place, date or name of printer. Signature: A 1r°-L 8r°. Available in Zürich, Zentralbibliothek. This copy is described in *Bibliography des martyrologes protestants néerlandais*, La Haye, 1890, Tome I, p. 203. (Thanks to a friendly note from Dr. J. F. G. Goeters in Bonn). Whether it came from the same printer as the copy described by F. Reichmann (M.Q.R., 1942, pp. 99-107) would have to be demonstrated by comparative study. It is my opinion that only the *Confessio* quat A 8v°-C 4 r° is by Thomas von Imbroich.

[135] B.R.N. X, pp. 69-79.

[136] Op. cit., quat B 8v°-C 4r°.

[137] quat. B 8v°-C 1v° = B.R.N. X, pp. 90-92.

[138] quat. C 1v° and 2r° = B.R.N. X, pp. 88, 93, 105.

[139] quat. C 2r°-3r° = B.R.N. X, pp. 93-95.

[140] quat. C 3v° = B.R.N. X, pp. 86-88. There also are some sentences in C3r°v° where Thomas writes down his own thoughts.

[141] quat. C 3v° and 4 r°.

[142] C. Krahn, op. cit., p. 94, already had this same idea; concerning H. Krufft see also Stiasny, op. cit., the index.

[143] B.R.N. X, p. 82 ff.

[144] B.R.N. X, p. 82. Menno Simons, *Opera*, 1681, fol. 468a, *Sommarie*, 1646, fol. 883a. See C. Krahn, op. cit., pp. 41, 43 ff., esp. note 120.

[145] W. A. *Die deutsche Bible*, vol. XI, 1st half. Weimar, 1960, p. 10, vs. 2-7 and p. 14, vs. 13-18.

[146] *Chonica Zeit//buch vnnd Geschichtsbibell von // anbegyn bisz in dis gegenwertig M.D. XXXVI. iar verlengt // ..., durch Sebastian // num Francken von Woerd*, Anno 1536, II. Teil, fol. 170v°, "Von der Tauff vnd gelübden Luthrns" = B.R.N. X, pp. 83, r. 14 v.b.-r2 v.o. In the manuscript of the *Geloofsboek*, p. F. 6v° in the margin is written "In libello de orando nog (as in Franck) 'Postill. Dominica iij post epipa.'"

[147] B.R.N. X, p. 100.

[148] *Chronica*, op. cit., fol. 140 v°, 142 r°.

[149] B.R.N. V, p. 322 and index.

[150] C. Krahn, op. cit., 40 ff.

[151] B.R.N. X, pp. 106-110.

[152] *Ibid.*, p. 107.

[153] A. Hegler, *Geist u. Schrift*, pp. 37, 118, note 2.

[154] B.R.N. X, p. 106.

[155] B.R.N. VII, pp. 307-310. Except for a booklet by David Joris, Nicolai quotes a writing of H. N.: "Van de Ghelatenheyt," p. 309, note 2. H. de la Fontaine Verwey, op. cit., p. 199, no. 58, says that "Eyn claer onderchseyt [sic, probably *onderscheyt*]" dates from 1552. J. Kimedoncius, *Vander Doope Onses Heeren Jesu Christi. Bekentenisse door Dierick Philips*, Middleburg, 1589, p. 165 is reminiscent of Schwenckfeld and Franck.

[156] B.R.N. X, p. 107.

[157] Chapter V, p. 30 ff.

[158] B.R.N. VII, pp. 307, 312, 359 ff.

[159] *Ibid.*, p. 311 ff. See, B. Becker, "Nicolai's inlassing over de Francisten," N.A.K.G.. XIX (1925), pp. 286-296. Nicolai apparently defended Franck.

[160] B.R.N. VII, p. 358.

[161] B. Becker, op. cit., p. 295.

[162] B.R.N. VII, p. 310. See also Nippold, *Z. f. histor. Theolgie*, 1862, p. 494.

[163] B.R.N. X, p. 108 ff.

[164] Joshua 5:2-9.

[165] B.R.N. X, pp. 111-134.

[166] *Ibid.*, pp. 113-121.

[167] This verse was the pillar on which Zwingli's doctrine of the Lord's Supper stood (Z V, p. 564, note 2). It was a shield in his defense against a literal interpretation (Z III, p. 341).

[168] An overview of the doctrine of Menno in C. Krahn, op. cit., pp. 139-142 and in H. W. Meihuizen, op. cit., pp. 116-121.

[169] *Sommarie*, 1646, fol. 56a-58a.

[170] Z IV, pp. 512-519; the first part is printed with translation in *Documenta Reformatoria*, Kampen, 1960, pp. 33-36.

[171] Z IV, p. 517. "Therefore not by this word 'This is my body' would the saving bread be transubstantiated, but it is given by the bread itself."

[172] *Chronica*, op. cit., fol. CXIII ff.

[173] The same in Menno, *Sommarie*, 1646, fol. 58a. Perhaps Franck copied this from Zwingli, Z IV, p. 807 ff. In many respects Dirk's doctrine of the Lord's Supper is in agreement with Zwingli's, Z IV, p. 807 ff. I had the opportunity to speak about this issue with Prof. Blanke. He agreed with me and cited several places from the works of Zwingli. I do not believe that Dirk read the writings of Zwingli.

[174] Dirk combined Matt. 26:26 and Luke 22:19 and takes the present passive participle as future: "shall be given to you."

[175] Seb. Franck, op. cit., fol. CXIIIb: "Understand what I have spoken spiritually. For you will not eat this body which you see here, nor drink the blood that will be poured out when I am crucified."

[176] Seb. Franck, *ibid*: "Whoever is not one with Christ does not eat his flesh nor drink his blood, even if he receives the sacrament (such a great matter) daily, to his eternal judgment."

177 These examples are already in Corn. Hoen's *Docum Reform*, p. 36. Zwingli gives other examples, Z V, p. 863.

178 This was already in Menno's *Sommarie*, 1646, fol. 58a. Seb. Franck, op. cit., "For the Lord is above until the end of the world, nevertheless the truth of the Lord is with us. For the body in which he was resurrected must be at one place and location. But his truth is poured out on everyone."
Zwingli thought this argument very important. Z IV, p. 831. "Christ has said, 'I leave the world, you will not always have me, and that must only be understood physically. For all facts and sense teach us that he wished to show us that he was going bodily to heaven to sit at the right hand of the Father until the last day." Further p. IV, *Christianae fidei expositio*, p. 51: "Augustine said that when we speak of Christ's body dwelling in another heavenly place, this is proper according to the true mode of bodily existence. And therefore, when we speak of Christ's body that was resurrected from the dead, we may properly speak of it dwelling in one place." See also p. 52.

179 Dirk alludes to Luther's doctrine of the ubiquity (omnipresence) of the body of Christ. Zwingli refuted this doctrine in *Christianae fidei expositio*, op. cit., p. 52. "For all learned men have rejected this view, in favor of a discredited and shameless one, which certain ones have dared to affirm, that Christ's body is equally everywhere and divine. It certainly cannot be everywhere unless it is infinite by nature; what is infinite is also eternal. The humanity of Christ is not eternal; therefore it is not infinite. If it is not infinite, it cannot be anything but finite. If it is finite, then it is not everywhere."

180 B.R.N. X, pp. 121-123.

181 The H.S. N 7r°v° has the better text: "All believers will be baptized into one body through one spirit, whereby they all become one body with Christ through faith..."

182 H.S. N 7v°: instead of "vermaent" [admonished] it says "verijnnert" [reminded].

183 E. Hennecke, *Neutest. Apokryphen*, Tübingen, 1924², p. 563.

184 H. W. Meihuizen, op. cit., p. 120.

185 B.R.N. X, pp. 123-125.

186 As already in Corn. Hoen, Z IV, p. 517, line 6 ff., line 11 ff.

187 B.R.N. X, pp. 125-128.

188 I Cor. 11:25; Matt. 26:28; Mark 14:24; Luke 22:20.

189 See above, pp. 75-76 and B.R.N. X, pp. 117 and 119.

190 *Ibid.*, pp. 128-134.

191 An allusion to the giving of communion to the ill among the Lutherans.

192 This refers to the practice of the priest taking communion by himself in the Mass, but also to that of the Lutheran preachers, who often did the same, even though it was forbidden by some church ordinances. R.E.³, vol. I, p. 72, R.G.G.², vol. V, p. 406.

193 This alludes again to Lutheran practice, R.E.³, vol. I, p. 71 ff. The Anabaptists followed the Zwinglin ordinance, op. cit., p. 75.

194 I think specifically about the article from the *Fundamentboek* printed by

Meihuizen, op. cit., p. 210 ff.

[195] B.R.N. X, p. 132.

[196] The derogatory name given by Lutherans to Anabaptists, Sacramentarians, and Zwinglians.

Chapter IX

[1] E. Krajewski, "The Theology of Felix Mantz," MQR, vol. XXXVI (1962), p. 84 ff.

[2] S. Cramer, BRN V, p. 591.

[3] Art. 2. See Beatrice Jenny, *Das Schleitheimer Täuferbekenntnis* 1527, Thayngen, 1951, p. 11 note 51 ff.

[4] Menno writes in the preface to the "Instruction on Excommunication" in CWMS. [J. ten Doornkaat Koolman calls it "Instruction Concerning the Apostolic Ban."]: "It is more than evident that if we had not been zealous in this matter [the ban] these days, we would be considered and called by every man the companions of the sect of Münster and all the perverted sects." [Trans. from CWMS, p. 962].

[5] K. Vos, *Menno Simons*, pp. 70, 97; from D. B., 1876, p. 22 ff.; Kühler I, p. 314 ff.

[6] BRN VII, pp. 444-448.

[7] H. W. Meihuizen, op. cit., p. 59.

[8] BRN VII, pp. 54, 59, 449, 532, note 2. What Nicolai says about Leenaert's attitude (BRN VII, p. 456 ff.) he probably heard in Emden.

[9] H. W. Meihuizen, op. cit., p. 57.

[10] BRN VII, pp. 448-450.

[11] *Ibid.*, p. 449.

[12] *Ibid.*

[13] *Ibid.*, p. 445.

[14] *Ibid.*, p. 446.

[15] Decision of Wismar § 3. K. Vos, *Menno Simons*, p. 124; BRN VII, p 235.

[16] BRN VII, p. 449.

[17] H. W. Meihuizen, op. cit., p. 57.

[18] BRN VII, p. 445. See also Nicolai's report, op. cit., p. 456.

[19] *Ibid.*, p. 446.

[20] *Ibid.*

[21] I Cor. 5:11; see also BRN VII, p. 465.

[22] I place Dirk's transition to Leenaert's party earlier than does De Hoop Scheffer, D. B., 1894, p. 40, note 1, on the basis of BRN VII, pp. 55, 465, 525, where it speaks of Leenaert and Dirk travelling together before the conference in Harlingen. Ottius, *Annales*, p. 119: "But in truth Leenaert Bouwens by his art of persuasion enticed Dirk Philips to his own position, from whom Menno, fearing excommunication, stepped back and yielded more closely to them." Perhaps the letter of Dirk to Menno belongs to this period, "Audi et alteram partem" [But listen to another side], BRN X, p. 571. This letter has been lost.

[23] BRN VII, p. 448..

Notes to pages 84-88

²⁴ Kühler I, p. 318. K. Vos, *Menno Simons*, p. 138, makes a credible case for six elder being present at Harlingen.

²⁵ Op. cit., p. 320. I agree with Krahn, op. cit., p. 92 ff., that the report from Alenson, BRN VII, p. 258 ff., is only second hand.

²⁶ That Menno was threatened with the ban is seen in BRN VII, p. 465 and p. 526. See also pg. 55. Menno himself says how much he feared the ban, *Sommarie*, 1646, fol. 357b; Kühler, I, p. 321.

²⁷ *Gesch. der Doopsgez. in Nederland*, p. 49.

²⁸ *Sommarie*, 1646, fol. 908b. See also, fol. 367b. Menno had not acquired enough experience.

²⁹ Op. cit., fol. 354; C. Krahn, op. cit., p. 93.

³⁰ *Sommarie*, 1646, fol. 372a, 908b, 920a. Therefore Menno could charge Zylis and Lemke not with slandering him, but the Holy Spirit, who had guaranteed his promise and led Menno to the full truth.

³¹ C. Krahn, op. cit., p. 93 and 151, made a start with this point of view. Meihuizen, op. cit., pp. 59, 62 ff., continued along the same path.

³² S. Cramer examined this thoroughly, BRN VII, p. 55, note 3; p. 223, note 1; p. 466, note 1.

³³ BRN X, p. 253.

³⁴ De Hoop Scheffer, "Het geslacht Sleutel," D.B., 1867, p. 58 ff.; BRN X, pp. 553, 567, 69; M.E., vol. III, p. 85 ff.

³⁵ BRN VII, p. 466.

³⁶ *Ibid.*, p. 227. Alenson prints the entire agreement.

³⁷ *Ibid.*, p. 228.

³⁸ See Chapter IV, notes 29 and 30.

³⁹ C. Krahn, op. cit., p. 94 ff., and Chapter VIII, note 142.

⁴⁰ One usually thinks of Hans Sikken from Danzig, C. Krahn, op. cit., p. 94.

⁴¹ *Ibid.*

⁴² D. B., 1894, p. 46, and note 1. Meihuizen, op. cit., p. 61, thinks that Menno shared a copy of the Wismar Articles with them.

⁴³ BRN VII, p. 526.

⁴⁴ Printed by de Hoop Scheffer, D. B., 1894, pp. 47-53. This letter is also found in the *Urkundenbuch der Gemeinde Heubuden*, pp. 15-20.

⁴⁵ This piece about shunning in marriage can also be found in Alenson, BRN VII, p. 222.

⁴⁶ For the title, BRN X, p. 30, note 4; for the booklet itself, see *ibid.*, pp. 249-265.

⁴⁷ Kühler, I, p. 326 misreads the meaning of this booklet, in my opinion. The signature D.P.I.B. (p. 265) signifies: Dirk Philips, your brother. Likewise, p. 529 D.P.V.B.I.H. = Dirk Philips uw broeder im Heren [Dirk Philips, your brother in the Lord].

⁴⁸ BRN X, p. 249. [Ts. note: In the original Dutch, the full and lengthy title is given. It begins with the words "A Lovely Admonition." In WDP the title used is simply "The Ban," p. 238].

⁴⁹ *Ibid.*, pp. 250-253.

[50] *Ibid.*, p. 253. Thanks to De Hoop Scheffer, D.B., 1894, p. 53 ff., one hears an allusion to the Upper Germans and Waterlanders. Menno used similar wording, *Sommarie*, 1646, fol. 356.

[51] BRN X, pp. 261-265.

[52] *Ibid.*, p. 264.

[53] *Ibid.*, pp. 253-258.

[54] *Ibid.*, p. 255.

[55] *Ibid.*, p. 259 ff.

[56] *Ibid.*, p. 258. The same three reasons are found in Menno Simons. See H. W. Meihuizen, op. cit., pp. 134-136.

[57] BRN X, p. 257.

[58] *Ibid.*, p. 256.

[59] *Ibid.*, p. 258 ff.

[60] *Ibid.*, p. 259.

[61] *Ibid.*, p. 261.

[62] C. Krahn, op. cit., p. 152, esp. note 215.

[63] BRN X, p. 261.

[64] *Ibid.*, p. 32 ff.

[65] In "Concerning the [True] Knowledge of Jesus Christ" (1557), *ibid.*, p. 159. Other places: p. 231 ff., 350, 366 ff. (The Song of Solomon is spiritually restored to Christ and his church). Further: pp. 408, 410, 636, 647. The image of Christ and his church as the bridegroom and bride was used already by Melchior Hoffman in "The Ordinance of God," BRN V, pp. 156-159.

[66] BRN X, pp. 159 and 410; *Remonstrance*, p. 157.

[67] In "[Concerning] the Sending of Preachers," (1559), *ibid.*, p. 229 ff.

[68] *Ibid.*, pp. 356-359, 366.

[69] *Ibid.*, p. 359.

[70] *Ibid.*, pp. 399-401.

[71] *Ibid.*, p. 399.

[72] *Ibid.*, p.400; see also p. 258.

[73] *Ibid.*, p. 400 ff.

[74] *Ibid.*, pp. 405, 406, 409, 413, 414.

[75] *Ibid.*, p. 413 ff.

[76] *Ibid.*, pp. 117, 174, 358.

[77] Dating in the separate printing, *Catalogus Doopsg. Bibl. Amsterdam*, 1919, p. 85 ff.

[78] *Sommarie*, 1646, fol. 368a and b.

[79] I Cor. 5:11; 2 Cor. 13:1-4; further I Cor. 6:10; Gal. 5:19-21; Eph. 5:5; Rev. 21:8, 22:15.

[80] See above, p. 85.

[81] *Sommarie*, 1646, fol. 361 ff.

[82] For the development of Menno's ideas regarding the ban, see Meihuizen's overview, op. cit., pp. 130-141; cf. also p. 62 ff.

[83] *Sommarie*, 1646, fol. 918b.

[84] *Ibid.*, fol. 374a. There is no discussion about making a confession to a fellow member.
[85] Menno used the Lutheran Lower Saxon [Nedersaksische] translation which the Lutherans followed, defended by Bugenhagen.
[86] W. Doskocil, *Der Bann in der Urkirche*, München, 1958, pp. 30-38. Prof. F. Blanke drew my attention to this book.
[87] *Sommarie*, 1646, fol. 368b-372a, 376a, b.
[88] *Ibid.*, fol. 371b; see Doskocil, op. cit., p. 80.
[89] *Sommarie*, 1646, fol. 370a, 377b; Doskocil, op. cit., p. 87 ff.
[90] BRN X, pp. 249, 258, 261; Doskocil, op. cit., p. 68 ff. Menno corrected this oversight in "Antwoord aan Zylis en Lemke" ["Reply to Zylis and Lemke"], *Sommarie*, 1646, fol. 912 ff.
[91] *Sommarie*, 1646, fol. 393-398. Meihuizen correctly prefers to call this "responsibility/accountability," op. cit. p. 62.
[92] May one ignore these and other explanations by Menno, as Kühler does? *Geschiedenis* I, p. 327.
[93] *Sommarie*, 1646, fol. 396.
[94] D.B., 1894, pp. 62-69. Therefore the statement by K. Vos, *Menno Simons*, p. 168 ff., that the "Reply to Zylis and Lemke" was only written in 1560, is correct in my opinion. It is improbable that Menno defended strict shunning in marriage only a few weeks after this letter.
[95] An unstable reed, an April shower [? Aprillen water]. [Translation is uncertain for "een fischefasch"]. *Sommarie*, 1646, fol. 908, marginal note.
[96] *Ibid*, fol. 916a.
[97] *Ibid.*, fol. 917b.
[98] *Ibid.*, fol. 916b.
[99] *Ibid.*, fol. 921b
[100] See J. T., *Een vriendelijcke Aenspraeck / aen alle Doopsghesinde over het Stuck ofte Puynct / der Echtmijdinghe / ende ghemeyne / Mijdinge*, no place, 1613, § 6-8, printed in part by de Hoop Scheffer, D.B., 1894, p. 59, note 1. The report of [Carel van Ghendt], BRN VII, p. 526, is somewhat of a summary because he does not distinguish between the meetings at Cologne in 1557 and 1559.
[101] *Sommarie*, 1646, fol. 908a ("while I myself cannot come personally").
[102] See § 8 of the just cited writing of I. T., not printed by de Hoop Scheffer. [Carel van Ghendt], op. cit., relates the case of a German brother at Franeker who refused to be rebaptized and although he was a minister [admonisher] was banned. See also, Kühler I, p. 328.
[103] BRN X, p. 507 ff.
[104] *Ibid.*, pp. 675-688.
[105] M.E., vol. IV, p. 918.
[106] The Upper Germans or Overlanders were sometimes called Swiss Brethren. See M.L. IV, p. 132 ff. Lemke was called "an excellent minister of the S[wiss] Br[ethren]" (*Sommarie*, 1646, fol. 911b in the margin.); "Overlanders were in the

overland and called Moravian Swiss Brethren," (*Ibid.*, fol. 922a in the margin). "A Confession ... of a Swiss Brother called Thomas Truckher." Written by Caspar Artlof in 1581. *Inventaris Archief Doopsg. Gem. Amsterdam*, I, no. 740. Thus the members of the Cologne congregation were also identified as Swiss brothers.

[107] In my opinion Dirk alludes to the "Rechenschafft vnserer Religion / Leer vnd Glaubens" by P[eter] R[iedemann]. The first printing is in the Zentralbibl., Zurich, written in 1540-41, later printed in Moravia. See my article in MQR, vol. XXXVI (1962), p. 169 ff. Riedemann wrote (Vom Ban, fol. 163b-165a), "If someone is found to have committed a great sin ... he is to be separated from the congregation without admonition, since the judgment of Paul has already taken place. (I Cor. 5:11)." What follows concerning shunning and reacceptance is also instructive.

[108] Obadiah 1:21. Obadiah is called Abdias in the Latin Bible (Vulgate).

[109] II Macc. 3:38, 39.

[110] "De Doopsgezinden te Antwerp in de zestiende eeuw," *Bulletin de la Commission Royale d'Histoire*, Tome LXXXIV, IVe Bulletin, Bruxelles, 1920, p. 340 ff. But Dirk may just as well have heard it from others.

[111] BRN X, p. 688. I doubt whether Jan B. is the elder Hans Busschaert.

[112] K. Vos made various guesses which he later improved upon: *Menno Simons*, p. 330, note 3, and *Doopsgezinden te Antwerpen*, p. 337 ff. See Van Braght, 1685, Vol. II, fol. 269. Laurens' first letter was written on May 25, 1559, to the brothers at Emden.

[113] K. Vos, *Doopsgezinden te Antwerpen*, p. 340, and *Antwerpsch Archievenblad*, published by P. Gérard, vol. IX, p. 17.

[114] BRN X, p. 675. For a description of the print see *ibid.*, p. 669, note 2.

[115] *Ibid.*, p. 687.

[116] *Ibid.*, 685.

[117] K. Vos wrote about him in *Doopsgezinden te Antwerpen*, p. 341 ff. See also, M.E., vol. III, p. 111a.

[118] "le prince souverain des Anabaptistes." K. Rembert, *Wiedertaüfer in Jülich*, p. 483, note 2.

[119] P. Gérard, op. cit., vol. II, p. 355.

[120] Van Braght, vol. II, fol. 329 ff.

[121] Alfr. Hegler and W. Köhler, *Beiträge zur Gesch. der Mystik in der Reformationszeit* (A.R.G., Texte u. Untersuchungen), Berlin, 1906, p. 84. Joachim den Suyckerbacker was in prison in Cleve, confessed by Michiel Gerritsz. under torture in 1571, D. B., 1912, p. 36.

[122] *Opera Parisiis*, 1616, pp. 673-674: "A certain one among the professors and teachers recanted this error, who on account of this error was held a prisoner in the territory of Cleve." Cassander instructed him; Joachim changed his mind. Fol. 674: "He condemend this error with some others in his own [Cassander's] sacred church in the same town of Cleve."

[123] loc. cit., p. 1151. See also Maria E. Nolte, *Georgius Cassander en zijn*

oecumenisch streven, Diss. Nijmegen, 1951, p. 128ff. I knew about the above mentioned citations already in 1915.

[124] Michiel Gerritsz. confessed in 1571 that he had been baptized six years earlier in Middleburg by J. den S., see note 121. Concerning Matth. Servaes, see Stiasny, *Verfolgung der Taüfer in Köln*, 1962, pp. 61-63 and the index. Two other short pieces of information: In Stiasny, op. cit., p. 53, Joachim van Antwerp was mentioned by an imprisoned Anabaptist as his baptizer (summer, 1562). J. F. G. Goeters, "Die Rolle des Täufertums, etc." (*Rhein. Vierteljahrsblätter*, 1959, pp. 217-236) shared on p. 232 that in 1563 Joachim Werner, the Sugarbaker in Emmerich, was imprisoned and converted by Cassander, without giving the source. 1563 seems to me incorrect and the name Werner is probably an error. J. de S. was also called Joachim Vermeer, K. Vos, *Doopsg. te Antwerpen*, p. 337 ff.

[125] See above, p. 85.

[126] His family name was "Yserman." Schijn-Maatschoen, *Gesch. der Mennoniten*, vol. III, 1745, pp. 1-41; Winkler Prins, *Encyclopedia*, vol. IX, 1950, p. 417; M.E., vol. II, p. 505; BRN X, pp. 553, 567, 692.

[127] This is a thesis which Van der Zijpp shared with me by word of mouth, and which I accept.

[128] *Sommarie*, 1646, fol. 905-925.

[129] De Hoop Scheffer, D. B., 1894, p. 57 ff. and Kühler, I, p. 327, call him a "Waterlander." See K. Vos, *Menno Simons*, p. 147 ff. and M.E., vol. II, p. 710.

[130] For the title, BRN X, p. 34, note 2.

[131] Preface, quat. A iijr°. I will pass over the part that was directed against Menno.

[132] BRN X, p. 259 ff. and H. Timmerman, op. cit., p. 8 and *passim*.

[133] BRN X, p. 261 and H. Timmerman, op. cit., p. 2 and *passim*, esp. p. 101 ff.

[134] quat. A iijr°-A v^{vo}.

[135] *Ibid.*, p. 102 ff.

[136] Timmerman set out to refute Dirk's arguments. BRN X, pp. 255-261 was subdivided into nine arguments, H. Timmerman, op. cit., pp. 77-105.

[137] *Ibid.*, p. 96.

[138] *Ibid.*, p. 105.

[139] BRN X, pp. 259, 261.

Chapter X

[1] Chapter IX, p 96.

[2] W. Keeney, MQR, vol. XXXII (1958), p. 185.

[3] Chapter VIII, note 18.

[4] Restitution according to Acts 3:21=the restoration of all things. "Concerning Spiritual Restitution" is printed in BRN X, pp. 339-376. Title: *ibid.*, p. 10, note 7.

[5] *Ibid.*, p. 341.

[6] See the instructive article "Restitution" in M.L. III, pp. 476b and 477.

⁷ A technical term used by Dirk (and Menno) for the Münsterite excesses.
⁸ Chapter VIII, pp. 61-62, 64.
⁹ BRN X, pp. 341, 375.
¹⁰ *Neudrucke deutscher Litteraturwerke des XVI. u. XVII. Jhs.*, No. 77 and 78=*Flugschriften aus der Reformationszeit*, VII, ed. by A. Knaake, Halle a. S., 1888, p. xii. For the contents see M.L. III, p. 552 ff. For the religious contents, see Kühler I, p. 126 ff.
¹¹ The "The Tabernacle of Moses" was quoted, BRN X, pp. 341, 351, 359.
¹² For example, p. 357 (Balaam and the donkey), p. 361 (the figure of Samson).
¹³ *Ibid.* p, 370 ff.
¹⁴ *Ibid.*, p. 372.
¹⁵ *Ibid.*, pp. 393-407; see also, p. 184 (Apologia).
¹⁶ *Ibid.*, p. 373, see chapter II, p. 9.
¹⁷ Chapter VIII, p. 59 ff.
¹⁸ Printed in BRN X, pp. 377-414; for the title, *ibid.*, p. 33, note 4.
¹⁹ *Ibid.*, pp. 379, 383.
²⁰ *Ibid.*, p. 388.
²¹ *Ibid.*, p. 394.
²² *Ibid.*, p. 400.
²³ *Ibid.*, pp. 380-393.
²⁴ *Ibid.*, pp. 393-408.
²⁵ *Ibid.*, pp. 408-414.
²⁶ A remarkable exegesis! Perhaps Dirk copied it from Luther, W.A., Bd. XXIV, (Weimar, 1900), *Predigten über das erste Buch Mose*, 1527, p. 98 ff.: "When Adam [Gen. 3:15] heard, he came out of hell again and was comforted again. It is a strong saying, that everything is struck to the ground that opposed to what is preached... It says there that Adam was a Christian long before Christ's birth. He did not see Christ with his eyes, but he had Christ in the word." The Latin text is more terse, on the same page. Dirk developed these thoughts independently.
²⁷ *Ibid.*, p. 392 ff. In the H.S. (see Chapter VIII, pp 59-60). K. shorter 4v°: "The Holy Spirit is the third person in the godhead, who proceeds from the Father through the Son and is for that reason one divine being with them."
²⁸ S. Hoekstra, *Beginselen en leer enz.*, p. 256.
²⁹ Other places concerning the Holy Spirit, BRN X, pp. 63 ff., 272 ff.
³⁰ Extracts are printed in *Documenta Reformatoria*, Kampen, 1960, p. 58 ff.
³¹ BRN X, pp. 205-248.
³² *Ibid.*, pp. 313-337, esp. p. 323.
³³ *Ibid.*, p. 397 ff.
³⁴ *Opera*, 1681, fol. 636b.
³⁵ *Sommarie*, 1646, fol. 353.
³⁶ Indicative, not imperative.
³⁷ See S. Hoekstra, op. cit., p. 286 ff.
³⁸ M.E., vol. II, pp. 347a-351b.

[39] Not in the "Reply" as Bender writes, but in the "Admonition" (*Gedenkschrift zum 400 jährigen Jubiläum der Mennoniten*, Ludwigshafen, 1925, p. 255, lines 7-23 and p. 255, line 33 p. 256, line 17). About the objections to footwashing, see Guy de Brés, loc. cit., p. 107. If not enough women were present the men certainly also washed the feet of the women. The writer asks, "is that proper?" Likewise Nicolai, BRN VII, p. 297.

[40] Chapter IX.

[41] H. W. Meihuizen, op. cit., p. 195 ff.; Kühler, I, p. 299.

[42] G. Grosheide, op. cit., p. 247 ff.

[43] BRN X, p. 393.

[44] *The Recovery of the Anabaptist Vision*, ed. G. F. Hershberger, Scottdale, 1962^2, p. 42 ff. See also the definition by H. Fast, R.G.G.^{2}, Bd. VI, p. 603.

[45] BRN X, p. 404. Kühler I, p. 335, mistakenly calls the commandment not to swear the sixth ordinance.

[46] Therefore I cannot agree with Kühler I, p. 338 when he says "D. P. includes the command for nonresistance in the ordinances of the church." Cf. H. S. Bender, loc. cit., p. 48 ff., "The concept of the suffering church," p. 51 ff., "The ethic of love and nonresistance."

[47] Pijper gives a good overview, BRN X, p. 12 ff.

[48] *Ibid.*, pp. 223, 394.

[49] *Ibid.*, pp. 420 ff., 424, 439, 445.

[50] *Ibid.*, p. 444.

[51] *Ibid.*, pp. 407 ff., cf. also p. 323.

[52] See Chapter IX, pp. 89-90.

[53] I only point to two mistakes: p. 407, line 11 where it says "a curse of the world and a burnt offering." This is copied from the old Lutheran translation, "We are always as a curse of the world and a burnt offering for all people." Also p. 411, line 12 where it says: "As a gate ['*Tuyn*'] for the vineyard." 7v° reads in the original, "as a '*thun*'=garden around the vineyard." Thus "*thun*"=*Zaun*=gate.

[54] Dl. II, p. 383.

[55] BRN X, p. 386 ff.

[56] *Ibid.*, p. 410.

[57] Literature: Bruno Schumacher, *Niederl. Ansiedlungen im Herzogtum Preussen z.Z. Herzog Albrechts (1525-1568)*, Lpz., 1903. Felicia Szper, *Nederlandsche Nederzettingen in West-Pruisen gedurende den Poolschen tijd*, Diss., Enkhuizen, 1913; H. G. Mannhardt, *Die Danziger Mennonitengemeinde, 1569-1919*, Danzig, 1919; Horst Penner, "Ansiedlung mennonitischer Niederländer im Weichselmündungsgebiet von der Mitte des 16. Jhds. etc." (*Schriftenreihe des Mennon. Geschichtsvereins*, Nr. 3), Weierhof, 1940; *idem*: "Westpreussische Mennoniten im Wandel der Zeiten," (M.G.Bl., 7, Jhg. 1950); M.E., vol. II, pp. 123a-125b, "East Prussia" (H. Penner); vol. IV, pp. 920b-926b, "West Prussia" (H. Penner); M.L., Bd. III, pp. 322a-325b, "Ostpreussen" (H. Penner).

[58] Schumacher, op. cit., p. 10 ff., notes 23 and 24.

[59] Szper, op. cit., p. 21 ff.; Schumacher, op. cit., pp. 33-37. H. G. Mannhardt, op. cit. pp. 41-43, note, tries to refute that Schottland was sold by the bishop to the city of Danzig, as Schumacher, op. cit., p. 36 ff. and Szper, op. cit., p. 23 report.

[60] Schumacher, op. cit., p. 37; Szper, op. cit., p. 38 ff.

[61] M.E., vol. IV, p. 922b; H. Penner, M.G.Bl., 1950, p. 21 ff.

[62] H. Penner, *Ansiedlung*, 1940, pp. 12 ff., 67 ff.

[63] C. Krahn, op. cit., p. 72 ff.

[64] K. Vos, "Twee brieven van Menno Simons" in *Geschr. ten behoeve v. d. Doopsg. in de verstrooiing*, no. 43, p. 7.

[65] H. G. Mannhardt, op. cit., pp. 25, 42, thinks that Menno went to Danzig a few times alone or in the company of Dirk Philips and Hans Sikken. H. Penner, M.G.Bl., p. 22 and M.E., vol. IV, p. 923a, thinks that Dirk remained there as leader.

[66] Chapter VII, p. 47.

[67] Printed by H. van Alfen in N.A.K.G., Dl. XXIV (1931), pp. 205-236. K. Vos copied a portion, D. B., 1917, p. 136 ff. I used the copy *Inv. Archief Amsterdam*, I, no. 364a and b.

[68] Melchior only came to Amsterdam in 1531, Kühler I, p. 65.

[69] I doubt whether this Jan van Sol is the same as Joham vom Soll Hollender, also Johann Solius (van Zoolen) who was mentioned by Schumacher, op. cit., p. 19, note 59; p. 67 ff., and *passim*. See also, H. G. Mannhardt, op. cit., p. 40.

[70] Nothing is known about this last person. H. G. Mannhardt, op. cit., p. 40, erred in his interpretation, in my opinion. Jan van Sol did not mean to say that these three were elders in Danzig.

[71] K. Vos read the manuscript hastily and made a minister of Herm. van Bommel. Herm. van Bommel appeared in the articles as an agent of Duke Albrecht, Schumacher, op. cit., p. 15, note 39, further note 266. He became a citizen of Danzig in 1550. As an agent of the duke and as a citizen of Danzig he can not have been a member of the Anabaptist congregation. He probably sympathized with the Anabaptists as had his previous lord, who had also taken refuge in Danzig and had settled in the neighborhood of the city. See Ubbo Emmius, *Rerum Frisicarum historia*, Leiden, 1616, fol. 885 sequ.; H. Penner, *Ansiedlung*, 1940, p. 67 ff.; *Mitteilungen der Niederl. Ahnengemeinschaft*, Hamburg, 1949, Bd. 2, Heft 1, p. 2 ff.

[72] Szper, op. cit., pp. 45 ff., 50, 236. Jan van Sol made the statement: Huyghe Mathyszoon worked as a tailor, weaver, and spoon maker and now is a peddler.

[73] *Bijdrage tot de gesch. der Anabaptisten*, Hilversum, 1938, pp. 155-165, 225 ff., 246 ff.

[74] According to S. Cramer, RE^3, p. 607, Dirk Philips lived in Schottland.

[75] Hans van Steen (1705-1781), elder from 1754-1779, put together a list of ministers of the congregation starting with 1667, somewhat complete. At the end the above mentioned notation is found. The "Gemeindebuch" is now in the Bethel College Historical Library, North Newton, Kansas, USA. A reproduction of the important information is in M.E., vol. I, Illustrations, p. 31.

[76] About Hans van Steen, see H. G. Mannhardt, op. cit., pp. 99-103.

[77] This book was available earlier in the Stadtbibliothek in Hamburg, which was burned in 1943. An explanation of the name "Clerken" is in H. G. Mannhardt, op. cit., p. 46. Concerning Georg Hansen and the disputation with the official of the bishop of Lesslau, see H. G. Mannhardt, op. cit., p. 77 ff.

[78] Georg Hansen, *Fondamentboeck*, p. 333.

[79] *Ibid.*, p. 430.

[80] Letter of July 28, 1914.

[81] Likewise cited by W. Keeney, loc. cit., p. 185.

[82] The oldest report of Menno's death was in the questioning of Anabaptists in Wismar in the spring of 1561, M.G.Bl., 18. Jhg., 1961, p. 36.

[83] K. Vos, "De dooplijst van Leenaert Bouwens," *Bijdragen en Mededeelingen van het Historisch Genootschap*, Dl. XXXVI, p. 41 ff.; J. O. *Onder verbeteringhe. Verclaringhe met bewijs etc.*, 1609, s.l. § 303, 306; K. Vos, M.E., vol. III, p. 305a, b proposes, in my opinion unjustly, the accusations that Leenaert was a drunkard and that he had accepted fifty half-crowns for his ministerial services in 1561. Cf. J. O. *Verclaringhe*, § 304 with K. Vos, *Dooplijst van L. B.*, p. 42.

[84] M.E., vol. II, p. 824.

[85] Letter from Dirk Philips to Hoyte Renix, Emden, July 7, 1567; see Appendix II. [Not reproduced here but translated in WDP, pp. 545-548].

[86] J. O. *Verclaringhe*, § 196; De Hoop Scheffer. D. B., 1893, p. 38, note 1.

[87] G. Grosheide, op. cit., p. 180 ff. Willem Janszn. said that he had been baptized 6 or 7 years earlier. According to the judicial sentence, however, it happened eight years earlier. See also p. 247.

[88] *Ibid.*, p. 185. Thijs Joriaensz., the later martyr, was "minister of the word" in Ransdorp in the sixties.

[89] Grosheide, op. cit., pp. 181, 236.

[90] *Ibid.*, p. 185. See also, BRN II, p. 538, note 1.

[91] *Ibid.*, p. 234.

[92] Kühler I, pp. 292, 294.

[93] S. Cramer, "De Doopsgezinde gemeente te Utrecht van 1560-1562," D. B. 1903, pp. 1-53.

[94] *Ibid.*, pp. 31 ff., 51.

[95] *Ibid.*, pp. 35, 37, 40.

[96] *Ibid.*, pp. 35, 40 ff.

[97] *Ibid.*, p. 42.

[98] *Ibid.*, p. 41.

[99] *Ibid.*, p. 34.

[100] *Ibid.*, p. 42.

[101] *Ibid.*, p. 34.

[102] *Ibid.*, p. 41. K. Vos, *Menno Simons*, p. 238 demonstrates that Brabants was the language used in the court of Brussels (pure Dutch) and refutes the opinion of Pijper that this indicates a stay of Dirk Philips in the Southern Netherlands. See BRN X, pp. 6 and 36, note 2, p. 653.

[103] S. Cramer, op. cit., p. 13.

[104] *Ibid.*, p. 50 ff. K. Vos, "Doopsgez. te Antwerpen," op. cit., p. 344, asserts that Joos Verbeek and Dirk Philips met each other and consulted in Utrecht about what needed to be done, shortly after the death of Menno. That is an error. Joos was in Utrecht during Lent, 1561, and was burned in Antwerp on June 26. Dirk only arrived around Christmas of 1561.

[105] I found these publications in the Stadtbibliothek in Hamburg in 1914/1915 and copied the title pages. They were burned in 1943. See chapter VIII, note 37.

[106] Concerning the printer Nic. Biestkens, see E. W. Moes, *De Amsterdamsche boekdrukkers en uitgevers in de zestiende eeuw*, Amsterdam, 1907, Dl. II, pp. 1-25; Paul Bergmans, *Les imprimeurs belges à l'étranger*, 1922, pp. 10, 16, 50; M.L., Bd. I, p. 220; M.E., vol. I, p. 341a.

[107] BRN X, pp. 415-459.

[108] MQR, vol. XXXVIII (1964), October, pp. 357-360.

[109] BRN X, p. 467.

[110] *Ibid.*, pp. 417-431.

[111] See chapter IX, p. 95.

[112] BRN X, p. 428 ff. One can go to the temples of the idols if one rejects false worship from the heart.

[113] *Ibid.*, p. 430.

[114] BRN II, p. 268, note 1 and p. 324, note 1. The sentence of the court of Friesland is dated March 14, 1559. The Spiritual superintendent or Heretic Master was Wilh. Lindanus, later bishop of Roermond. M.L., Bd., II, p. 657.

[115] BRN X, p. 428 ff.

[116] *Ibid.*, pp. 444-459.

[117] *Ibid.*, pp. 445, 454, 457.

[118] *Ibid.*, pp. 451-457. In "A Short but Fundamental Account," *ibid.*, pp. 557-561, this is developed. On p. 523 he also speaks of the covenant of God.

[119] *Ibid.*, pp. 445, 457; cf. p. 253 and above, chapter IX, pp. 87-88.

[120] *Ibid.*, p. 444.

[121] *Ibid.*, pp. 432-444.

[122] *Ibid.*, pp. 434-436.

[123] *Ibid.*, pp. 436-438.

[124] Cf. *ibid.*, p. 428 ff. For the reborn not being able to sin the writer appeals to I John 3:9.

[125] *Ibid.*, pp. 438-441. Perhaps Dirk was thinking about Joos Verbeek, martyred on June 21, 1561, and Joachim the Sugarbaker, who lay in prison in Cleve and whose desertion was not yet known; perhaps also about the brothers and sisters in Utrecht who had been captured.

[126] *Ibid.*, pp. 441-443.

[127] *Ibid.*, p. 459; see above, pp. 111-112.

[128] *Ibid.*, p. 444. Would his travel companion perhaps have been Hans Sikken, who also accompanied Dirk Philips in 1567 and who was known to the writer of the "Beginsel der Scheuringen?" BRN VII, p. 542.

[129] Cf. p. 250 ff. (Psalm 79:1-3) = p. 439; p. 252 (be peacemakers) = p. 443; p. 253

(Guard against the rash and bragging spirits) = p. 435 ff.; p. 263 (2 Peter 2:22) = p. 435; p. 357 (the Balaamites) = p. 440; p. 368 (the golden calves) = p. 440.

[130] D. B., 1893, p. 1.

[131] BRN X, p. 444, cf. 2 Cor. 7:5.

[132] *Ibid.*, p. 605. During the Frisian-Flemish struggle Leenaert wrote a letter to Danzig to Dirk's opposition in which he complained: "The spirit which brought sorrow to Joseph in the well and to me in Emden still reigns here." J. O. *Verclaringhe*, § 305, 306.

[133] K. Vos, *Dooplijst van L. B.*, pp. 51, 55.

[134] See chapter VIII, pp. 58-59, and my article in MQR, October, 1954. Perhaps the name *Enchiridion* was chosen by Dirk with Erasmus' book in mind, the *Enchiridion oder handbüchlein*, printed in 1518 by J. Froben in Basel.

[135] The first one who did this for the whole Bible was Nic. Biestkens in his Bible of 1560.

[136] BRN X, p. 469 [trans. from WDP, p. 440].

[137] Amsterdam, 1919, p. 95.

Chapter XI

[1] The second letter, BRN X, pp. 432-444, esp. p. 432 ff.

[2] *Ibid.*, p. 433.

[3] J. G. de Hoop Scheffer, "Het verbond der vier steden," *Doopsg. Bijdragen*, 1893, pp. 1-90; F. Pijper, BRN X, pp. 36-43, 511-516, 537-543, 585-587; W. J. Kühler, *Geschiedenis der Nederlandsche Doopsgezinden*, Dl. I, Haarlem, 1932, pp. 395-435.

[4] *Ibid.*, p. 399, note 4.

[5] The figures from K. Vos, "De Vriesch-Vlaamsche twisten," *De Zondagsbode*, August 16 and 23, 1914, esp. p. 171, note 6.

[6] J. O[uterman], *Onder verbeteringhe. Verclaringhe met bewijs / wt den droevighen handel / van Vr. ende Vlam.*, 1609, § 304.

[7] *Ibid.*, § 303, 306.

[8] *Ibid.*, § 12.

[9] *Ibid.*

[10] *Verclaringhe*, § 12. "Many ministers from Holland and Friesland surrendered the matter to the previously mentioned ministers."

[11] M.E., vol. II, p. 824; BRN X, p. 602.

[12] M.E., vol. II, p. 135; BRN X, p. 604. Perhaps other ministers from Harlingen were present, for example Jacob Feeriks.

[13] BRN X, p. 604. About the dull-headedness of Ebbe Pieters Dirk wrote, *ibid.*, "the less he says the better, for his word has no power." About Ebbe's attitude, see also J.O., *Verclaringhe*, § 12.

[14] BRN VII, p. 533. The baptism list of Leenaert Bouwens reports no baptisms

between 1565 and 1568. K. Vos, in *Bijdragen en Mededelingen van het Historisch Genootschap*, Dl XXXVI, pp. 36-39.

[15] BRN X, pp. 530-534 (following the "Epistle to Four Cities").

[16] BRN X, p. 32, note 5.

[17] Printed in the *Enchiridion, ibid.,* pp. 205-248.

[18] Kühler, I, p. 408, assumes that Dirk returned to Danzig immediately after the controversy with L. B. and then later made the difficult trip to Franeker once again. I believe with K. Vos that Dirk remained for some time in Emden to restore peace in the congregation. K. Vos, "De Vriesch-Vlaamsche twisten," op. cit., p. 166b and "Een bisschop in Appingedam." Reprint from the *Gron. Volksalmanak*, 1916, p. 15.

[19] J. O. *Verclaringhe*, § 12. Ebbe complained that "the fountain had been stopped, but he considered Leenaert Bouwens to be his beloved brother and minister."

[20] BRN VII, p. 534.

[21] *Ibid.*, p. 533 ff.: [Syvaert Pieters], "Corte aenwijsinghe / voorgestelt in eenighe Vraghen / vande voornaemste mishandelinghen der Vlamingen ende Vriesen" Hoorn, 1624, p. 14. I used the copy of the Doopsg. bibliotheek in Hamburg-Altona.

[22] J. O. *Verclaringhe*, § 14. In my opinion Leenaert did not accept the invitation but returned to Emden when he heard that Dirk would come to Franeker.

[23] BRN VII, p. 534 ff.

[24] Kühler, I, op. cit., p. 403.

[25] [Syvaert Pieters] = Corte aenwijsinghe," p. 3.

[26] De Hoop Scheffer, op. cit., p. 11, note 1; BRN VII, p. 537.

[27] M.E., vol. III, p. 844.

[28] M.E., vol. I, p. 485 and vol. II, p. 648 ff.; K. Vos, *Menno Simons*, Leiden, 1914, p. 145 ff.

[29] The names of the four ministers are in J.O. *Verclaringhe*, § 17. That only four ministers were called, instead of seven, as was normal in "difficult cases," shows in my opinion that they did not consider the conflict to have been serious.

[30] J. O., *Verclaringhe*, § 17 and 21. On this occasion Dirk made peace with the Harlingen ministers about the suspension of Leenaert, BRN X, p. 604.

[31] The detailed account concerning this covenant by [Syvaert Pieters], *Corte aenwijsinghe*, p. 3 ff. K. Vos, *Zondagsbode*, Aug. 23, 1914, p. 170, assumes that the covenant was already established in 1557 as a consequence of the Harlingen assembly. De Hoop Scheffer, op. cit., p. 1 says, "around the year 1560"; Pijper, BRN X, p. 37 and Kühler, op. cit., p. 397, accept this dating.

[32] De Hoop Scheffer, op. cit., p. 3 ff., reconstructed the most important articles from J.O., *Verclaringhe*, § 30 and [Syvaert Pieters], loc. cit.

[33] The charge against Ebbe Pieters was that although he had been chosen, he did not accept the office of elder. He excused himself on the grounds that he first wanted to visit the congregations with Dirk and Leenaert in the hope that God would confer on him a greater boldness, [Syvaert Pieters], *Corte aenwijsinghe*, p. 14. The members were satisfied with that, J. O. *Verclaringhe*, § 12 and 13. For Dirk Philips' thoughts, BRN X, p. 604. See also, K. Vos, *Zondagsbode*, Aug. 23, 1914, p. 170b.

[34] J.O., *Verclaringhe*, § 31. Later the Frisians discontinued the support because

the Flemish denounced the covenant, [Syvaert Pieters], *Cort aenwijsinghe*, p. 18 ff.

[35] De Hoop Scheffer, op. cit., p. 1

[36] Op. cit., p. 4.

[37] *Verclaringhe*, § 17.

[38] Besides, in a different part of Friesland, with Bolsward as the center, the "Zuiderhoekse" (South corner) ordinance existed. J. O. *Verclaringhe*, § 139, § 124, and Kühler I, op. cit., p. 398 ff.

[39] J. O. *Verclaringhe*, § 17 and § 313. Outerman quoted the testimony of Hertman Sijbrants who had learned this saying from Dirk Philips from nonpartisan ("middelmatiche") brothers of Harlingen. Pijper passed over these references in silence; apparently he attached no value to them.

[40] [Syvaert Pieters], *Corte aenwysinghe*, p. 7; J. O., *Verclaringhe*, § 21, 37.

[41] See for this, De Hoop Scheffer, op. cit., pp. 16-36; Kühler I, op. cit., pp. 408-412; Pijper, BRN X, pp. 39 ff., 511-514.

[42] "The Frisians sometimes looked at the Covenant as God's Word. They declared, 'What ministers and teachers ordain is proven to be scriptural, and one must therefore discipline those who rebel against it.'" J. O. *Verclaringhe*, § 28. The Frisians in the Bishopric ['t Sticht] claimed, "The Covenant is so divine, that what teachers and ministers have ordained and instituted is equal to Holy Scripture, so that all those who oppose it must be disciplined as 'trouble makers.'" [Syvaert Pieters], *Corte aenwijsinghe*, p. 19. The Flemish at first tolerated the observance of the Covenant, but later they compared it to a human ordinance. J. O. *Verclaringhe*, § 29.

[43] Op. cit., I, p. 408.

[44] [Syvaert Pieters], *Corte aenwijsinghe*, p. 28.

[45] *Ibid.*, p. 19 ff.

[46] Op. cit. I, p. 401, note 2.

[47] J. O., *Verclaringhe*, § 54.

[48] De Hoop Scheffer, op. cit., p. 35, see also note 4.

[49] [Syvaert Pieters], *Corte aenwijsinghe*, p. 20 ff.; De Hoop Scheffer, op. cit., p. 36, note 3.

[50] BRN X, pp. 521-529; the letter, with a preface, was published in 1567. Pijper made an error on p. 40. The signature D.P.V.B.I.H. signifies "Dirk Philips Uwe Broeder im Heeren" [Dirk Philips Your Brother in the Lord].

[51] De Hoop Scheffer, op cit., p. 36 ff. The admonition for peace was worded so generally that it clearly shows how little he had yet heard of the details of the dispute.

[52] BRN X, p. 522. This offer was repeated at the end, p. 528 ff.

[53] *Ibid.*, p. 523.

[54] The title of the letters in *ibid.*, p. 517.

[55] Kühler I, p. 413. In my opinion, what Kühler concluded further from the letter, however, missed the point. The battle with the Amelekites was quoted (Exod. 17:11) in the letter, op. cit., p. 522; on the other hand in "A Short...Account" op. cit., p. 567, Dirk alluded to I Sam. 15 where Saul spared Agag and the valuable possessions of the Amelekites. The comparison is not sufficiently developed to warrant drawing a

parallel with "the business in Friesland." In the letter, op. cit., p. 522, Dirk names various examples of turmoil among the Israelites, among others the making of the golden calf, without hinting at the Covenant of the four cities. But in "A Short...Account", op. cit., p. 560 ff., the Covenant was indeed compared to the golden calf (Exod. 32, I Kings 12:28 ff.).

[56] BRN VII, p. 539 ff.

[57] Kühler I, op. cit., p. 414.

[58] Hendrik van Arnhem, elder in Antwerp, M.E., vol. II, p. 699a. See also De Hoop Scheffer, op. cit., p. 31, note 1 and K. Vos, *Menno Simons*, p. 146.

[59] Jan Willems, 1533-1588, M.E., vol. III, p. 85 ff., chosen elder in Hoorn in 1557 and ordained by Dirk Philips. Lubbert Gerrits was born in Amersfoort in 1534, fled to Hoorn in 1559 because of the persecution in his birth place, and in the same year became an elder and was ordained by Dirk Philips, M.E., vol. II, p. 505. See also De Hoop Scheffer, op. cit., p. 39, note 2, and Kühler I, op. cit., p. 396.

[60] M.E., vol. II, p. 519; Vos, *Menno Simons*, p. 146.

[61] These were called "Landsdienaren" [district ministers] and always dealt with important matters together, "just as was their custom and was recommended to them by Dirk Philips," J. O. *Verclaringhe*, § 196.

[62] J. O., *Verclaringhe*, § 192-197.

[63] I conclude this from the letter of Job Jansz., written on March 31, 1568 from prison in the Hague to Jan Willems and Lubbert Gerrits (*Urkundenbuch der Gemeinde Heubuden*, mss.) pp. 30-33, esp. p. 33: "You know well how you have acted and spoken at Amsterdam, why you were uncomfortable being judges. And when you received the letter in the assembly [congregation] (Hoyte's writing) your heart was changed. It made Hoyte proud in Bolsward, when he said, 'I can not make it clear to you but I can certainly make it clear to the men from Holland. See to it indeed how you are motivated.'"

[64] BRN X, p. 554; see also De Hoop Scheffer, op. cit., p. 37 ff.

[65] From this comes the name "The Compromise." The agreement is printed in BRN VII, p. 62 ff, with an improvement from the Emden Protocol by S. Cramer and De Hoop Scheffer, op. cit., p. 40 ff.

[66] For the names of the judges, see De Hoop Scheffer, op. cit., p. 39, note 1.

[67] The phrase "ende sy en hebben niet daer af gehouden" means "they did not stick with it," i.e., "keep their promise." BRN X, pp. 564 and 603. Job Jansz. comments, op. cit., p. 32, "For although we submitted to the Compromise, we gave it [no] further [authority] than so far as one judges according to God's Word. We would have complied on behalf of peace, although that is not clear in the Compromise. One nevertheless ought to follow only God's Word." See also J. O. *Verclarighe*, § 199.

[68] Already before the signing of the Compromise the Frisians had objected to giving an account, in the presence of the opposite party, of the ban pronounced over the Flemish. Hoyte also refused to meet this requirement. De Hoop Scheffer, op. cit., p. 38 ff.

[69] J. O. *Verclaringhe*. § 200.

[70] *Ibid.*, § 210-213, 232.

Notes to pages 122-124

[71] Kühler I, op. cit., p. 415 ff.

[72] J. O., *Verclaringhe*, § 215; Gillis Schrijver signed the Compromise, BRN VII, p. 264, and was one of the twelve judges, but later recanted everything, De Hoop Scheffer, op. cit., p. 39, note 1, pp. 44, 51. See also, BRN X, p. 565.

[73] The date is from De Hoop Scheffer, op. cit., p. 44, note 3.

[74] [Carel van Ghendt] gives a detailed description of it, BRN VII, p. 540 ff.

[75] J. O., *Verclaringhe*, § 216.

[76] BRN VII, p. 540.

[77] Perhaps they had received "instructions" beforehand, *ibid*.

[78] *Ibid*., p. 540 ff.

[79] Only a few met the requirement. Among them was Job Jansz., the (later) martyr, BRN VII, p. 541 ff. In the letter quoted above he wrote (p. 31): "I have confessed my guilt with your knowledge ... I did it on behalf of peace," and p. 32: "Now since it is not directed according to God's Word, but according to the Compromise, I can no longer stay with you." If "you asked the Lord in the highest, he would attribute injustice to your act."

[80] See note 63.

[81] Once again it is Job Jansz. who sheds some light on this, op. cit., p. 33: "I know for certain that you were influenced by the Frisians, as they influenced Leenaert Bouwens. I feel sorry for you in my heart that you were so deceived. For you were driven by them just as foam is driven by wind on water." See also, *Bespreck binnen Hoorn tusschen Jan Lues van die Vlaemsche mennichte ende Peter Jansen Twisk van die Oude Vriesen*, 1622 [Mss. in the Archief der Doopsg. gemeente te Amsterdam, Inventaris, Dl. I, no. 558, 1]. Especially § 58, "With such pronouncements, they [the Frisian ministers] confirmed all of Hoyte's unjust judgments which were laid on the Flemish, to call them apostates, as Hoyte Renix acknowledged in the letter written to Dirk Philips on April 17, 1567." This statement is not present in the fragment of the letter known to us.

[82] I, op. cit., pp. 408, 411.

[83] Op. cit., pp. 18, 68.

[84] BRN VII, p. 542.

[85] Dirk Philips accused them, BRN X, p. 565, "They have broken bread here and there, but we cannot say it was the Lord's bread."

[86] For example, Jacob de Roore (Candlemaker), J. O., *Verclaringhe*, § 359. An extract of his 12th letter in P. V[er] K[indert], *Brief, Dienende om te bewijsen, dat niemand in een ander behoort te straffen een Daedt, die hy aen hem selven, ofte aen den sijnen, pooght te verschoonen*, Haarlem, 1634, p. 24 ff.; M.E., vol. II, p. 62 ff.

[87] BRN VII, p. 542.

[88] Dirk Philips mentions several statements in the "A Short but Fundamental Account," BRN X, p. 555.

[89] Jeroen had said already at the time of the dispute with Ebbe Pieters, "there must first be a Timothy, that is, a minister present." See [Syvaert Pieters], *Corte aenwijsinghe*, p. 10. Also Rosevelt made the proposal to ask Dirk Philips. See De

Hoop Scheffer. op. cit., p. 26 ff.

[90] BRN X, p. 553. The last words were not noticed by De Hoop Scheffer, op. cit., p. 34, note 1. Therefore he related Hoyte's negative answer with the earlier proposal of Rosevelt, op. cit., p. 26, note 4.

[91] BRN X, p. 552 ff.; Dirk says this can be proven.

[92] The letter is printed in *Corte aenwijsinghe* (Syvaert Pieters), p. 21 ff. by De Hoop Scheffer, op. cit., p. 53 and by Kühler I, p. 420. The date is in *Bespreck binnen Hoorn*, 1622, § 58.

[93] Letter from Dirk Philips to Hoyte Renix of June 7, 1567, in *Urkundenbuch der Gemeinde Heubuden*, pp. 20-25, on p. 21 (Appendix II). See also BRN X, p. 573 and *Bespreck binnen Hoorn*, 1622, § 48.

[94] [Syvaert Pieters], op. cit., p. 23.

[95] M.E., vol. II, p. 651. He was already present in Wüstenfeld in April, 1556, at the meeting with the Upper Germans. He sent a letter from the Netherlands to the elder Steven Vader in Danzig and conveyed greetings from D.P. [Carel van Ghendt] knew Hans Sikken, BRN VII, p. 542.

[96] G. H. Mannhardt, *De Danziger Mennonitengemeinde, ihre Entstehung und ihre Geschichte von 1569-1919*, p. 43.

[97] J. O. *Verclaringhe*, § 90. According to the same source, § 262, the letter was transmitted by several messengers, who had to explain the Frisian position.

[98] BRN X, p. 550.

[99] Letter to Hoyte Renix, op. cit., p. 21. Dirk Philips had already written extensively about God's covenant in the third letter, BRN X, pp. 451-457.

[100] BRN X, p. 572.

[101] See above, pp. 118-119.

[102] K. Vos, in *Zondagsbode*, Aug. 16, 1914, p. 167b; concerning the Covenant, D.P. "spun around like a top." Kühler, op. cit., p. 413 ff.; "D. P. changed fronts in bewilderment; it was an unprincipled about face."

[103] See above, note 30.

[104] J. O., *Verclaringhe*, § 18.

[105] *Zondagsbode*, Dec. 6, 1925, p. 55 ff. and *Gesch. der Nederl. Doopsgezinden* I, pp. 399, 408, 413 ff.

[106] Kühler I, op. cit., p. 402.

[107] *Ibid.*, p. 414, see above p. 125.

[108] De Hoop Scheffer, op. cit., p. 55 ff.

[109] BRN X, p. 554, "They made the two youngest ministers judges, who certainly at their age would not have had any difficult assignments before."

[110] BRN X, p. 554 ff.: "But they did not do that because they were not trustworthy and did not keep their promise." Did D. P. mean that the judges had promised to ask him? This is not known from any other source. See also, De Hoop Scheffer, op. cit., p. 39, note 1.

[111] Letter to Hoyte Renix. Dirk was prepared to reply to it.

[112] In the only part of Hoyte's letter (April 17, 1567) that is known, this prehistory

is missing. See also De Hoop Scheffer, op. cit., p. 55, note 1.

[113] The entire issue was treated in *Bespreck binnen Hoorn*, 1622, § 29-33; the quotation is § 33. See also De Hoop Scheffer, op cit., p. 55, note 2.

[114] *Bespreck binnen Hoorn*, 1622, § 29 and BRN X, p. 553 ff.

[115] The printed letters in BRN X, p. 692, are only fragments. See also BRN X, p. 554, note 2.

[116] BRN X, p. 550.

[117] BRN X, p. 569: "We have always desired, according to God's Word and our commission from our congregation, that the quarreling parties might come together." BRN X, p. 572, "we did not come to judge, but to make peace, in as much as was possible by the Lord's grace." [Syvaert Pieters], op. cit., p. 22 ff. wrote in the same spirit, probably supported by these statements. What De Hoop Scheffer, op. cit., p. 54 and Kühler, op. cit., p. 420 ff. wrote about Dirk Philips' charge are statements without any proof.

[118] BRN X, p. 540. Kühler generally neglected Pijper's explanations, which certainly deserve our attention.

[119] *Ibid.*, p. 56.

[120] K. Vos, *Menno Simons*, p. 329; idem., *Zondagsbode*, Aug. 16, 1914, p. 167a. Kühler, op. cit., p. 421; De Hoop Scheffer already alluded to it, op. cit., p. 60, note 3.

[121] BRN X, pp. 444, 459 at the end of the 2nd and 3rd epistle; p. 483 in the Preface to the Refutation, probably written in Emden; p. 549, in the Christian greeting for the "A Short but Fundamental Account."

[122] H. Reimers, *Ostfriesland bis zum Aussterben seines Fürstenhauses*, Bremen, 1925, p. 166. In the beginning of the sixties of the 16th century the grain business with Danzig was temporarily displaced from Amsterdam to Emden.

[123] BRN X, p. 570.

[124] I follow Kühler's description here, op. cit., p. 421, but I would deny that Dirk had anything to do with it. His name is nowhere mentioned in the sources.

[125] See above, p. 116 ff.

[126] J. O., *Verclaringhe*, § 306.

[127] *Ibid.*, § 309.

[128] *Ibid.*, § 310: "The ones in Emden began to side with the Flemish." See also Kühler, op. cit., p. 421, note 1.

[129] J. O., *Verclaringhe*, § 311.

[130] *Ibid.*, § 310.

[131] Later Dirk was accused by the Frisians of not shunning the banned Flemish. See [Syvaert Pieters], op. cit., pp. 26 ff. and 68 and and the yet to be mentioned letter to the congregation in Groningen of July 12, 1567, BRN X, p. 586.

[132] [Syvaert Pieters], op. cit., p. 22, says that this was his right; also that Hoyte and his party were obligated "concerning these actions and judgments to give account to their opponents." See also J. O., *Verclaringhe*, § 344.

[133] It is too bad that Dirk did not indicate Bible texts. I suspect that he would mention proofs such as Deut 17:8; 19:15-21; further Acts 22-25 (the trial of the

Apostle Paul), and above all, Acts 25:16. Thus he acted indirectly according to Roman law.

[134] BRN X, pp. 569-571; further pp. 550 ff., 556 ff., 565, 593 ff., 601, 608.

[135] *Bespreck binnen Hoorn*, 1622, § 26.

[136] *Ibid.*, § 26 mentions four letters which have been lost. The two letters which are reprinted in BRN X, p. 692 and p. 690 ff. (June 30, 1567), respectively p. 692 ff., the 5th and 6th letter are mentioned, *Ibid.*, § 28. De Hoop Scheffer, op cit., p. 56, suspects that the accusation that Jan Willems was a liar was already present isted in the first letter. See also BRN X, p. 554.

[137] BRN X, p. 671.

[138] See p. 124-125, note 1. According to the "Urkundenbuch," p. 25 this letter was written on June 7, 1567; in the *Bespreck binnen Hoorn*, § 48, June 8 is given.

[139] Kühler, op. cit., p. 420. [Syvaert Pieters], op. cit., p. 21, condemned these threats; likewise J. O., *Verclaringhe*, § 264, 265.

[140] This part of the letter, unknown until now, is printed in BRN X, p. 689 ff.

[141] [Syvaert Pieters], op. cit., p. 22 ff.; J. O., *Verclaringhe*, § 264. The letter from Hoyte Renix "proves after all that [the Frisians] were not inclined to try to win over their opponents to their cause in the presence of Dirk Philips."

[142] J. O., *Verclaringhe*, § 265. Dirk Philips wrote in the "A Short but Fundamental Account," BRN X, p. 573: "If we had wanted to accept the human Covenant, the Compromise and Judgment, 'we would have been the dearest friends.'"

[143] *Verclaringhe*, § 266: "D. P. had not underestimated the excesses of Hoyte's actions, consequently he ordered him to stop his activities not just in the form of advice, but on pain of punishment." Also Pijper, BRN X, p. 41 ff., admits that these letters "would have done little to calm the emotions. Rather they threw oil on the fire."

[144] BRN X, p. 550; with almost the same words in the "Appendix," *ibid.*, p. 593.

[145] P.V.K. Brief, *Dienende om te bewijzen*, pp. 23 and 44; see also, De Hoop Scheffer, op. cit., p. 75.

[146] This is the general opinion of the second generation. P.V.K., op. cit., pp. 21, 23, 44: D. P. "in his own name banned the fellow ministers without the congregation." Likewise, [Syvaert Pieters], op. cit., p. 13, J. O., *Verclaringhe*, § 269, 273, 274, 347. Pijper tried to defend Dirk's position, BRN X, p. 671 ff. He emphasized the conditional aspect of the suspension and asserted that Dirk acted according to the charge he had received from his congregation. This cannot be proven. Pijper does not address the conditional ban (the withdrawal of brotherhood).

[147] J. O., *Verclaringhe*, § 270, who also notes "but we do not believe that he would have been free from guilt when he wrote such a threat to Dirk Philips; that is not our understanding."

[148] *Ibid.*, § 271.

[149] Printed from P.V.K., op. cit., § 21, by Pijper, BRN X, p. 691 ff.; also in De Hoop Scheffer, op. cit., p. 58 ff.

[150] Somewhat later Dirk wrote, BRN X, p. 567: "Indeed we regret that we ordained the two H[olland] M[en] into the ministry."

[151] J. O., *Verclaringhe*, § 271 and 272; BRN X, p. 569 ff.

[152] When it speaks of Frisians in this connection, it means a delegation from Friesland.

[153] BRN X, p. 569.

[154] Dirk made this proposal "so that our meeting and discussion might not therefore be detained." BRN X, p. 570.

[155] BRN X, p. 569.

[156] BRN X, p. 690 ff. and 692 ff.

[157] [Syvaert Pieters], op. cit., p. 23.

[158] De Hoop Scheffer, op. cit., p. 61, note 1.

[159] Thijs Joriaensz. from Rarop = Ransdorp, N[orth] H[olland], the later martyr (see M.E., vol. IV, p. 712 ff.) wrote a letter on July 10, 1567 to J. W. and L. G. See *Urkundenbuch der Gemeinde Heubuden*, pp. 25-30. The quoted gibes are also in, *Bespreck binnen Hoorn*, 1622, § 77 and 78. The letter from Thijs Joriaenez.is printed in *Twee Brieven, den eenen van Thijs Joriaens ... ende den ander van Job Jansen*, printed in the Year of our Lord, Anno 1609, no place. Available in the Bibl. der Doopsg. Gemeente te Amsterdam. But only A 1-8 remain; the rest is missing. Also missing is the important letter of Job Jansz., which fortunately was kept in the *Urkundenbuch*. See note 63.

[160] *Ibid.*, p. 26.

[161] *Ibid.*, p. 27. This is the opinion of a contemporary.

[162] [Syvaert Pieters], op. cit., p. 23. *Ibid.*, in J. O., *Verclaringhe*, § 276, 283.

[163] It seems improbable to me that Hoyte Renix was delegated by the assembly of the North Holland congregations, as De Hoop Scheffer, op. cit., p. 63, assumes. He probably joined the delegation in Friesland, as did the other Frisians, Egbert Kuiper and Jacob Freeriks of Harlingen. See de Hoop Scheffer, op. cit., p. 65, and BRN X, p. 607.

[164] [Syvaert Pieters], op. cit., p. 23, "as if it had been decided by a worldly court of seven sheriffs." For the date, see de Hoop Scheffer, op. cit., p. 63, note 3.

[165] The entire statement is printed by De Hoop Scheffer, op. cit., p. 66 ff., from J. O., *Verclaringhe*, § 285 and 343.

[166] *Urkundenbuch*, op. cit., p. 27. In a letter from Thijs Joriaensz. of July 10, 1567, he says, "you replied to the man from the Danzig congregation without authority," and p. 28, "you answered Dirk Philips in the name of all the congregations: and that without the power or word from all the congregations. So it is presumptuous, that you used the names of the ministers of the congregations, and did not have the power and truth of the congregations."

[167] J. O., *Verclaringhe*, § 276, 283, printed by De Hoop Scheffer, op. cit., p. 63, note 1. *Ibid.*, § 286: "As was shown before, the Dutch and Frisian men had not met with their congregations to say farewell to Dirk Ph, as they themselves acknowledged in the 't Sticht, but they decided with an inappropriate authority." Several congregations from the Oversticht (now Overijssel) tried to bring about a reconciliation. [Syvaert Pieters], op. cit., p. 23 has the same information.

[168] Even Kühler I, op. cit., p. 424, had to acknowledge this.
[169] J. O., *Verclaringhe*, § 277.
[170] BRN X, p. 569.
[171] J. O., *Verclaringhe*, § 277, 287.
[172] Especially *ibid.*, § 286. Outerman discovered that the Dutch elders misused their authority by transferring an authority which they had not received from their congregations to their messengers. The date is from De Hoop Scheffer, op. cit., p. 63, note 3.
[173] J. O., *Verclaringhe*, § 287.
[174] *Ibid.*, § 278. There is no doubt that this signified the ban. The following paragraph begins, "When word of the banning of Dirk Ph. got around..." See also § 287: Dirk Philips "said to some of their messengers, 'If their men would not reply in the presence of the parties they could go,' which accords with the words of Hans Sickes when he said that he would not accept the message of Dirk Philips' dismissal any further than coming from an apostate."
[175] De Hoop Scheffer, op. cit., p. 65 ff. and p. 66, note 1; Kühler, I, op. cit., p. 424.
[176] *Zondagsbode*, Aug. 16, 1914, p. 167a.
[177] "Een bisschop te Appingedam," *Gron. Volksalmanak*, 1916, reprint, p. 16.
[178] J. O. *Verclaringhe*, § 278, 287.
[179] De Hoop Scheffer, op. cit., p. 67 and p. 63, note. 3.
[180] Dirk Philips argued in the same way, BRN X, p. 572: "They wanted to judge us and thereby they have judged themselves." See also, p. 571 below and p. 572 above. He therefore took them to be apostate. *Ibid.*, and p. 573 ff., he calls them "audacious, boasters, haughty spirits," p. 576 ff.
[181] J. O., *Verclaringhe*, § 285, 343.
[182] BRN X, pp. 545-581; De Hoop Scheffer, op. cit., p. 69, places it later. Pijper does not say what the date of appearance was. He only placed the "Appendix" after the sentence of the ban and after the epistle to Groningen, op. cit., p. 586.
[183] See note 177.
[184] BRN X, p. 580. His haste is obvious from the many repetitions and germanisms.
[185] BRN X, p. 571 below to p. 587; also p. 566, r. 12 ff., vo were inserted later.
[186] *Ibid.*, pp. 552-557.
[187] *Ibid.*, p. 565 ff. This refers to the banning of the Flemish who rejected the Compromise, although they had signed it; perhaps also to the ban pronounced over the Flemish at Harlingen and Franeker by Hoyte Renix.
[188] *Ibid.*, p. 556 ff.
[189] *Ibid.*, p. 451 ff. (in the third letter) and p. 523 ff. (in the letter to the four cities). Now, *ibid.*, pp. 557-561.
[190] On covenant theology, see M.E., vol. I, pp. 726a-727a, and also the literature. G. Schrenck's article, R.G.G.^{2}, Bd. I, Sp. 1364-1367, shows how the concept of "covenant" played a large role for the first Anabaptists, but was misused by the revolutionary Anabaptists. Anabaptist opponents, Zwingli and Bullinger, used it as a weapon. Bullinger in particular developed a doctrine of the covenant: *De testamento*

seu foedere Dei unico et aeterno. Later also in the "Hausbuch" (Walter Hollweg, *Beiträge zur Gesh. u. Lehre der Reform. Kirche,* Bd. VIII, Neukirchen, 1956). Dutch translation: *Huysboec,* Emden, 1563, fol. 105, 4-106, 2, "Van den verbonde Gods ende der menschen." But the "covenant" in Pilgram Marbeck is also important (Jan J. Kiwiet, *Pilgram Marbeck, sein Kreis und seine Theologie,* Kassel, 1957, pp. 84-148.) What influence it may have exercised on Dirk I cannot say. For the Bullinger citations I thank Dr. Joachim Staedtke of Zurich.

[191] *Ibid.,* pp. 361. Dirk rejected the accusation that in an earlier letter to the four cities he had praised the human covenant and recognized it as a good ordinance. He said that in his *writings* he only spoke about the divine covenant and not about the human one. But how does that square with the extract from Dirk, quoted above (p. 119) from J. O., *Verclaringhe?* Apparently he had forgotten it or did not want to be reminded of it.

[192] *Ibid.,* pp. 561-564. especially p. 561.

[193] *Ibid.,* p. 564, see also above pp. 121-122.

[194] *Ibid.,* pp. 563, 572 ff.

[195] *Ibid.,* pp. 564-568.

[196] *Ibid.,* pp. 568-575.

[197] *Ibid.,* pp. 575-581.

[198] *Ibid.,* p. 596. Dirk wrote, "a more horribly scandalous letter we have never seen nor read in all our days, not to mention the other scandalous letters about us."

[199] "Bespreck binnen Hoorn," op. cit., § 59, 64-68. These paragraphs were printed by Pijper, BRN X, p. 586.

[200] [Syvaert Pieters], op. cit., p. 26 in the margin: "Read Hoyte R., Letter and Statement about D. P." and further, p. 27, "And he boasted that primarily because of this [not shunning the banned Flemish] Dirk Philipsz. and several others from Groningen-land were separated from the church of God."

[201] They were, among others, Gillis Schrijver, Hendrik van Rosevelt, and Jacob Jansz. See De Hoop Scheffer, op. cit., pp. 49, 51.

[202] Dirk Philips defended them in the "Appendix," BRN X, p. 603. H. R. with his adherents "so horribly portrayed, depicted, and described [them] in his letter that it is too inhuman and scandalous to repeat or write about."

[203] De Hoop Scheffer, op. cit., p. 66 ff. See also, BRN X, p. 573: "After that they scolded us for being trouble makers, disturbers of the peace, and destructive of God's church."

[204] [Syvaert Pieters], op. cit., p. 26 ff. Hoyte Renix in his epistle called Dirk Philips a blasphemer against God's holy sacraments and ceremonies because he "[will] not shun his named apostates," and p. 68: "because he [will] not shun all his separated ones on account of the dispute." Syvaert Pieters probably quoted here from the "epistle."

[205] BRN X, p. 593.

[206] *Ibid.,* p. 593 ff. This sequel to the dispute was only noted by Pijper (*ibid.,* p. 586 ff.) and not by de Hoop Scheffer or Kühler.

[207] *Ibid.*, pp. 589-613.
[208] *Ibid.*, p. 594.
[209] *Ibid.*, pp. 595, 610.
[210] *Ibid.*, 601, 610.
[211] *Ibid.*, pp. 593-601.
[212] *Ibid.*, p. 608.
[213] *Ibid.*, p. 606 ff.
[214] *Ibid.*, p. 547.
[215] This probably was the case with Job Jansz. He wrote (*Urkundenbuch*, p. 32), "I cannot blame the members who did not keep the Compromise ... although, because you have so defamed the members in your horrible epistle, I am so tormented on account of it that I am scarcely a person." On the basis of the epistle he was taken prisoner and tortured.
[216] The comments about the first trial against Leenaert Bouwens were already quoted above, p. 115 ff.
[217] BRN X, p. 553; see also De Hoop Scheffer, op. cit., p. 27, note 2; p. 33, notes 1 and 2, and p. 37 ff.
[218] BRN X, p. 602.
[219] *Ibid.* Dirk asked for information from Hoyte's brother.
[220] *Ibid.*, p. 608.
[221] See chapter X.
[222] BRN X, p. 604 ff.
[223] J. O., *Verclaringhe*, § 343, also § 281.
[224] See above, pp. 121-122.
[225] BRN X, p. 595. The Frisians "pretended that it was unreasonable to deal with the apostates."
[226] *Ibid.*, p. 593, "we have not doubted even once as to whether we are right"; p. 600, "By God's grace we are sure of our cause."
[227] *Ibid.*, p. 580.
[228] *Ibid.*, p. 608.
[229] *Ibid.*, pp. 605, 611.
[230] *Ibid.*, p. 611.
[231] *Ibid.*, p. 592.
[232] *Ibid.*
[233] *Ibid.*, p. 599.
[234] *Ibid.*, p. 580.
[235] J. O., *Verclaringhe*, § 265, 286, 287, 343, 344; [Syvaert Pieters, *Corte aenwijsinghe*, pp. 13, 21-24; P. V. K., *Brief dienende om te bewijsen*, p. 21 ff., 44. I summarize: The Frisians threatened Dirk Philips and wanted to force him to accept the Harlingen sentence without investigation. Later they banned him without authority from their congregations and without Dirk's congregation knowing about it. For his part, Dirk placed Hoyte Renix and the Dutch judges under a conditional ban without being empowered to do it by the Danzig congregation and without appearing

before the congregations of the Frisians as an accuser.

²³⁶ At the conferences of the Waterlanders in Emden (Jan. 17, 1568) such rules were established. D. B., 1877, pp. 69-73. Whoever compares himself to another will appear in a favourable light.

²³⁷ Pijper defends Dirk Philips' position and makes the case that he could not have acted otherwise. But he also admits that his behavior in the dispute was not admirable. BRN X, pp. 537-543.

²³⁸ De Hoop Scheffer has written extensively about it, op. cit., pp. 69-90.

²³⁹ BRN VII, p. 544 ff.

Chapter XII

¹ BRN X, p. 573.
² *Ibid.*, p. 580.
³ *Ibid.*, pp. 593, 595.
⁴ *Ibid.*, pp. 483, 549, 627, 647, 649. Premonitions of his approaching death: *ibid.*, pp. 444, 459; "Remonstrance de l'excommunication," pp. 155, 156, 169 (Appendix III).
⁵ Several Latin words were adopted in part from Sebastian Franck. Pijper sums them up: BRN X, p. 5, note 6. As a supplement: *ibid.*, p. 332, *propositum*; p. 489, *gradus, oppositum*; p. 494, *Joannes Baptista, Ibidem, forma*; p. 503: *in genere-in specie.* See p. 635: *causa et effectus*; p. 637, *proprietates*. For Latin words at the end of a treatise, pp. 134, 376, 414, 534.
⁶ From the Vulgate, p. 593, Isa. 30:15; p. 611, Zechariah 11:17. From the Latin translation of the N.T. by Erasmus (1530), "Remonstrance," p. 166, Matt. 19:9, *quicunque repudiauerit*, etc. BRN X, p. 558, I Tim. 1:5, *fide non simulata*. Dirk altered the text in connection with the preceding.
⁷ *Ibid.*, p. 571, "Audi alteram partem." Here "our L.B.M.S." (= Menno Simons) was called "of good memory" [onse L.B.M.S. goeder gedacheniss]. Actually, "*Audiatur et altera pars*" (Seneca, *Medea*, 199), already in Augustine in a shorter form. *Ibid.*, p. 606, "*Obsequium amicos, veritas odium parit*," Terentius, *Andrias* I, 1, 41. "Remonstrance," p. 156, "*Fortissima omnium veritas*."
⁸ BRN X, p. 606; see K. Vos, *Menno Simons*, p. 328, and also BRN VII, p. 556, where this proverb is combined with the other ("*Obsequium amicos*" etc.) and is translated into Dutch.
⁹ BRN X, p. 607 ff., *Ars poetica Horatii*, v. 78: *Grammatici certant et adhuc sub judice lis est.*
¹⁰ K. Vos, *Menno Simons*, p. 328. Des. Erasmi. R. in *novum testamentum Annotationes*, Basileae, 1519, pp. 354, 486.
¹¹ *Biblia: Dat ys: De gantze Hillige Schrifft*. Verduedtschet dorch D. Marti. Luth. Gedruckt tho Magdeborch dorch Hans Walther. MDXLV. The publication was

overseen by Bugenhagen. At I Cor. 15:33 in the margin: *Menander poeta*, and at Titus 1 in the margin: *Epimenides*. Available in the Doopsges. Bibl., Amsterdam.

[12] Nic. Blesdikius, *Historia Davidis Georgii*. Dav., 1642, p. 6. *Erat hic (Theodoricus) graecae et latinae linguae peritus.*

[13] BRN X, p. 63. The Holy Spirit is the *Paracletus*; p. 138. That Word (in the Greek *Logos*, in Latin *Sermo* or *Verbum*), cf. Adam Pastor, BRN V, p. 530; BRN X, p. 503, the explanation of *Ecclesia* and *Ecclesiastes*; p. 648, *Paedobaptisten* or infant baptizers.

[14] *Ibid.*, p. 60, a God *Schadai*, that is an Almighty (Gen. 17:1), also pp. 270, 451, 557, 678. Further, p. 160, the name Lord is the tetragrammaton for the Jews.

[15] *Ibid.*, p. 571. According to Ludw[.] Koehler, *Lexicon in veteris testamenti libros*, Leiden, 1953, sp. 31 and 1037 *Achitophel* = my brother who does not speak intelligently. Dirk or his spokesman must have been thinking about a form of *naphal* = apostate, Sp. 625 a.

[16] See chapter VII, pp. 48-49 concerning the Flemish Anabaptist refugees at Emden. Laurens van der Leyen wrote on May 25, 1559, "grace and peace to all the brothers who live in Emden, especially to my two brothers and Tonijntgen, Lievens' wife," van Braght, fol. 262.

[17] In the hearing he explained that he had been baptized about a year and a half before in Friesland by Dirk Philips, an old man, along with six or seven persons. P. Génard, *Antwerpsch Archievenblad*, Dl. XII, p. 346 ff. and p. 369.

[18] *Ibid.*, p. 369, note 1. They also bound them with a cloth around the mouth; "these muzzles were terrible to behold and never before been seen in Antwerp."

[19] Nicolai only calls it the *banboeck* [Ban Book], BRN VII, p. 443 ff. It must have appeared already in 1567 for Nicolai, who died already in 1567 or 1568 (*Ibid.*, p. 271), quoted several sentences from it. That edition has been lost. I found the treatise in the French translation of the "Enchiridion or Manvël" where it was printed on pp. 153-169. See Appendix III [not reproduced here; for an English translation, see WDP, p. 590 ff.].

[20] "Enchiridion ou Manvël," pp. 155, 156, 169, 170.

[21] BRN X, p. 586.

[22] If the time period is correct, Dirk alludes to the ban on David Joris and his followers and to the dispute with Adam Pastor, Antonius van Cologne, and Hendrik van Vreden.

[23] See Chapter IX, pp. 87-91.

[24] Loc. cit., pp. 155, 156, 169.

[25] BRN X, pp. 249-265.

[26] *Ibid.*, p. 169.

[27] *Ibid.*, p. 157.

[28] *Ibid.*, 158.

[29] *Ibid.*, p. 159.

[30] Lev. 20:2-5; Ezra 2:8; Jer. 15:19 ff.

[31] *Ibid.*, pp. 159, 160.

Notes to pages 146-151

[32] BRN X, pp. 258, 400; see Chapter IX, pp. 88-91.
[33] Loc. cit., pp. 161, 162; see also BRN X, p. 660.
[34] BRN VII, p. 444.
[35] Loc. cit., p. 162. The image of the mangy sheep and of the strong and biting medicine is also in BRN X, p. 660.
[36] For the ban as a work of love in Menno, see Kühler I, pp. 239, 306, and Meihuizen, op. cit., p. 139 ff.
[37] Loc. cit., p. 163.
[38] *Ibid.*, pp. 163-169.
[39] Loc. cit. pp. 163, 164; see also, BRN X, p. 660 ff.
[40] Loc. cit., pp. 164, 165; see also BRN X, p. 661 ff.
[41] Loc. cit., p. 165; see also, BRN X, p. 662 ff.
[42] Loc. cit., pp. 165, 166; see also, BRN X, p. 663 above.
[43] Loc. cit., pp. 166, 167; see also, BRN X, p. 665 ff.
[44] Loc. cit., p. 167. In the "Omitted Writing about the [Evangelical) Ban and Avoidance" nothing is to be found that agrees with this.
[45] Loc. cit., pp.. 167-169; see also BRN X, p. 664 ff., only there everything is more aptly said.
[46] *Ibid.*, p. 169 ff.
[47] Chapter IX, p. 90. Pijper guesses that this is a result of the admonition of Herman Timmerman. BRN X, p. 654.
[48] Chapter IX, pp. 87-88.
[49] Appendix I, § 5 and Chapter VI, p. 44.
[50] Appendix I, §1 and 3, Chapter VI, p. 43.
[51] See above pp. 146-147.
[52] BRN X, p. 45 ff., 370 ff.
[53] *Ibid.*, p. 655; see also J. H. Wessel, *De leerstellige strijd etc.*, pp. 83, 339.
[54] Chapter IX, p. 84.
[55] BRN X, pp. 657-666. In French: "Enchiridion ou Manvël," 1626, pp. 171-176. *Autre petit traité touchant l'Excommunication.*
[56] Loc. cit., p. 171: *Le quel a esté trouvé à part en escriture à la main par Théodore Philippe.*
[57] Chapter IX, pp. 93-94. BRN X, p. 653, note 1. See also, Appendix IV, Bibliography I, no. 21. Something similar happened with Menno's "Reply to Zylis and Lemke" (D.B., 1905, p. 78).
[58] BRN X, p. 663.
[59] See above, pp. 147-148 and BRN X, p. 664 ff.
[60] BRN X, p. 665.
[61] BRN X, pp. 481-506.
[62] Chr. Sepp, *Bibliographische Mededelingen*, Leiden, 1883, pp. 183-187.
[63] Concerning de Zuttere (P.H.G. = Petrus Hyperphragmus Gandavensis = Pieter Overd'hage from Gent), see N.N. B.W., Dl IV, 1049 ff. Article by P. Bockmühl, and the literature there. Prof. B. Becker of Amsterdam drew my attention to this.

[64] Bruno Becker, "Nederlandsche vertalingen van Seb. Franck's geschriften," N.A.K.G. XXI, 1928, p. 153 ff., esp. p. 154, note 1.

[65] The letter to Campanus (Feb. 4, 1531) is printed (the Lower German and the High German text) by M. Krebs and H. G. Rott in *Quellen zur Gesch. der Täufer*, Bd. VII, 1959, pp. 302-325; see esp. p. 325: literature. See the important critical textual comments of Hegler-Koehler, *Beiträge zur Gesch. der Mystik*, Berlin, 1906, pp. 90-97. The letter to Campanus was translated into modern German by H. Fast in *Der linke Flügel der Reformation*, Bremen, 1962, pp. 219-233. An English translation by G. H. Williams is in *Spiritual and Anabaptist Writers*, London, 1957, pp. 145-160. As Prof. Becker reported to me, a copy of a fragment of the Latin letter is in Vienna: *Epistola impia impii Sebastiani Franck ad impium Joannem Campanum ex autographo descripta* (no date). See J. Chmel, *Die Hss, der K.K. Hofbibl. in Wien*, Bd. II, p. 231 (Vienna, 1874). This fragment was published by Prof. Becker separately in the N.A.R.G., Dl. XLVI.

[66] Hegler-Koehler, op. cit., pp. 67, 96 ff.

[67] *Ibid.*, pp. 88-90.

[68] See BRN X, pp. 474-476.

[69] Hegler-Koehler, op. cit., pp. 62-88; B. Becker, "Nicolai's inlassching over de Franckisten," N.A.K.G. XIX, 1925, p. 286, note 1.

[70] The title: BRN X, p. 17, note 1 and p. 478, note 2. In addition to the publication of 1602, there is a second after the *Enchiridion* of 1627. See Appendix IV, no. 19.

[71] BRN X, p. 483.

[72] Therefore the many Germanisms. See *ibid.*, p. 6, note 3 and p. 478, note 1. But this is no reason to assume that the booklet was originally written in German; the writings about the Frisian-Flemish quarrel also contain Germanisms. In the last years of his life Dirk was in contact with Nedersaksisch and German speaking people.

[73] BRN X, pp. 484-492.

[74] I used the Zurich copy of the letters for the preface. The text of the letter to Campanus follows the Krebs-Rott print; the letter to the brothers in the Eifel follows the Leiden copy.

[75] Op. cit., Aijr° and v°.

[76] BRN X, pp. 493-505.

[77] *Ibid.*, p. 493 = "Eyn Brieff van S. Franck tho Joh. Campaen," A 4v-6r. 7v-8r. Dirk made extracts from the letters and formulated theses. The numbering is mine.

[78] *Ibid.*, p. 495 = Eyn Brieff van S. Franck tho Joh. Campaen," A 5r, B 2v-3r.

[79] *Ibid.*, p. 496 ff. = "Eyn Brieff van S. Franck tho Joh. Campaen," A 7v, 8r.

[80] *Ibid.*, p. 498 = "Eyn Brieff van S. Franck tho Joh. Campaen," A 5r and v; A 7v, 8r.

[81] "Eyn Brieff van S. Franck tho Joh. Campaen," B 2v.

[82] *Ibid.*, p. 500 = "Eyn Brieff van S. Franck tho Campaen," A 7v, 8r, B 1r. See also. Seb. Franck, *Chronica*, 1536, II, fol. 134a, 144a, b; 145 b, and A. Hegler, *Geist u. Schrift*, pp. 256 ff., 266, note 1.

[83] BRN X, pp. 205-248.

[84] *Ibid.*, 227 ff.

[85] *Ibid.*, pp. 233-236. See also the *Chronica*, 1536, II, fol. 145b. I cannot support what Pijper, BRN X, p. 476 ff., writes about Dirk's attack on Franck in other writings. In my opinion Dirk was opposing the Davidjorists.

[86] Prof. Becker shared with me as a place of proof *Paradoxa ducenta octoginta*, 1559 (no place) p. 238a, b. I could not find any other places.

[87] *Ibid.*, p. 502 ff. = Eyn Brieff van S. Franck tho Joh. Campaen," A 5v, 6r, B3v and "Eyn Brief S. Franck an etlicken in der Eyfelt," B 8 v.

[88] BRN X, p. 231 ff.

[89] *Ibid.*, p. 503.

[90] *Ibid.*, p. 504 the kingdom of heaven is equated with the visible church. See Chapter X, p. 103.

[91] *Ibid.*, p. 504 ff.

[92] *Ibid.*, p. 505 ff.

[93] *Ibid.*, p. 497 ff.

[94] *Ibid.*, p. 497.

[95] "Epistola Sebastiani Franck ad inferioris Germaniae fratres, geschreven te Bazel 15 Mei 1541 or 1542." Johan van Bekensteyn lived at that time in Oldersum near Emden. Dirk Philips probably stayed in East Friesland also during those years. See Chapter III, p. 18. Further, see Hegler-Koehler, op. cit., pp. 88, 31-37.

[96] The Latin letter was speedily translated into German in an abbreviated and revised form. This translation was probably distributed in manuscript form and copied often. A copy appeared in Eifel, and was translated and published by de Zuttere in Middle Dutch. Hegler-Koehler, op. cit., pp. 93-96. The particular place is "Eyn Brief S. Franck an etlicken in der Eyfelt," B 8r, v, and Hegler-Koehler, op. cit., p. 89.

[97] BRN X, p. 498.

[98] B. Becker, N.A.K.G., Dl XIX, 1925, pp. 286-296.

[99] See Franck's song, "Von vier zwieträchtigen Kirchen" [About four discordant churches], H. Fast, *Der linke Flügel der Reformation*, pp. 246-248.

[100] A. Hegler, *Geist u. Schrift*, p. 287 and note 2.

[101] See above, p. 143, note 4.

[102] BRN X, p. 478.

[103] *Ibid.*, p. 25, note 4.

[104] *Ibid.*, p. 55, also all the following editions of the *Enchiridion, ibid.*, p. 50 ff.

[105] A. Hegler, *Geist u. Schrift*, pp. 55, 59.

[106] Hegler-Koehler, p. 58 ff.

[107] Chr. Sepp, *Drie Evangeliedienaren*, Leiden, 1879, p. 85 ff.

[108] BRN V, p. 4 and p. 40, note 4.

[109] *Chronica*, 1536, II, fol. 167a-176a.

[110] See Chapter VIII, pp. 71-75.

[111] BRN X, pp. 623-649. [Carel van Ghendt] called this his "last jewel," BRN VII, p. 532. The booklet was printed in 1569, BRN X, p. 623.

[112] *De leerstellige strijd enz.*, pp. 338-341.

[113] BRN X, p. 623.

[114] *Ibid.*, p. 625 ff.
[115] *Ibid.*, pp. 634, 640.
[116] See Chapter VII, pp. 51-52.
[117] D. B., 1877, pp. 74, 78. See also, J. H. Wessel, op. cit., pp. 57-60.
[118] BRN X, p. 345 ff.
[119] *Ibid.*, pp. 628, 631 ff., 647.
[120] *Ibid.*, p. 641 ff.
[121] *Ibid.*, pp. 640 ff., 643, 648.
[122] *Ibid.*, 637, 649. The same in "(Concerning) the Ban," *Ibid.*, p. 259.
[123] *Ibid.*, p. 646. It is a misunderstanding when Pijper speaks about divorce, *Ibid.*, p. 619. Dirk means shunning in marriage.
[124] See Chapter VII, p. 53, note 52.
[125] D. B., 1877, p. 74.
[126] BRN X, p. 645.
[127] *Ibid.*, p. 646. Dirk meant the Frisian-Flemish fight, of course, where one person had kept him outside in the beginning.
[128] *Ibid.*, p. 621. Kühler had a different judgment about it, *Geschiedenis* I, p. 343.
[129] BRN X, p. 649.
[130] BRN VII, p. 462.
[131] *Ibid.*,, pp. 271, 277.
[132] K. Vos, *De dooplijst van Leenaert Bouwens*, p. 59. Vos came to the same conclusion in "Een bisschop in Appingedam" (*Gron. Volksalmanak*, 1916, p. 17, from the off-print). The Danzig "Gemeindebuch" likewise says, "Dirk Philips died in Friesland [East Friesland] in 1568." This was incidentally confirmed by two reports. At the attempt at reconciliation in Sept., 1568 "an empty chair" was placed for Dirk and the Flemish appeared ready to defend his position (*Besprek binnen Hoorn ...*, 1622, § 192). The judges from the Bishopric said in their pronouncement (1569), "Concerning the improper ban of D. P. against the Dutch and Frisian men we will commend it to the heavenly Father, 'seeing that he cannot repent now.'" (P. Verkindert, *Brief, Dienende om te bewijsen etc.*, p. 23).
[133] BRN VII, p. 544.
[134] All the dead of Falder were buried there. The former village got its own cemetery only in 1574 (Report from Prof. F. Ritter at Emden, July 5, 1914).
[135] BRN VII, p. 543.
[136] *Geschiedenis* I, p. 425.
[137] Re: small gift, BRN X, pp. 157, 182, 296, 337, 379, 446, 459. "Remonstrance," p. 155. Re: poor, useless servant, BRN X, pp. 157, 310, 330.
[138] *Ibid.*, p. 182.
[139] Chapter XI, p. 140.
[140] BRN X, pp. 580, 637.
[141] *Ibid.*, p. 170 ff.; also pp. 66, 320, 450.
[142] *Ibid.*, pp. 67, 170, 275 ff., 320, 450.
[143] *Ibid.*, p. 396 and *passim*.

[144] The places quoted by Pijper, *ibid.*, p. 48, note 13, only treat the keeping of God's commandments, the doing of His will, the avoidance of sin, and the attempt to be sanctified.

[145] *Ibid.*, pp. 58, 292, 330.
[146] *Ibid.*, pp. 169, 217.
[147] *Ibid.*, pp. 220, 231.
[148] *Ibid.*, pp. 370 ff., 379 ff., 407, 414.
[149] *Ibid.*, pp. 396, 495.
[150] *Ibid.*, pp. 79, 347. Cf. Kühler, *Geschiedenis* I, p. 303 ff.
[151] Review of BRN X in *Theol. Literaturzeitung*, 41, 1916, p. 407 ff.
[152] BRN X, p. 232, also p. 231.
[153] *Ibid.*, pp. 68, 81, 179, 182, 202 ff., 371.
[154] *Ibid.*, pp. 369, 500.
[155] *Ibid.*, pp. 347, 369.
[156] *Ibid.*, pp. 79, 216, 242.
[157] *Ibid.*, p. 409, see Kühler I, p. 331 ff.
[158] John Horsch, MQR, VII, 1933, p. 119.
[159] Kühler, I, p. 280.

Postscript

[1] Werken, Amsterdam, 1630, I, pp. 377-383vo. For the date, see Bruno Becker, "Nogmaals datering van Coornherts dialogen" in *Spiegel der Letteren*, vol VII (1963-1964), 2. Antwerp, pp. 119-128.

[2] *Geschiedenis* I, p. 361.
[3] W.W. I, pp. 353-364vo.
[4] W.W. III, p. 302 ff.
[5] W.W. III, pp. 342-355.
[6] B. Becker, *Bronnen tot de kennis van het leven en de werken van D. V. Coornhert*, 's Gravenhage, 1928, p. 232 ff.

[7] Chr. Sepp, *Drie Evangeliedienaren uit den tijd der Hervorming*, Leiden, 1879, p. 1 ff.; Cornelia Boer, *Hofpredikers van Prins Willem van Oranje*, (Diss. Leiden), 's Gravenhage, 1952; R.G.G.^{3}, Bd. VI, p. 604.

[8] The Dutch publication: Haarlem, 1590, pp. 102-164 "Concerning the Baptism of Young Children of Christians" [*Van den Doop der jonghe kinderen der Christenen*].

[9] C. Boer, op. cit., p. 166.

Index

À Lasco, Johan .... 21, 172, n. 36
Adriaentgen, Wife of Jochem the Sugarbaker 95
Ahlefelt, Bartholomew van 58
Alenson .... 68, 179, n. 20, 193 n. 25
Althamer, Andreas 66
Altona .... 180, n. 34
Alva, Duke of 128
Amsterdam .... 102, 105, 122, 209, n. 122
Anna van Oldenburg 20
Antonius van Cologne .... 26, 32, 39, 42, 216, n. 22
Antwerp 49, 95
Appingedam 4, 5, 7, 108, 134, 138
Aquilomontanus, Hermannus 20
Aschendorpe 29
Athanasian Creed .... 178, n. 6
Augustine .... 75, 215, n. 7

Barbier, Thonis 106
Barentsdr, Aleid, daughter of Claeszn, Jan .... 172, n. 38
Barentszn, Otto 58
Basel, David Joris moves there 30
Batenburg, Jan van .... 10, 12, 18, 166, n. 2
Batenburgers 10, 22, 31, 39
Beatris Jansdr. 109
Bekensteyn, Johan van 152
Bender, Harold S. .... 102, 199, n. 39
Bengevoirth, Dyrich ten .... 181, n. 23
Biestsken, Nicolaes .... 110, 202, n. 106, 203, n. 135
Blanke, F. .... 190, n. 173
Blankenham, Peter Jenss van .... 170, n. 50
Blesdijk, Nicolas .... 9, 12, 13, 30, 31, 48, 60, 144, 166 n. 2, 175, n. 15
Bloemkamp 8
Bocholt 13
Bockmühl .... 217 n. 63
Bogaert, Pieter Willems 133
Bolsward .... 117, 131, 205, n. 38, 206, n. 63

Bommel, Herman van 105, 106
Bookbinder, Bartholomew 3
Bos, P. B. .... 168, n. 37; nn. 1, 7
Bouwens, Leenaert .... 31, 48, 49, 52, 53, 55, 82, 83, 85-87, 91, 93, 95, 97, 107, 108, 114, 115, 116, 118, 124, 126, 128, 139, 140, 161, 182 n. 38, 192, n. 8, n. 22, 201, n. 83, 204, n. 19, 22, 205, n. 33, 214, n. 216
    Bouwens' Baptism list .... 204, n. 14
    Wife of Leenaert Bouwen 51
Brabants .... 201, n. 102
Brandsma .... 171, n. 27, 173, n. 6, 177, n. 53, 181, n. 10
Bruinsma, A. J. .... 166, n. 3
Bucer 21, 24
Bugenhagen .... 144, 195, n. 85, 216, n. 11
Bullinger, Heinrich .... 10, 20, 156, 212, n. 190
Burgman, J. C. 11, 19
Busschaert, Hans .... 117, 121, 123, 182, n. 43
Buwo, Bernardus 61
Buyser, J. de 68

Campanus, Joh. .... 67, 99, 151, 218, n. 65
Cassander, Georgius .... 60, 96, 196, n. 122, 197, n. 124
Charles V 7, 15
Claeske Gaeledr. 111
Clara Jansd. 108
Cleve 25, 35, 41, 47, 96, 196, n.121
Cologne .... 70, 87, 94-96, 117, 195, n. 100
Cologne Debate at 94
Compromise .... 206, n. 65, 207, n. 68, 210, n. 142, 214, n, 215
Coomen, Jasper van 127
Coornhert, Dirck Volckerzoon 165
Costerus 10
Count van Hoogstraten 15
Count Enno II 16, 20
Countess Anna 21
Covenant .... 205, nn. 42, 50, 55, 208, n. 102, 210, n. 142, 213, n. 191
Covenant Theology .... 213, n. 190
Cramer, S[amuel] .... 49, 181, nn. 19, 27, 186, n. 59, 193, n. 32, 200 n. 74
Cranesteyn 109

Cruiningen, Quirijn Pieters . . . . 171, n. 14
Cuiper, Frans 47
Cuyper, Dierick . . . . 3, 167, n. 21

D'Auchy, Jacques 111
Danzig . . . . 47, 104, 106, 107, 110, 112-114, 116, 119, 125, 141, 143, 193, n. 40, 200, nn. 59, 70, 74, 203, n. 132, 204, n. 18, 208, n. 95, 209, n. 122
Davidjorists 29-31, 52, 72, 81, 111, 162
de Bres, Guy . . . . 61, 165, 166, n. 2, 180, n. 34, 185, n. 53, 199, n. 39
Denck, Hans 66
Deventer . . . . 4, 168, n. 5, 175, n. 8, 178, n. 77
Doetinchem . . . . 178, n. 77
Dokkum . . . . 117, 118, 121, 167, n. 28
Duchess of Parma 95

East Friesland . . . . 219, n. 95
Ebbink, Heinrich (nickname Dr. Klumpe) . . . . 49, 181, n. 23
Edam 108
Eilkeman, Gerdt . . . . 7, 10, 12, 169, n. 28
Elijah 3
Emden . . . . 16, 18, 20-22, 32-34, 39, 41, 43, 44, 47, 50, 58, 66, 81-84, 104, 107, 112, 114, 116, 117, 127-129, 132, 134, 138, 143, 144, 152, 158, 161, 182, n. 55, 192, n. 8, 203, n. 132, 204, n. 18, 209, n. 121, 215, n. 236, 225, n. 235
Emken, Henrick, and wife Anna 109
Emmerich . . . . 197, n. 124
Enoch 3
Epimenides 143
Erasmus . . . . 24, 66, 71, 143, 203, n. 134, 215, n. 6
Ewich, Joh. 152

Faber, Gellius . . . . 17, 39, 52, 55, 57, 169, n. 38
Falder . . . . 48, 143, 161, 220, n. 134
Feeriks, Jacob . . . . 107, 116, 117, 119-122, 125, 134, 138, 140, 144, 203, n. 12
Flemish . . . . 205, n. 34, 207, n. 68, 213, n. 187, 216, n. 16

Florisz, Theunis 105
Franciscans 1, 21, 161
Franeker .... 82, 87, 113, 117, 118, 120, 121, 124, 195, n. 102, 204, nn. 8, 22, 213, n. 187
Franekers 66, 67, 70, 71, 82, 85, 143, 151, 153, 155-157
Franck, Sebastian .... 75, 190, n. 173, 215, n. 5, 219, n. 85
Freeriks, Jacob .... 133, 211, n. 163
Frerichs, G. E. .... 179, n. 45
Fresenburg 58
Friesland .... 206, n. 55
Frisian-Flemish 108, 158
Frisians .... 117, 119, 120, 122, 125, 126, 136, 140, 141, 205, nn. 34, 42, 207, n. 81, 210, n. 141, 211, nn. 152, 163, 214, n. 225

Garbrantszn, Claes .... 20, 172, n. 38
Garcaeus, Johannes .... 17, 166, n. 9
Garten, Danzig suburb 104
Garthen, Johan 1
Geelen, Jan van 7
Gelre, Karel van 7, 8, 15, 96, 106, 120-124, 127, 129, 132-134, 136, 138
Germanisms .... 218, n. 72
Germans, Upper (or Overlanders) .... 87, 194, n. 50, 196, n. 106, 208, n. 95
Gerrits, Lubbert .... 121-122, 206, nn. 59, 63
Gerritz, Michiel .... 196, n. 121, 197, n. 124
　　　Baptized by J. den S. 96
Gheerts, Jan 61
Ghendt, Carel van .... 8, 125, 219, n. 111
Gillis van Aken (or Gieles) .... 10, 26, 31, 32, 49, 51, 52, 81, 182, n. 36
Goch .... 26, 34, 36, 39, 41, 42, 50, 57, 173, n. 4, 174, n. 33, 176, n. 42, 183, n. 4
Goeters, J. F. G. .... 189, n. 134
Govert 41
Grauinne, Anna .... 175, n. 2
Groningen .... 5, 7, 13, 15, 18, 138, 139, 179, n. 20
Grosheide, Greta 106

Hamelmann 25
Hansen, Georg .... 107, 201, n. 77
Harlingen .... 85, 87, 91, 92, 111, 112, 117, 118, 120-122, 124, 127, 128, 136, 140, 161, 193 n. 24, 204, n. 12, 205, nn. 30, 31, 211, n. 163, 213, n. 187, 214, n. 235
Harms, Geert 125, 134
Hartwerd 8
Hastenrath, Theunis van .... 26, 174, nn. 29, 31
Hegler, A. 152
Hendrik van Arnhem 121-124
Hendrik Euwesz. 111
Henegouwen 117
Hero, nobleman 17
Herrison .... 52, 182, n. 38
Heyns, Joriaan 86
Hilmers, J. H. .... 168, n. 36
Hoekstra, S. 62, 101
Hoffman, Melchior .... 2-4, 8, 12, 19, 33, 64, 65, 86, 100, 167, n. 14, 186, nn. 59, 76, 194, n. 65
    Hoffman: Bridegroom and bride 90
    in Amsterdam .... 200, n. 68
Hoffmanites 86
Hoorn .... 96, 108, 122, 129, 131, 133, 206, n. 59
Horatius 143
Houtzager, Peter .... 3, 4, 167, n. 24
Huyghe Mathyszoon .... 200, n. 72

Illikhoven .... 26, 174, n. 29
Imbroich, Thomas van .... 70, 71, 96, 189, n. 134
Jacob (from Herwerden) 4
Jan van Sol .... 200, nn. 69, 70, 72
Jan Quirynszn. 108
Janssen, Henrick 59
Jansz, Jacob .... 138, 213, n. 201
Jansz., Job .... 122, 124, 133, 139, 206, nn. 63, 67, 207, nn. 79, 81, 211, n. 159, 214, n. 215
Janszn, Willem .... 108, 201, n. 87
Jerome 143

Jeroen .... 207, n. 89
Joachim van Antwerp .... 197, n. 124
Joachim Werner, the Sugarbaker .... 95-96, 196, nn. 121, 122, 197, n. 124, 202, n. 125
Joriaensz, Thijs .... 133, 134, 201, n. 88, 211, nn. 159, 166
Joris, David .... 5, 13, 19-21, 23, 29-31, 39, 60, 72, 145, 166, n. 2, 175, n. 2, 187, n. 92, 190, n. 155
    Johan van Brugge as alias 30
    Joris, Tanneke, daugther of David Joris 31
Jorists 22
Julich 26, 35

Kanneghieter, Jan .... 167, n. 28
Keeney, William .... 42, 179, n. 18, 180, n. 1
Kessel .... 173, n. 20
Kettner, Fr. Theophil .... 180, n. 34
Kiewit, Jan .... 167, n. 16
Kimedoncius, Jacobus 165
Kistemaker, Anthony 7
Koehler, Walther 163
Koning, C. .... 166, n. 1
Krahn, Cornelius .... 71, 87, 189, n. 142, 193 nn. 25, 31
Krechting, Hendrik 19
Kremer, Jacob 7, 8
Kremer, Lambrecht (see Lemke)
Krufft, Heinrich .... 71, 87, 96, 189, n. 142
Krüsi, Hans 70
Kühler, W. J. .... 23, 47, 53, 57, 85, 115, 119, 120, 124, 128, 135, 160, 161, 177, n. 68, 180, n. 34, 183, n. 4, 193, n. 47, 199, n. 45, 204, n. 18, 205, n. 55, 209, n. 118, 119, 220, n. 128
Kuiper, Willem de .... 167, n. 21
Kuiper, Egbert .... 127, 130, 133, 135, 140, 211, n. 163
Kuiper, Frans Reines 32, 33, 39
Kükenbieter (Nossiophagus), Joachim 1, 17, 18

Index

Las, Virgile de 145, 150
Laurens van der Leyen .... 95, 144, 196, n. 112, 216, n. 16
Leeuwarden 1, 3, 118, 121
Lemke(Lambrecht Kremer) .... 26, 84, 87, 93, 97, 193, n. 30, 190, n. 106, 174, n. 29
Lemsius, Wilhelm 17
Libertines 72
Lievens, Tonijntgen .... 216, n. 16
Lindanus, Wilh. .... 202, n. 114
Lipke, Nette 117, 121, 122, 139
Lippe 8
Lower Saxon .... 195, n. 85
Lübeck .... 30, 31, 34, 49, 51, 55, 79, 175 nn. 18
Luther, Martin .... 6, 71, 76, 101, 157, 191, n. 179, 198, n. 26
    On ubiquity 76
Lutheran .... 191, nn. 192, 193, 192, n. 196

Maatschoen, Schijn .... 104, 166, n. 1
Malet 161
Mander, Carel van .... 94, 150, 183, n. 56
Mannhard, H. G. .... 47, 107, 200, nn. 65, 70
Mantz, Felix 81
Marpeck, Pilgram 102
Maria of Hungary 15, 20
Martens, Roelof (see Pastor, Adam) 29
Mathyszoon, Huyghe 106
Matthijs, Jan 3-5, 8, 19
Mecklenburg 52
Meihuizen, H. W. .... 170, n. 50, 171, n. 27, 172, n. 46, 176, n. 34, 179, n. 38, 183, n. 63, 193, n. 31, 195, n. 91
Melanchthon 24
Melchiorites 5, 106
Melchizedek .... 68, 188, n. 119
Mellink, A. F. .... 11, 167, n. 21
Menander 143
Mennisten 21

Menno Simons 12-21, 23-26, 29-34, 36-39, 42, 43, 47, 49, 51-53, 55,
    57, 58, 60, 61, 71, 74, 77, 79, 81, 84-87, 91-93, 97, 101, 102,
    105-107, 111, 124, 143, 147, 160, 162, 177, n. 64, 179, nn. 9, 10,
    180, nn. 27, 28, 34, 181, n. 23, 182, n. 43, 186, n. 59, 192, n. 4,
    193, nn. 26, 42, 194, nn. 56, 82, 195, nn. 85, 93, 95, 198, n. 7,
    200, n. 65, 201, n. 82, 202, n. 104, 215, n. 7, 217, n. 36
    On infant baptism and salvation 69
Mennonist 55
Michiel Janszoon 106
Micron, Martin .... 45, 52, 180, n. 34
Monnikendam 133
Mudder family .... 169, n. 26
Mudder, Jan 4, 5, 7, 9, 11, 18, 67, 77, 81, 105
Münster .... 186, n. 59
Münsterites 5, 7, 8, 39

Naaldeman, Hendrik 86
New Galilee Cloister 1
Niclaes, Hendrik 65, 66, 72
Nicolai, Gerardus .... 10, 35, 43, 72, 84, 144, 147, 156, 161, 184, n. 23,
    190, n. 155, 192, n. 8, 216, n. 19
Noerich, Peter van 4
Norden .... 17, 171, n. 17

Obbe Philips .... 1-5, 8-14, 16, 18-20, 23, 39, 55, 162, 166, n. 2,
    167, n. 21, 183, n. 60, 186, n. 76
    called Aelbrecht .... 171, n. 21
Obbist 55
Obbenites 10-12, 20
Ohling .... 171, n. 11
Oistwart, Michiel 24
Old Cloister 8, 10
Oldersum .... 17, 20, 156, 170, n. 50, 171, n. 11, 172, n. 38, 219, n. 95
Olieslager 41
Ommelanden 5
Outerman, J. O. .... 118, 120, 135, 205, n. 39, 212, n. 172

Index

Overd'haghe (Hyperphragmus), Pieter Anastasius 151
    Also known as Suttere, Pieter de 151
Overdam, Hans van 48
Overflakkee 48
Overlanders (see Germans, Upper)

Pastor, Adam 25, 26, 29, 30, 31-35, 41, 42, 49, 50, 52, 55, 61, 72, 145,
    175 nn. 2, 6, 19, 176 n. 44, 177, nn. 49, 56, 64, 178, nn. 76, 77,
    181, n. 27, 182, n. 30, 216, n. 22
    Actual name: Roelof Martens 29
Persijn, M. Hippolytus 39
Philips, Obbe (see Obbe Philips)
Pierson, Pierken 117
Pieters, Syvaert 118, 138
Pieters, Ebbe .... 116-118, 120, 122, 124, 126, 203, n. 13, 204, n. 33,
    207, n. 89
Pijper, F. 7, 18, 53, 67, 68, 90, 110, 119, 121, 129, 131, 136, 142, 143,
    150, 160, 176, n. 30, 179, n. 18, 182, n. 47, 188, n. 107, 199, n. 47,
    201, n. 102, 205, n. 39, 209, n. 118, 210, n. 146, 212, n. 182,
    215, n. 237, 217, n. 47, 219, n. 85, 220, n. 123
Polderman, Cornelis 3
Praet, Claes de 49
Prussia 104, 107

Ransdorp 108
Reichenberg 105
Reitsma, J. .... 1, 9, 167, n. 14
Rembert, K. 25
Renix, Hoyte 6, 97, 108, 114, 116, 117, 120-127, 129, 130, 131, 133,
    136-138, 140, 141, 201, n. 85, 206, nn. 63, 68, 207, n. 81,
    208, n. 90, 209, n. 132, 210, n. 141, 211, n, 163, 212, n. 187,
    213, nn. 202, 204, 213, n. 235
Reynckcuper, Frans 23, 26
Roore, Jacob de 124
Rosevelt, Hendrik van .... 124, 125, 138, 213, n. 201
Rostock 18, 19

Rothmann, Bernhard 7, 62-64, 99
Ruebsam, Tewes 25
Rutgers, Swaen 82, 84, 85, 115

Sacramentarians 2, 4, 105
Sattler, Michael 81
Schagen, M. 58, 86
Scheerder, Hans .... 3, 8, 167, n. 22
Scheffer, J. G. de Hoop .... 1, 38, 39, 87. 113, 114, 120, 128, 135, 181, n. 19, 194, n. 50, 204, n. 32, 208, n. 90, 210, n. 136, 211, n. 163
Schenck, Gov. van Toutenburg .... 4, 8, 15, 168, n. 5
Schleitheim 81
Schoenmaker, Harmen 7
Schotland .... 105, 200, nn. 59, 74
Schrijver, Gillis .... 121, 122, 123, 138, 207, n. 72, 213, n. 201
Servaes, Matth. .... 96, 197, n. 124
Servet, Michael .... 50, 182, n. 30
Sicke Freriks Snijder 2
Sicke [Sikke?], Hans .... 107, 135, 212, n. 174
Sijbrants, Hertman .... 119, 205, n. 39
Sikken, Hans .... 47, 87, 113, 125, 134, 136, 193, n. 40, 200, n. 65, 202, n. 128
Sol, Jan van 105, 106
Sommelsdijk 48
South Flanders 49
Staedtke, Joachim .... 212, n. 190
Steen, Hans van .... 95, 106, 200, n. 75, 201, n. 76
Stollaert, Isaac 60
Strasburg 2, 3, 19, 86, 87
Swart-Pot, Y. de 6
Swiss Brethren .... 195, n. 106

Tafflen, Jean 165
ten Cate, Blaupot .... 26, 35, 58, 172, n. 46
ten Bosch, A. S. M. 6
Theunis van Jüchen 24
Tielt, Herman van .... 52, 87, 182, n. 43

Timmerman, Herman de .... 97, 144, 150, 165, 182, n. 43, 197, n. 136, 217, n. 47
Tinnegieter, Jeroen 117, 119, 120, 124, 126
Titelman, Inquisitor Pieter 95
Tollenaar, Joos de 68
Trinity 50
Tripmaker 2

Ulrich van Dornum 17
Utrecht .... 108, 109, 202, n. 125

Vader, Steven .... 107, 125, 208, n. 95
van Bekenstein, Johan .... 219, n. 95
van Ghendt, Carel .... 123, 161, 195, n. 100
van Vreden, Hendrik .... 32, 39, 181, n. 23, 217, n. 22
van Campen, Jacob 4, 5
van Leiden, Jan 5, 7
van Braght, T. 95
Velsius, Gerard 96
Veluanus, Anastasius 156
Verbeek, Bede .... 166, n. 10
Verbeek, Joos .... 108-110, 112, 202 nn. 104, 125
Verlongen, Pieter 144
Verwer, Jan de 106
Verwey, H. de la Fontaine 6
Visschersweert 26
Visser, Barent 107
Von Wied, Elector Herman 24, 26
Von Rennenberg, Wilhelm 25
Voordt, Cornelis van 109
Vos, Karel .... 5, 10, 128, 135, 166, n. 13, 168 n. 15, 177 n. 68, 180 n. 34, 196, nn. 112, 117, 200, n. 71, 201, n. 102, 202, n. 104, 204, nn. 18, 31, 208, n. 102, 220, n. 132
Vreden, Hendrik van 26, 145
Vulder 58
Vulgate .... 215, n. 6

Waldfeucht .... 174, n. 29
Walloon Protestants .... 173, n. 20
Warfum 8, 11
Waterlander .... 197, n. 129
Waterlanders .... 82, 85, 86, 158, 194, n. 50, 215, n. 236
Wesbusch, van 94, 150
Wessel, J. H. 53, 157
Westerburg, Gerh. .... 174, n. 27
Weyer, Johannes 25
Wezel .... 173, n. 20
Wijer (also Wyer), Matthijs .... 25, 60, 165, 173, n. 20
Wijer, Jan 60
Wilhelm, Duke of Julich, Cleve and Berg 24, 25, 27
Wilhelmi, Hieronymus 29
Willem Willemsz. 109
Willems (Bogaert), Pieter 138
Willems, Jan .... 86, 97, 108, 120-124, 127, 129, 132-134, 136, 138, 206, n. 63, 210, n. 136
Williams, George Hunston 165
Winsum 7
Wismar .... 182, n. 43, 201, n. 82
Wüstenfeld .... 33, 52-55, 57, 58, 79, 81-84, 87, 91, 114, 160, 208, n. 95

Zandt, 't 4, 11
Zijpp, N. van der 6, 85
    about Hans Busschaert at Wismar 52
Zillis (in the Eifelgebergte) 26
Zillis van Aken, baptized Thomas van Imbroich 70
Zurich 20
Zutphen .... 178, n. 77
Zuttere, Pieter de .... 152, 156, 157, 217, n. 63, 219, n. 96
Zwingli, Ulrich .... 74-76, 137, 190 nn. 167, 173, 191, n. 193, 192, n. 196, 212, n. 190
Zylis (also Sylis) .... 84, 87, 93, 97, 193, n. 30

About Pandora Press

Pandora Press is a small, independently owned press dedicated to making available modestly priced books that deal with Anabaptist, Mennonite, and Believers' Church topics, both historical and theological. Our books are typeset and printed using desktop technology. This allows us to produce short-run titles at a relatively low cost, while maintaining a high level of print quality. We welcome comments and suggestions from our readers.

Also Available from Pandora Press

Sarah Dyck, ed. and trans., *The Silence Echoes: Memoirs of Trauma and Tears* (Kitchener, Ont.: Pandora Press, 1997). xii, 236pp., 2 maps. Softcover. ISBN: 0-9698762-7-0
$17.50 U.S./$19.50 Canadian. Postage: $4.00 U.S./$5.00 Can.
[First person accounts of life in the Soviet Union, translated from German]

Wes Harrison, *Andreas Ehrenpreis and Hutterite Faith and Practice* (Kitchener, Ont.: Pandora Press, 1997). xxiv, 274pp., 2 maps, index. Softcover. ISBN 0-9698762-6-2
$26.50 U.S./$32.00 Canadian. Postage: $4.00 U.S./$5.00 Can.
[First full biography of this important seventeenth century Hutterite leader. Volume 36 of the *Studies in Anabaptist and Mennonite History* series]

C. Arnold Snyder, *Anabaptist History and Theology: Revised Student Edition* (Kitchener, Ont.: Pandora Press, 1997). xiv, 466pp., 7 maps, 28 illustrations, index, bibliography. Softcover. ISBN 0-9698762-5-4
$35.00 U.S./$38.00 Canadian. Postage: $5.00 U.S./$6.00 Can.
[Abridged, rewritten edition for undergraduates and the non-specialist]

Nancey Murphy, *Reconciling Theology and Science: A Radical Reformation Perspective* (Kitchener, Ont.: Pandora Press, 1997). x, 103pp., index. Softcover. ISBN 0-9698762-4-6
$14.50 U.S./$17.50 Canadian. Postage: $3.50 U.S./$4.00 Can.
[Lively exploration of the supposed conflict between Christianity and Science]

C. Arnold Snyder and Linda A. Huebert Hecht, editors, *Profiles of Anabaptist Women: Sixteenth Century Reforming Pioneers* (Waterloo, Ont.: Wilfrid Laurier University Press, 1996). xxii, 442pp. Softcover. ISBN: 0-88920-277-X
$28.95 U.S. or Canadian. Postage: $5.00 U.S./$6.00 Can.
[Biographical sketches of more than 50 Anabaptist women; first of its kind]

The Limits of Perfection: A Conversation with J. Lawrence Burkholder. Second edition, including a new epilogue by J. Lawrence Burkholder. Edited by Rodney Sawatsky and Scott Holland (Kitchener, Ont.: Pandora Press, 1996). x, 154pp. Softcover. ISBN 0-9698762-2-X
   $10.00 U.S./$13.00 Canadian. Postage: $2.00 U.S./$3.00 Can.
[J.L. Burkholder reflects on his life experiences; eight Mennonites respond]

C. Arnold Snyder, *The Life and Thought of Michael Sattler* (Scottdale, Pa: Herald Press, 1984). viii, 260pp., hardcover. ISBN 0-8361-1264-4
   $10.00 U.S./$12.00 Canadian. Postage: $4.00 U.S./$5.00 Can.
[First full-length biography of this central Anabaptist leader and martyr]

To order, contact:
Pandora Press   Telephone: (519) 578-2381
51 Pandora Avenue N.   (519) 742-1876
Kitchener, Ontario   Fax: (519) 578-2381
Canada N2H 3C1   E-mail: panpress@golden.net
                    Web site: www.golden.net/~panpress

Pandora Press books are also available through
Herald Press   Orders: (800) 245-7894
616 Walnut Avenue   E-mail: hp%mph@mcimail.com
Scottdale, PA
U.S.A. 15683   Web site: www.mph.lm.com